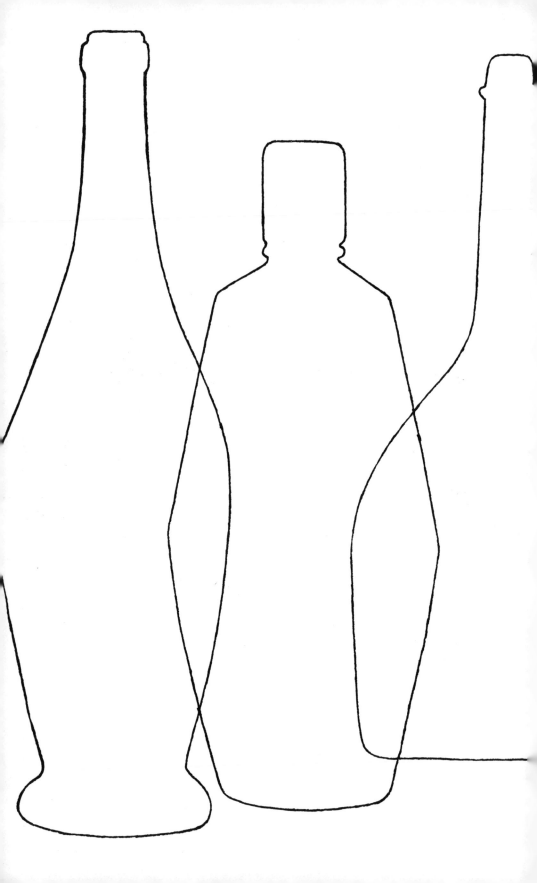

Massee's
Guide to
Wines
of America

BOOKS BY WILLIAM E. MASSEE

Wines and Spirits

Wine-Food Index

Wine Handbook

Wines of France
(IN COLLABORATION WITH ALEXIS LICHINE)

The Art of Comfort

SATURDAY REVIEW PRESS · E. P. DUTTON & CO., INC.

WILLIAM
E.
MASSEE

*Massee's
Guide to
Wines
of America*

NEW YORK · 1974

MAPS BY
DOROTHY IVENS

Library of Congress Cataloging in Publication Data

Massee, William Edman.
Massee's guide to wines of America.

First published in 1970 under title:
McCall's guide to wines of America.
1.   Wine and wine making—United States.   I.   Title.
II.   Title: Guide to wines of America.
TP557.M38 1974   641.2'2   73-22412

ISBN: 0-8415-0300-1   (cloth)
ISBN: 0-8415-0303-6   (paper)

Printed in the United States of America
Designed by The Etheredges

For Phil Wagner
and
Frank Schoonmaker,
who take time
to get things right.

Contents

Part Three: The Kinds of Wine

*Massee's
Guide to
Wines
of America*

PART ONE

Discovery

New World
of
Wines

It takes a long time to get things right.

A dozen centuries ago Charlemagne stood where the Rhine crooks west, gazing across to snowy slopes that glistened in a pale spring sun. One patch was bare. "Secure the heights and set a vineyard where the ground is clear," said he. And it was done.

The Schloss of Johannisberg was built above the vineyard, and ever since, Johannisberg wines have carried the legend around the world. Their labels show the castle and its vines from the place where the emperor is said to have stood.

Hoping to match the wonder farther south, Swiss vintners took cuttings from the old vines and planted them in the Valais on the upper Rhone, calling the wines from them Johannisberger Riesling. Although the wines from the new setting lacked the brilliance of their northern sires, they were good.

Old lore is early lost, only to be found again. Any Rhinelander could have told the Swiss that it was all very well to honor the legend, but one had to match the climate and the soil as well.

Almost a thousand years have passed since Leif set sail westward to see what he could find — through the fogs, beyond the bergs. The land he came upon was forest that stretched beyond his will for sailing, but what he marked most were the vines. Vines looped through the trees, tangled along the beaches, choked the river mouths. The grapes had a musky taste. He made wine in the hollow of a stone. It was musky too. Still, he called the country Wineland.

More than a score of generations passed. Virginia's first settlers caught the scent of grapes while still at sea and one among them crushed the round, bronze berries — enough from a single vine to fill a cask. The wine, though bitter, tasted somewhat like plums when enough sugar was added — not at all what they'd hoped for. They called it Scuppernong. At all the colonies, settlers took the time to see what could be wrung from other native grapes. But all the wines were strange, musky. One of these settlers, Thomas Jefferson, even sent to Europe for cuttings but the vines spindled in the new soil and soon died. What wine was made was bad. However, the desire for good wine was growing — surely something could be made from these strange grapes.

Around the same time Franciscan fathers came up the western valleys to raise a new kingdom in the wilderness, planting missions and vineyards on the way from Mexico along El Camino Real. The Royal Road lay behind the coastal ranges, where winding rivers watered rolling country. To Spanish eyes, the land was one for orchards and for vines. Fra Junípero Serra brought cuttings from Mexican haciendas, offshoots from vines that had come on early Spanish galleons. Not knowing what the vines were, he called their fruit Mission grapes. The wines they made were not much good. Good wines cannot be made from poor grapes. In *Wine Grower's Guide* (Knopf, 1965), Philip M. Wagner says:

> The wonder is not so much that they were satisfied with a single mediocre variety of wine grape as that they got any wine at all. Few missions had proper wine presses and few had adequate cooperage or other wine-making equipment. Thus at one mission, Santa Gertrudis, the German Jesuit Jorge Retz solved the problem by hollowing out

some huge rocks which he used first as fermenting vats, and then, by filling with new wine and sealing with pitch, as "casks." Ordinarily the crushing of the grapes was done by "well-washed Indians," their hair tied up and wearing only a *zapata,* whose hands were covered with cloths to wipe off perspiration, and who thrashed about in the mass of fresh grapes until these were sufficiently macerated, the fresh must being then caught and, with the help of God, fermented into wine in big leather bags.

Empire builders came after the Church, but were too busy with pelts and gold to follow Noah's example and tend a vineyard. Yet Californians have always been a thirsty lot. Once the first fortunes were made, there was an urge to celebrate. What was needed was a Charlemagne, and he came to the Sonoma Valley soon after the Gold Rush. He was Hungarian, and his name was Ágoston Haraszthy.

Haraszthy found a hillside with a lovely view, so he called his vineyard Buena Vista. His wines soon became the delight of San Francisco.

Just as Roman legions had preceded Charlemagne with plantings along the rivers of the Empire from the Crimea to Iberia, so had others in America planted cuttings before Haraszthy. Vineyards had flourished around Monterey and Santa Barbara, and a man from Bordeaux — aptly named Vignes — had planted a hundred acres of imported vines in what was to become downtown Los Angeles. But Haraszthy had the touch, as well as a cooler climate for his grapes, and in 1861 the governor of California, enthusiastic about his wines, commissioned Haraszthy to tour Europe and bring back cuttings from its vines.

Seven months later Haraszthy returned with one hundred thousand cuttings, of several hundred varieties, from the great vineyards of Europe — those of the Rhine and the Danube, the Rhone and the Loire, Burgundy and Bordeaux, Jerez and Oporto. All were neatly done up, with labels and notes about handling their grapes in vineyard and in vat. But the Civil War had come to California by then, and nobody cared about vines.

Haraszthy planted some of the cuttings and got his neighbors to let him set out others in their grounds so the strains would not be lost. He sent his three sons around the countryside — up into Mendocino, over east into Napa, south of San Francisco to Livermore and Santa Clara and San Benito — to plant vines anywhere they could.

Identifying tags were lost. Maybe wayward bees caused strange pollinations. Odd mutations occurred in the foreign soils. And the state refused to pay Haraszthy for his troubles. Disgusted, he sailed off for Nicaragua to make a new fortune from rum and coconuts. He was riding across a ford one day — it is said — when his horse reared and tossed him into the stream, where he was eaten by alligators.

It was 1869, hardly a century ago, when Haraszthy — lift a glass to him and to his sons — disappeared. Other winemakers came to California, and some prospered. Most used the vines on hand, those meant to provide raisin or table grapes; a few experimented with imported varieties. The wines were mainly red, rough, and unbalanced, their defects hidden with sugar.

What was lacking in taste was made up for by the heavy addition of grape brandy. What was lacking in fame was made up for by calling the wines Port and Sherry, Burgundy and Bordeaux — any name that was recognizable and popular. A vigorous printing trade sprang up, counterfeiting European labels. The state put a stop to this eventually, but there was great curiosity in Paris and London about California Burgundy, and about sparkling Catawba from Eastern vineyards. The exotic wines from the New World were a threat, or might be. The strange grapes were worth exploring.

Now wines are wonders; great wines are magical; and winemakers are mad. Like horse fanciers, they are always trying to improve the breed. The best wines come from what are called noble vines, on which are grown grapes with the proper balance of sugar and acidity to produce a pleasing taste, plus enough tannin so that the wines can live long enough to develop all their qualities. This happens most advantageously when grapes are grown as far north as possible, at the limit of their range.

Grapes need just enough sun to ripen well, but not so much that the sugar overpowers the fruit acids in the juice. When noble vines are raised in warm climates, fruit acids are not retained, and the juice is mostly sugar and makes a bland, dull wine. Grown too far north, the grapes may not mature completely, their juice being mostly acid, with little sugar, making a thin, sharp wine.

The harder a vine works, it is said, the better the wine. Vines grown at the extremity of their range are called shy bearers, yielding little fruit. Wines of high quality can be produced from this fruit, but the quantity is low. Winemakers are always experimenting — to increase yield, to raise quality.

All European vines are of a single species, *Vitis vinifera,* the wine bearer. There were dozens of species in the New World — *Vitis labrusca, Vitis rupestris, Vitis riparia,* among others — and, in the 1870s, hoping that some of these species might be resistant to ills that were crippling European vines, limiting yields, French vineyardists imported American cuttings to see how they would do in French soils. They did devastatingly, for the roots of these vines harbored a burrowing louse called *Phylloxera vastatrix,* which invaded every European vineyard, and within twenty years, destroyed all but a few isolated vines. There was one solution: Since native American roots were impervious to the louse, great European stocks had to be grafted to roots from American vines.

Grafting was expensive, and European growers were forced to face an awful truth: Only the best vines are worth planting, and these only in places where they grow best. Noble vines belong in northern vineyards, where they can produce grapes for wines that live a long time and mature well. This ability to develop came to be considered a characteristic of every great wine, which must also be true to the type of grape from which it was made and to the region from which it came. Some of them can live for decades.

Various good vines grown in milder latitudes will produce acceptable quantities of grapes, whose wines are characteristic and true to type, but not particularly distinctive — good wines that do not last a decade and rarely achieve any special excellence. Other vines can be grown all over the countryside, producing plenty of grapes, and wines that are delicious when drunk young — within a year or two of the vintage. Called *vins du pays,* and usually poured from a pitcher or carafe, these country wines typify their grapes and their districts; they vary from one district to another and are seldom exported. Still other vines, grown in hot-weather vineyards, produce mountains of grapes and floods of ordinary wines, *vins ordinaires,* that are generally used as everyday wines for the table, more quenching than water.

Such distinctions have always been pretty well understood in South America, settled mostly by people from the Mediterranean, where wine was a daily drink and quantity counted more than quality. A desire for better wines eventually led to the introduction of noble vines, in Chile particularly, but local demand kept the wines from being shipped abroad.

North Americans took a while to learn the lesson. In the East, native vines were cultivated over and over again, always producing wines with a musky taste. Accidental crosses occurred, and some of these led to palatable wines, still strange in taste but with the wild tang muted enough to make them interesting. Where the growing season was right for noble vines, the winters were too harsh, but perseverance in New York State and the Niagara peninsula resulted in some good wines from white grapes, and experiments with hybrids — usually French vines carefully crossed with native stock — led to other wines with distinctive tastes.

Californians persisted in using table and raisin grapes and inferior varieties like Mission for making wines, mostly because the vines bore well in the hot climate. Big-producing European varieties were tried, with foul result. Noble vines were planted in warm areas, where the grapes matured too rapidly and lost their fruit acids, producing bland and flabby wines. But gradually the counties around San Francisco Bay began to yield; the vineyards were cool enough to produce fair grapes and fair wine, with hope of better to come.

Wine has three lives: in the vineyard, in the vat, and in the bottle. More than two thousand years went into the establishment of the great European regions; the counties around San Francisco Bay had been discovered in a scant one hundred years. Around the turn of the century, each great European region had a score or more of outstanding vineyards; search was continuing to seek out such around the Bay. Meanwhile, there were the secrets of fermentation — what happens to wines in the vats — for scientists to explore.

Around the middle of the last century Louis Pasteur discovered that fermentation is governed by the action of yeasts. Not until nearly the middle of this century were the steps involving the conversion of grape sugar to alcohol by yeasts fully understood. The time since then has seen more changes in winemaking than did the previous two thousand years.

Many of the discoveries have been made in California, which has been the first region to put the new knowledge to practical use. One discovery — perhaps the most important — was that fermentation temperatures should be kept from rising too high. During the 1960s the fermentation process was perfected in California wineries, and the knowledge began to affect winemaking practice around the world. At the same time, experimentation with vineyard techniques was proving so successful that shy bearers could be brought to ripeness at the end of the growing season (and not before), with the right balance of sugar and fruit acid to make superior wines. During the 1970s these changes in vineyard management will travel around the world. Right now they are resulting in the production of some exceptional American wines, particularly in California. These wines are light and elegant, well balanced, superbly made. At first there were few bottles, because only a few hundred acres were planted in the noble vines, and also because Californians, quick to discover what they had in their midst, bought many of the wines direct from the wineries, which kept supplies short. During the past decade, as new vineyards were planted, more and more wines became available. Unfortunately most of them were lost in the flood of more commonplace wines on the market. But gradually the good wines are being distributed, competing with European vintages that become scarcer and more costly as increasing numbers of Americans take to drinking wines.

As the seventies began, table wines were starting to outstrip other types in popularity — almost as if the public had been waiting for good ones all the time. Within the decade, three out of every four bottles sold will probably hold table wine — good wines with names like Mountain Red or Mountain White, fine ones named after noble vines like Cabernet Sauvignon or Chardonnay.

It has taken a long time — almost a thousand years since Leif found the land, two hundred since Franciscan fathers first planted grapes in California, more than a hundred since wines were made from Haraszthy's grapes, twenty-five since the secrets of fermentation were at last unraveled, just ten since the techniques of growing vines were mastered and put into practice in the vineyards. Only now are the best wines being produced in quantities large enough to get far beyond state borders. Some of the best California wines have, even now, rarely been tasted much beyond San Francisco.

Names unknown as the decade began will be famous by its end. There are dozens of wines to discover now; there will be scores in the next few years. American wines have come of age, to delight us all. Haraszthy would have been pleased.

The Four Kinds of Wine

People who do not know the first thing about wines get confused when they walk into a shop and see all those bottles on the shelves. What they may want is just a bottle of red or white to have with dinner, preferably not sweet and not expensive. The choice is simple if you know a little bit about the kinds of wine there are.

The first thing about wines is that they are made by fermenting the juice of freshly squeezed grapes. The result is *table wine,* mostly drunk with food, and containing between 9 and 14 percent alcohol by volume. Man complicates it by adding things.

Sparkling wines, like Champagne, are made by adding bubbles. *Fortified wines,* like Sherry and Port, are made by adding brandy, so that they contain as much as 21 percent alcohol. *Aromatic wines,* like Vermouth and aperitifs, are made by adding flavors from herbs, roots, flowers, and spices; they are usually fortified as well.

These four are all the kinds of wine there are. But fermentations of berries and fruits — cider from apples, perry from pears, and so on — are often called "fruit wines."

Each kind ranges from dry to sweet, and the wine enthusiast quickly focuses attention on dry table wines, because these are the ones he drinks most often. These are also the ones America makes best.

Ranging in color from deep ruby red through garnet and all the shades of pink, from bright gold to the paleness of lightly tarnished silver, and ranging in taste from young and fruity to old and silky or velvety, they are a new world exciting to explore. The best of them reflect the grapes from which they come, the soil and climate in which their vines grow, their years in cask and bottle. Such elegant concern for this happy link between nature and man comes later. In the beginning all anybody wants is a wine that tastes good. And not too expensive, please.

Table Wines: Varietals, Generics, and Jug Wines

All one really needs to know are the names that wines are sold by. They are marketed under grape names, place names, or type.

American winemakers identify their best wines by grape variety. These form a class called *varietals,* and just by knowing the names of the best grapes, a buyer can start out by drinking the best wines America produces. For details, see pages 16 through 33, and accounts of the various winemakers. For now, here is a list of the best varietals.

VARIETAL RED WINES	VARIETAL WHITE WINES
Cabernet Sauvignon	*Pinot Chardonnay*
Pinot Noir	*Johannisberg Riesling*
Zinfandel	*Pinot Blanc*
Gamay Beaujolais	*Chenin Blanc*

Where the wine comes from can make a great difference. Substantial quantities of excellent varietals come from the counties around San Francisco Bay, the center of California quality production, the North Coast counties — the Napa and Sonoma valleys, Mendocino and Alameda, Santa Clara, San Benito, and Monterey. Small quantities of white varietals come from New York State, but most of the wines are blends.

Blended wines are patterned after European types or take the names of European districts. They are called *generics.* Here, confusion lies.

When the types of blended wines are those marketed with place names or brand names, there is no trouble. California producers call some of their best blends Mountain Red or Mountain White, but they have devised few others. Some wines are called Vino da Tavola or Château this-or-that, the foreign words doing no harm and perhaps even lending a certain cachet. Such wines are generally soundly made and are sold by the bottle or the gallon. They are called *jug wines,* rarely distinguished but usually good, and those from producers in the San Francisco area are generally better than European wines at the same price.

American winemakers have shown a lack of imagination in naming most of their generics, however. They have simply borrowed famous European names and stuck them on any sort of wine. These types are what the trade calls generics.

Such generics are a nuisance wherever in the world they appear on the market, glutting it and confusing the buyer. All are meant to match the popular idea of what such wines — Burgundy or Chablis, for example, or Rhine wine — should be. Usually it is a vague idea, so vague that a generic wine can be anything a blender chooses to make it.

Also, a generic wine can come from any sort of grape. Thus, while a red Burgundy from France must be made from Pinot Noir or Gamay grapes grown in the region, a California Burgundy may be made from Concord grapes or any others (as long as 75 percent of them are from the state). French Chablis must, by law, use only Chardonnay grapes grown in the Chablis district of France; California Chablis can be anything. And so it goes.

There is no way at all to tell what a generic wine will taste like — except that it probably won't taste like much, and it may be slightly sweet. In the eyes of producers, Americans talk dry and drink sweet, but not too sweet; to producers, this means that a dry wine should not be too dry, and a sweet one should be only moderately sweet. Producers try to give the public what it wants, even when it does not know.

Sauternes is the French district that produces sweet wines — the sweeter the greater. The California version of the French Sauternes is called sauterne — the final *s* being dropped as confusing — and is usually watery and not very sweet. So-called dry sauterne is generally equally watery, and it generally drinks sweet.

Italian Chianti comes from vineyards near Florence and is sprightly and refreshing; California versions are usually bland, "mellow" rather than dry. German Rhine wine, from the valley of the Rhine, is flowery and sharp from fruit acids, but California versions are usually sweetish and watery. A Rhine wine produced in California may come from the same vat as the Chablis. Only the names are changed to beguile the innocent.

Argument is made that Sherry and Port — and in the United States, which does not recognize the international agreement to the contrary, Champagne — are types of wine, and by long tradition, nothing more. The argument is stretched to include table wines, and it certainly seems odd to get a Rhine wine from California. Such names popularly identify the worst wines, not the best.

Top U.S. producers are apt to make clean generic wines — fairly dry ones, with no off tastes — but even these are rarely more than ordinary, with little character. When a good producer has a wine with some character, he is likely to give it a varietal name if he can — if, that is, at least 51 percent of the wine is from a single variety of grapes. United States wine laws are patterned after those for whiskey, which say that 51 percent of the grain going into bourbon must be corn, and 51 percent of rye whiskey must come from rye; hence 51 percent of a varietal wine must come from the variety of grapes the wine is named for — 51 percent of Chardonnay wine from Chardonnay grapes, for example, and 51 percent of Cabernet Sauvignon from grapes of that name. In practice, most producers use 75 percent or more of a grape variety, for 75 percent is about the minimum needed to make a wine typical of a grape variety.

If the good producer of a good wine can't give it a varietal name, he is apt to call it Mountain Red or Mountain White or to give it a brand name and sell it at a low price to compete with the nondescripts. Good producers hate the practice of using generic names because it downgrades their blends.

Much of the blame for the confusion about wine names can be placed on the Wine Advisory Board, a state bureau formed at the turn of the century to promote and legislate for California wines. The board collects a small levy on each case of California wine, using the money to support its advertising, public relations, and educational programs. One of its efforts is to avoid international agreements in order to preserve for producers the right to use generic names any way they please. Helping things along is the Wine Institute, a California trade association that also conducts a public relations program, and hires a public relations firm to do still more. The Board runs an excellent test kitchen to provide wine recipes, and the Institute sends reporters around with guides to make sure they see what they should.

Some Notes on Tasting: Nose, Body, Depth, and Balance

Once you have bought a bottle of Zinfandel or a jug of Mountain White, only taste will tell you whether it is good or not. You can tell at once. A good wine will have nothing unpleasant in the taste, however unfamiliar that taste may be.

Some of the main taste characteristics are listed below, and there are more in the Glossary. One often takes the unfamiliar to be unpleasant, and some acquaintance with the way a wine may taste can help in surmounting that psychological barrier.

Taste a glass of good wine. The wine has *nose*. That is a taster's term for a developed bouquet, which is the collection of smells, mostly flowery or fruity, given off by the alcohols and esters in a wine. The *original bouquet,* consisting of fresh smells, comes from life in the cask; the *acquired bouquet,* of subtler smells that develop when a wine's alcohols break down into higher alcohols, comes from life in the bottle. Acquired bouquet may remind one of attics, or old velvet or cool moss by a brook — hard to define, but easy to recognize.

The wine has *body*. This means that the wine does not taste of water, but tastes of wine. A wine too light in body may taste watery, but with a difference — some extremely light wines (with perhaps 10 percent alcohol, or even less) have been called glorious water. A full-bodied wine fills the mouth, and some are so full they can almost be chewed. Somewhere in the middle is best.

The wine has *depth*. This is related to body, but suggests a complexity of taste, one that lasts into the aftertaste, seeming to be an echo of the first sip. The taste is long and subtle, not obvious and quickly over.

The wine has *balance,* meaning that the elements of the wine are in equilibrium. The nose is somehow related to the taste, and this is carried over into the moments after the wine is swallowed. It is experienced as all one thing — a unity, not a collection of separate qualities. One speaks of the acid-tannin balance, meaning that the bitter taste from tannin is matched by the fresh taste of fruit acids. You can't say sour, because the sour taste in wine comes from the development of acetic acid as a result of contact with air, turning the wine to vinegar — *vin aigre* in French, sour wine.

There are other things, too. A *good* wine tastes good. A *great* wine has all the elements so completely balanced, and so well, that it can live long enough — three years or so for white wines, six or so for reds — to develop secondary characteristics. A great wine must also be characteristic of the grapes from which it was made and of the soil in which those grapes were grown. It is something unique, something not to be duplicated anywhere else in the world. Such wines now come from California, but few people outside California believe it — rarely spending the effort to seek them out.

Noble Vines for Reds, Whites, and Rosés

As confusing as the language and labeling of wines may seem, one basic truth, which wine growers and wine lovers discovered generations ago, is simple: Only the best grapes make the best wines. The grapes come first, and the novice wine drinker who familiarizes himself with the names and characteristics of the traditional grape varieties is halfway home.

"The more you know, the better you're off," an excited friend once said, regretting that his increasing familiarity with good wines had made him impatient with cheap, ordinary ones. But this did not really matter, he said, given the widening awareness, even joy, that came with much tasting. That may well be. A wine expert has little sympathy.

A wine expert is a person who has tasted more bad wines than most. But he has tasted more good ones, too. He is able to notice subtle differences that may be missed by the inexperienced. These differences can add to the excitement and pleasure of drinking in much the way that unnoticed overtones add to the wonder of listening to music. To know wines you have to drink a lot of them. Regularly.

A novice tasting at random begins to make some of the same distinctions and to compare wines in some of the same ways an expert does when he is tasting the products of a particular grape variety or a particular district. Wines, and their producers, gain reputations because repeated tastings and endless discussion finally lead to a conclusion that one or another is better than the rest. It is an oral tradition, this rating of wines, based on tasting and talking that may extend over generations, even centuries.

At least a score of expert tasters, many books, articles, and producers — and many bottles — have been consulted and considered in making the lists of selections for the wines discussed below.

A maker of Chardonnay, for instance, can be asked who makes outstanding Chardonnays — in addition to himself, of course. After one has talked to a dozen or so such producers, a list begins to take shape. Often, however — as is the case with Chardonnays — a list of *all* the good wines of a particular variety would be so long that the reader might get the idea that all are pretty much the same. They are not, and for that reason, I have chosen to use shorter lists — ones that indicate a level of excellence, against which other wines of the same variety may be judged. More than a few good wines — as is the case, again, with Chardonnays — are thus not included in the basic lists. References to some, which a reader can seek out and taste for himself, appear in the later accounts of the various districts and producers.

In one sense, a critic is an explorer who describes what he has found out so that others may find out for themselves. An expert may also be an explorer, searching in familiar territory but still seeking what has been missed. A stranger can use a map to find his way.

The lists that follow indicate distinctive peaks in the range, while the later accounts of districts and producers point out summits that can be found with a little searching. Every man, after all, must explore for himself. One of the pleasures of wine is that there are so many ranges, so many peaks.

Red Wines

CABERNET SAUVIGNON

*California had at least 6,000 acres in bearing by the 1974 vintage, with an additional 6,000 acres coming into fruit by 1976.**

Cabernet Sauvignon is the informing vine of Bordeaux, so called because its grapes give the wines of France's greatest region their distinctive character. The English call them *claret,* supposedly because the first wines shipped from Bordeaux were pale blends of white and red called *clairet.*

The Cabernet Sauvignon produces wines that are light, subtle, and balanced. Retaining a fresh and forestlike character of woods in spring, even when very old, it produces the finest wines of California. The best of these are from the North Coast counties, particularly in the Napa Valley, where special reserves that may have been kept four years in oak before bottling, may begin to reach their peaks only after fifteen years.

Cabernets bottled after three years in wood, or slightly less, often require five more years in the bottle before developing thoroughly. Before that they are hard, that is, they have a bitter taste from the tannin in the wine. This changes to a pleasing firmness in time. Its presence in the young wine is a sign that the wine will have a long life. Wines lacking in tannin when young have a softness on the tongue, and they are apt to be short-lived. Wines pick up some of their tannin from the oak in which they are stored, so Cabernets left less than three years in wood are usually marketed during the fourth year after the vintage. They are then considered to be drinkable, but wise buyers lay them aside for at least two more years, and preferably twice that long, because the wines continue to improve.

The Cabernets, which is what both vines and wines are familiarly

* Yield from noble vines varies from two to four tons of grapes per acre. A ton produces about 150 gallons of wine, or some sixty cases of twelve bottles each. A great vineyard of Bordeaux like Château Haut-Brion produces even less in a normal year, only about 11,000 cases from 92 acres.

called, are the slowest to mature of all the great red wines. For more than a century Bordeaux growers have been planting part of their vineyards in varieties that produce fast-maturing, soft wines, particularly Merlot and Malbec. Such grapes are crushed along with the Cabernets and may account for more than half of each pressing. Something like a thousand acres of Merlot are planted in the North Coast counties, plus a few acres of Malbec, and cautious attempts are being made to use them with the Cabernets. Top producers hesitate to tamper much with the elegant splendor of their Cabernets, which are the best bargains in the world of wines today.

There has been some experiment with Cabernet Franc, a close relative of Cabernet Sauvignon, which matures quickly and produces a soft wine. That cousin is now extensively planted in the Bordeaux districts of St. Émilion and Pomerol, as well as along the Loire, where it produces the reds of Chinon and Bourgueil and some excellent Anjou rosé. The grape has not distinguished itself in California.

At a San Francisco exposition in 1939, only a single varietal wine was presented, a lone Cabernet. At least two score varietals are marketed today, and there are now some fifty producers of Cabernets. Several are so small that they sell only to winery visitors; others do not ship their wines outside the state.

Of the Cabernets that can be found in some metropolitan centers at outstanding wine shops, expert opinion agrees that the following producers, listed in no particular order, offer exceptional wines.

Beaulieu Vineyard
Louis M. Martini
Inglenook Vineyard
Charles Krug Winery
The Christian Brothers
Mirassou
Korbel
Parducci

SERVING CABERNET: This elegant, dry red wine complements roasts and grillades, particularly those with rich sauces, and contrasts superbly with more delicate chicken and veal dishes. A classic wine to serve with cheese, it is also excellent to serve after a heartier or younger wine has been presented with a preceding course.

PINOT NOIR

At least 3,000 acres in bearing in 1974; with an additional 2,000 acres coming into fruit within the next couple of years. *

All the great red Burgundies, from the lordliest Chambertin to the lightest Mercurey, are made from Pinot Noir, perhaps the shyest bearer of all the noble vines. Superbly balanced, fruity, and light when well made, it is ready to drink three or four years after the vintage and generally well past its prime ten years after the vintage.

California Pinot Noirs reflect this elegant fruitiness, more so than many fine, French Burgundies, to which sugar is added to the fermenting grape juice, increasing the alcoholic content of the wine and adding to it a fullness considered to be traditional. The process, called chaptalization, is not permitted in California, so that North Coast county wines reflect the classic lightness of a true Pinot Noir, and not the heavy imbalance that flaws so many Burgundies but gives them a long and lingering taste. Few people have ever tasted the lovely lightness of a true Pinot Noir, except perhaps in the rare estate-bottling from a smaller producer, so the California Pinot Noirs are usually a surprise. Even so, many of the wines from older vineyards lack distinction, having been planted from mediocre stocks. The new certified vines now beginning to bear should produce better wines. Outstanding producers include:

> *Louis Martini*
> *Beaulieu Vineyard*
> *Robert Mondavi*
> *Freemark Abbey*

SERVING PINOT NOIR: This fragrant, fruity wine complements stews, broiled meats, particularly beef, and fowl served with rich sauces,

---

* Yield in the greatest Burgundy vineyards is limited by law to 321 gallons of wine per acre; while those wines bearing township names are permitted a yield of 374 gallons per acre.

especially duck and wild fowl. It is a fine wine to serve with cheese, particularly as a second wine, following a Zinfandel or one of the Gamays.

ZINFANDEL

About 21,000 acres in bearing.

Zinfandel is unique. The most widely planted grape in California, it is a wayward scion of some European parent as yet unknown, producing exceptional wines in cool vineyards of the North Coast counties and the most ordinary wine, good for nothing but blending, in the hot valleys. In good hands it produces a full wine with considerable fruitiness that is ready to drink within two years of the vintage. In the Napa Valley the wine has a deep color and light, fresh taste that reminds some of wild raspberries and others of blackberries. This might lead one to believe that it is related to wines of the Rhone, but experts deny this.

What makes Zinfandel so unusual is that when a bottle is allowed to age for six years or so, it develops an elegant, balanced quality easily confused with a Cabernet Sauvignon — a definite claretlike taste with a certain woodsy quality, perhaps reminiscent of the smell of fresh mushrooms. This might lead one to expect that the Zinfandel is related to wines of Bordeaux, but experts also deny this.

Despite the mystery of its origin, Zinfandel produces two of the best wines of California, outranked only by the Cabernets and Pinot Noirs — but only when grown in cool North Coast vineyards. When drunk as a young wine, it is probably unsurpassed in California, and only equaled by the Gamay Beaujolais. When drunk as an old wine — perhaps ten years after the vintage — it is like no other, resembling Cabernets in dryness and elegance, but retaining a richness all its own. Zinfandel is a wine to buy regularly, hoping that a bottle will be overlooked so that it can be drunk when old.

Expert opinion agrees that the following producers offer outstanding wines:

Louis Martini
Charles Krug

Buena Vista
Inglenook
Simi

SERVING ZINFANDEL: The wine for all seasons — but only from a top producer of the North Coast counties — Zinfandels complement all meats and fowl that are roasted or stewed. Young Zinfandels go well with all manner of sauced dishes — the pastas and risottos of Italy, the ragoûts of France, the roasts of Spain, the American barbecues. Old Zinfandels complement delicately sauced meats and grillades, particularly duck and wild fowl. A young Zinfandel is an excellent first bottle to precede an old Cabernet Sauvignon. An old Zinfandel can be served the same way, after a young one, to confound the wine lover, who will appreciate the revelation.

GAMAY NOIR OR NAPA GAMAY, GAMAY BEAUJOLAIS

*Some 1,400 acres of Gamay Noir in bearing, another 1,000 acres coming in; while 1,200 acres of Gamay Beaujolais are producing, the number will be doubled by 1976.**

The *Gamay Noir à jus blanc* produces Beaujolais, the fruitiest and most delightful young wine of France, best drunk within a year or so of the vintage. A close relative called the Napa Gamay, grown in the Napa Valley, produces a softer and fuller wine, from a similarly large bunch that ripens late. Producers believe it needs a year in cask plus a year in bottle to develop properly, but when so made it does not have the fruitiness or freshness characteristic of Beaujolais. The wine is sometimes more properly called Gamay Noir in California.

Gamay Beaujolais is a grape that produces red juice from a tight bunch that ripens early, so named by Paul Masson who brought back

* Gamay comes into its own in the Beaujolais district of Southern Burgundy, where yield of some 428 gallons per acre is permitted for wines bearing township names; some 480 gallons are permitted when the wines are labeled Beaujolais-Villages or Beaujolais Supérieur; wines simply labeled Beaujolais come from vineyards with permitted yields of 535 gallons, about 3½ tons of grapes per acre, or some 220 cases.

cuttings from Burgundy. It is now considered to be related to the Pinot Noir and should be so called. There is confusion in the vineyards, the small-yield "Gamay Beaujolais" producing a wine with perhaps more distinction than its big-producing cousin.

When experts cannot agree, the orderly are confused and the casual are delighted. What we have are two wines where there was one before — both soft and rounded, pleasingly fruity, consistently acceptable. Some will prefer the softness of the Napa Gamay at one time, the subtlety of the Gamay Beaujolais at another. Expert opinion cannot agree on the best producers, nor can they decide who makes the best rosé from Napa Gamay. My preference is for a Napa Gamay made available as young as possible, within months of bottling, and for a Gamay Beaujolais when it is nearer three years old. A casual drinker will be happy with either. The names should be changed, however.

SERVING GAMAY: As presently vinified and offered on the market, after a year in wood and another in the bottle, the Gamays are practically interchangeable, going well with dishes that are rich and full of taste. Such simple young wines go best with hearty foods. They have a particular affinity for pork dishes and for pastas with spicy sauces. A younger Napa Gamay, just bottled, would serve well with cold cuts, delicatessen, and buffet dishes like chili and macaroni and cheese. An older Gamay Beaujolais, in the bottle for two years or so, serves well with barbecues, roasts, or stews.

RED WINE GRAPES FOR THE FUTURE

For the North Coast counties, *Merlot* may prove to make an astonishing wine, but present opinion is that its use may be concentrated on improving blends. *Petite Sirah,* as it is spelled in California, produces an exceptional wine of great depth and body in the Livermore Valley, Mendocino, and elsewhere in the counties around the Bay, but most experts feel that the wines lack distinctiveness. Experts do not consider it to be the great grape of the Rhone called Syrah or Petit Syrah; it may even be related to an ill-considered grape called the Duriff. I feel that the Petite Sirah has been underrated, in any case, having been seduced by its fullness. There are 7,500 acres planted.

What a grape does in the New World is not always the same as what it has done in Europe; a not particularly distinguished Italian grape of the Piedmont, *Grignolino,* produces an exceptional light and fruity wine on some 30 acres of the Heitz vineyard. A grape of similar origin, *Charbono,* is the pride of Inglenook, although expert opinion rates it as a wine of full body and fruit, but without subtlety. *Barbera* is one of the best grapes of the Piedmont, and does even better in Napa or Sonoma, where it produces a full, fruity wine with a pleasing sharpness that is the best of the Italianesque wines of California. Much of the production from some 13,000 acres goes into blends.

In the warm vineyards of California's interior valleys, 10,000 acres of *Ruby Cabernet* show promise of producing a full and fruity wine. It is a cross between the Cabernet Sauvignon and the heavy-yielding Carignan of southern France. There are some 29,000 acres of the latter grape — spelled Carignane in California — producing an ordinary but sound wine used in blends, perhaps worth bottling as a varietal when it comes from Sonoma vineyards.

In the past couple of decades, experimental plantings of hundreds of strains of European vines have been tried, such as the *Nebbiolo,* the greatest of Piedmont grapes. Only those listed here have proved particularly successful so far. There is a feeling that all successful grapes have already been discovered, but there is also an undercurrent of excitement as various crossbreedings and special selections of successful grapes are being tested. Seven of them, so far identified only by number, show great promise for the warm valleys. For the record, they are numbers 1160, 1178, 6–F, 25–F, B–15, 842, and 986. Some of them may become new wonders by the end of the decade.

For now, the following producers of such red varietals have produced wines that have attracted the attention of experts.

PETITE SIRAH
Concannon
Parducci

CHARBONO
Inglenook

RUBY CABERNET
Rubion of Paul Masson

GRIGNOLINO
Heitz

BARBERA
Louis Martini
Sebastiani

SERVING UNFAMILIAR VARIETALS: There is often a tendency to discount unknown wines simply because they are unfamiliar. Perhaps the way to enjoy them most is to treat them casually, searching for their good points and not for similarities to familiar favorites. Familiar foods that are simple in taste and not too highly seasoned will present the stranger in the best light. Such wines should be tried a few times with various meals so that there will not be too much novelty demanding attention. Steaks or chops or a roast of beef or chicken, even a savory stew or pot roast, will bring out the best of a wine. Simplest of all would be crusty bread and cheese, for almost any dry table wine tastes fine with a Brie or Camembert or Cheddar. In wine countries, when a producer wants to make his wines shine, it is common practice to serve a strong bouillon or consommé before the wine because the alkalizing effect makes just about any wine taste marvelous.

White Wines

CHARDONNAY

At least 2,000 acres in bearing in the 1973 vintage, with 2,000 more acres coming in by 1976.

The graceful, rounded wine from the Chardonnay, which produces all the fine white wines of Burgundy — from Chablis to Pouilly-Fuissé, and is part of every Champagne Cuvée — produces wines in

California that rank with the reds made from Cabernet Sauvignon. Chardonnay is the shyest of bearers, bottled about a year after the vintage, and is ready to drink a year after that. It is generally past its prime five years after the vintaging.

The grape, and its wine, is often called Pinot Chardonnay, but it is not of the Pinot family. It is most properly called, simply, Chardonnay. Some Chardonnay has been planted successfully in the Finger Lakes region of New York and the Niagara peninsula of Ontario, and these occasionally rival the soft elegancies from California. Expert opinion ranks the following as outstanding, although most producers make excellent wines:

> *Hanzell Vineyards*
> *Stony Hill*
> *Beaulieu Vineyard*
> *Charles Krug Winery*
> *Wente Bros.*
> *Robert Mondavi*

SERVING CHARDONNAY: Elegant and fruity Chardonnay, the best white wine of California, graces almost any dish made with fish, seafood, or cheese, or goes with cold dishes from the buffet. It is unsurpassed with lobster or crab and with dishes that have a rich cream sauce. Many prefer it to a red wine when it is served with simply cooked chicken or turkey, with ham or other spiced meats, and with pork chops or roasts. This versatile wine is excellent with curries and with many dishes of the Oriental cuisines.

RIESLING, WHITE RIESLING, JOHANNISBERG RIESLING

About 2,000 acres in bearing; plus 600 acres coming into production by 1976.

A confusion of names sharply limits popular awareness of this light, dry, flowery wine that has a beautiful balance of freshness and fruit. The Riesling grape produces all the great wines of the Rhine and Moselle. When it was transplanted elsewhere, it came to be called Johannisberger Riesling, after the famous Rheingau vineyard. In Switzerland, the grape so called was actually the Sylvaner.

A lesser grape of the Rhine, the Sylvaner is also called Franken Riesling in Germany, partly to identify the informing vine planted in Franconia and partly to cash in on the reputation of the true Riesling. Other vines have Riesling tacked onto their names, so California legal minds decided that it was lawful to market wines from the Sylvaner as "Riesling."

California growers took to calling the great Rhineland grape Johannisberg Riesling, so identifying it on labels. To clear things up, experts at the Davis research center of the University of California decided the best name for wine and grape was White Riesling; this is now the authorized name. Producers market the wine as Johannisberg Riesling but call it White Riesling in discussions.

No matter what one chooses to call it, the wine is ready to drink two years after the vintage and past its prime after five years. It ranks close to the Chardonnay in excellence, and expert opinion ranks the following as outstanding:

> *Beaulieu Vineyard*
> *Souverain Cellars*
> *Charles Krug Winery*

SERVING RIESLING: The elegant freshness and floweriness of the true Riesling makes it one of the few table wines that is drunk by itself as a refreshing drink. It is the wine to open when something different is wanted, the way one opens a bottle of Champagne, but without the to-do. No wine seems to go so well with hearty sandwiches from the delicatessen, a light lunch or a fancy one, a late snack or an evening party. It is delicious with ham and other smoked or spicy meats or salty foods. Creamy dishes with pronounced tastes, and many Oriental dishes are complemented by a well-chilled Riesling. It is particularly enchanting with fish or seafood served with sauces, particularly those that have a sweet savor, like scallops or shrimp or lobster. It is an excellent wine to serve with aspics or mousses, with hot hors d'oeuvres and with vol-au-vent. No wine tastes better with sausages or with picnic foods, particularly when these have some lightness or delicacy; heartier versions might call for Sylvaners or Gewürztraminers.

SAUVIGNON BLANC AND SÉMILLON

About 1,100 acres of each in bearing, with perhaps twice as much coming into fruit by 1976.

Together, these two grapes produce the flowery Graves and the rich Sauternes and Barsacs of Bordeaux. Alone, the Sauvignon Blanc produces the flowery, fresh wines of the Upper Loire, where the grape is called the Blanc-Fumé. Both produce dry and excellent wines in cool vineyards of the North Coast counties; the Sémillon is somewhat softer than most white wines, the Sauvignon somewhat drier and more distinctive. In overall quality, they rank with the red wines from Zinfandel. Both are ready to drink two years after the vintage and are past their primes when five years old. When picked late and vinified together, they produce a light and flowery sweet wine with some of the richness of Sauternes, which is always sweet. Because of this, wines from these grapes are usually designated as dry or sweet on the label; when no such identification appears, the wines are dry.

Expert opinion identifies the following as outstanding producers of Sauvignon Blanc:

> *Wente Bros.*
> *Christian Brothers*
> *Concannon*
> *Mirassou*
> *Robert Mondavi (as Fumé Blanc)*

Expert opinion identifies the following as an outstanding producer of Sémillon:

> *Wente Bros.*

SERVING SAUVIGNON BLANC AND SÉMILLON: Wines from these two grapes are soft and flowery, with a springlike freshness that lends itself to foods with a certain delicacy or lightness of flavor, such as simply cooked fish or seafood and dishes served with light sauces. They are excellent wines for luncheon or the buffet, good to serve with a delicate first course that might be followed by a roast and a bottle of Cabernet Sauvignon or Pinot Noir. They are particularly good with dishes that incorporate ham, tongue, or other lightly smoked or spiced meats.

PINOT BLANC AND SYLVANER

Perhaps 600 acres of Pinot Blanc in bearing, with another 200 acres coming into fruit by 1976. Perhaps 1,200 acres of Sylvaner in bearing, with another hundred acres producing by 1976.

The Pinot Blanc is a secondary grape of Burgundy, producing a superior white wine in California, with a good bouquet and distinctive fruitiness. The Sylvaner is a secondary grape of the Rhine, producing an excellent and fruity wine in California that is light, fresh, and short-lived, best drunk within two or three years of the vintage.

The wines are quite dissimilar but are on a par, ranking in overall quality perhaps just below the red wines from the Zinfandel. The Pinot Blanc is slightly longer-lived, still sound after four years, and perhaps somewhat superior to the Sylvaner, which is usually called "Riesling" on its labels.

Expert opinion lists the following as an outstanding producer of Pinot Blanc:

Wente Bros.

Expert opinion lists the following as outstanding producers of Sylvaner:

Buena Vista
Louis Martini
Mirassou

SERVING PINOT BLANC AND SYLVANER: These attractive wines complement fish and seafood dishes particularly, the Pinot Blanc enhancing those of simple taste, the Sylvaner enhancing those with heartier flavors. They are excellent with cold meats when the more distinctive and authoritative tastes of the Chardonnay or Johannisberg Riesling might be considered too pronounced. They are fine for casual drinking, when the urge comes for a glass of wine. They are good wines to serve when you cannot make up your mind — with a choucroûte garnie, for instance, or spaghetti with clam sauce or tuna fish salad.

CHENIN BLANC OR WHITE PINOT

About 5,000 acres in bearing, with an additional 7,500 acres coming into fruit by 1976.

Chenin Blanc produces the fruity and flowery wines of the middle Loire — Vouvray, Anjou, and Saumur — and in California the grape produces fresh and flowery wines. For no good reason, it is often called White Pinot in California and is so marketed. It is extensively used in blends, particularly those marketed as "Chablis," under which name it has established such demand that producers hesitate to switch over to the varietal name. The grape is also known as Pineau de la Loire, and is so marketed by The Christian Brothers. Expert opinion lists the following producers as outstanding:

> *Inglenook White Pinot*
> *Louis Martini Mountain Dry Chenin Blanc*
> *Charles Krug Chenin Blanc*
> *Robert Mondavi*
> *Mirassou*

SERVING CHENIN BLANC: Here is a white wine for any time. Drunk often in blends but rarely under its grape name, it is the perfect wine to have when some white wine will taste good. The wine complements all sorts of fish and seafood and other light dishes, particularly those with spicy savors or those incorporating ham or other smoked meats.

OTHER WHITE WINE GRAPES

In the early sixties, California produced few white wines of much distinction. The wines lacked acidity and were bland, with little freshness and light bouquets. Wente Bros. produced superior wines from the Sauvignon Blanc and Sémillon, others had perhaps 600 acres planted in Sylvaner for use in blends or to be marketed as "Riesling." All other top varietals together numbered less than 500 acres.

Producers in the Napa Valley, like the Mondavi Brothers at Charles Krug, Louis Martini, and a few others became convinced that good white wines could be made, and extensive plantings were begun in 1959. More than 800 acres were planted that year, a third in Chenin Blanc, and the effort continued throughout the decade. Results were spectacular. California was thirsty for dry white wines, so much so that few bottles were getting out of the state by the end of the decade, and most of it is still drunk there. Planting continues.

A few other white wines have West Coast popularity. There are now some 1,000 acres of *Gray Riesling,* a misnamed grape that is probably the Chauché Gris, of small acclaim, which produces a pleasant little wine that is fashionable in San Francisco. There is a similar grape called *Emerald Riesling* and another of indefinite origin called *Green Hungarian.* These are of passing interest.

The *Folle Blanche* of the Loire makes a fresh light wine in California; the *Veltliner* of Austria is pleasantly spicy, but plantings are less than 300 acres.

There are almost 1,000 acres of the Traminer grape of Alsace, now mostly called *Gewürztraminer* (which means "spicy Traminer") and coming from a strain that produces a particularly spicy, fruity wine.

Wines vary widely from vintage to vintage and are exceptional from time to time. Any of these may become nationally popular during the seventies, but emphasis is more apt to be concentrated on the varieties described in detail above. There is extensive experiment with crossbreeds and special strains, and by the end of the decade, at least one of these may be successful, to become the sensation of the eighties.

Rosé Wines

GRENACHE ROSÉ

Some 13,000 acres in bearing, with an additional 300 acres coming into fruit by 1976.

The Grenache produces the best pink wine of France, Tavel, and does spectacularly in cool districts of California, where its rosé is the match of any in the world. The wine is light, fresh, and fragrant. Almadén was instrumental in making the wine popular nationally, and now there are several good producers.

The red grapes are crushed and then separated from the skins before the fermenting wine picks up too much color. Several of the grapes that do well in California are made into pink wines, following European practice. These include the Gamay, Cabernet Sauvignon, Zinfandel, and Grignolino. All of them are invariably superior to blends from other grapes that are simply marketed as rosés, although some houses make blends of superior grapes. All of them are best drunk when young, within a year or two of the vintage.

The following selections are outstanding:

GRENACHE ROSÉ
Almadén
Souverain Cellars

GAMAY ROSÉ
Inglenook Navalle
Martini Mountain

GRIGNOLINO ROSÉ
Heitz Winery

CABERNET ROSÉ
Beaulieu Beaurosé
Buena Vista Rose Brook

ZINFANDEL ROSÉ
Nichelini
Concannon

SERVING ROSÉ: Considered an indeterminate wine by most wine buffs, possessing little of the distinction of reds or whites, rosés are pleasant enough to drink when others cannot be found. They are touted as going well with all sorts of food, but they serve best as substitutes for white wine.

The Professors

The world of wine spins around winemakers, but in recent years a new group has been heard from. They are causing a revolution, and you will find them at Davis, the town around the spread of the University of California's branch campus, a little west of Sacramento. This hotbed is a crosshatch of streets edged with an irrigation of greenery, and behind the parking lots, surrounded by new buildings, are offices and labs of the wine research center.

Here, a gaggle of professors leads an international group of some thirty students through a three-year course in enology. The old buildings are not covered by vines — there are some experimental plantings nearby and others all over the state — but beside one of them is a still, the only American college to be so endowed. There is also a winery, a cellar containing thousands of different wines, and a nursery for vines. Staff and students taste wines every day as part of their work.

There is a similar wine college at Geisenheim in Germany, another at Montpellier in France, and others of less renown elsewhere in Europe, Australia, and South Africa. The professors are forever traveling from one to another, telling what they know, finding out what they do not know. At graduation the students scatter to every major wine region on earth, but the majority finally settle down with the vines of California.

The vines were the first big problem in California. With them, the revolution began.

Many vineyards disappeared during Prohibition. Many of those that did not switched to growing Alicante Bouschet, a grape that makes nasty wine but has a tough skin that makes it easy to ship. Proper wine grapes have thin skins (slip skins), but bootleggers in the East preferred the tough variety. Their dark skins could color so much water that as many as 700 gallons of liquid could be obtained from a ton of grapes, according to Maynard Amerine, long the professor of enology at Davis.

With Repeal, there was much replanting, often in nondescript varieties. Amerine and associates scrambled around the state to persuade growers to plant the best vines. Few listened. By 1938 there was a glut. The state bailed out the growers by fostering a distilling program. This would have led to a glut of brandy but the flood was used up during World War II, saving many from bankruptcy. After the war, growers began to hearken to the professors — not that there was much to hear.

A. J. Winkler, professor of viticulture, had done what he could, classifying the havoc in the wake of Haraszthy, trying to make sense of the odd varieties he found everywhere. Stocks of the best vines were started in the nurseries, beginning with a single bud, or clone, to get superior vines. But there weren't enough to go around.

At least two years are needed to get such an initial planting going. This becomes the foundation block, the single source of cuttings for mother blocks, which then become the single source for increase blocks, cuttings from which are used to establish a vineyard. Getting your planting stock can take as much as a decade.

Once the stocks are in the vineyard, they take four years to come to bearing, and they may need six before producing a crop of mature grapes. If they are red wine grapes, another two or three years in cask and at least as long in bottle will be needed before anyone can tell whether the wine will be good. And this takes time, perhaps another decade from planting the new vine to tasting the maturing wine. Clones set out in the fifties have produced scions going into vineyards in the seventies. Growers had to put a lot of faith in Winkler, Amerine and friends to allow planting of mother blocks on their land. Suppose the vines weren't right for the climate? For years, everybody had been saying California had no vintages because the climate was so nice. Unlike Europe, grapes ripened every year — and then some. Grapes from noble vines ripened too much, losing their fruit acids, making bland wines with little bouquet. The interior valleys were so hot that only ordinary vines would grow there. New varieties were needed to match the climate, and for that a breakdown of the state into viticultural zones was needed.

California stretches for nearly 800 miles, about as long as Italy and much like it in climate, ranging from almost tropical desert to alpine cold. Growing areas had to be matched to European equivalents.

Region One, with daily temperatures averaging between 62° and 65° during the four-month growing season, was like the Rhine or Moselle, Champagne or Chablis.

Region Two, three degrees warmer — up to 68° — was like Bordeaux or Burgundy's Côte d'Or.

Regions Three and Four, with temperatures up to 74°, were like Italy.

Region Five, 74° to 80°, was like Algeria.

The professors said it was all a matter of heat summation, measured in degree days. The vine needs 50° temperatures in which to grow during its four-month season. What you did was to note the number of degrees over that and add them up. Suppose June averaged 60°. This excess of 10° multiplied by the days of the month gives you 300° days. Region One averaged out to under 2,500° days over a seven-month growing season; Region Two was not much over that. The noble vines grow best in these regions, the climates of the North Coast counties.

All such particularity stirred up the growers, but what really moved them were the nematodes. These were worms that sucked juice out of the roots, giving the vines viruses in the same way mosquitoes transmit malaria. This reduced yields. The professors found they could kill the virus by keeping root stocks in a mist chamber at 100° for as long as a hundred days. Cabernet, which had a low yield of less than three tons an acre, might double production if the vines were virus free. The clincher came in 1968, when the price of Cabernet rose to nearly four hundred dollars a ton. Everybody who could began planting the new vines — and counting on large yields.

Meanwhile, back at the wineries, even better things were happening. In the fifties few winemakers really understood the volatile changes that occur during fermentation. Scientists claim to have known all about them for fifty years, of course, but the knowing was locked up in the laboratories or in journals. In the fifties, winemakers were just getting around to chemical analysis and precise control of fermentation.

Pasteur described fermentation a century ago as taking place without the presence of air, anaerobically; the process was later described as the action of enzymes by which sugar is changed to alcohol and water, releasing carbon dioxide as a by-product. This is the use by yeast organisms of carbohydrates, something called the Embden-Meyerhof pathway. Dr. Amerine once described fermentation as "essentially a process of reversible inter- and intra-molecular oxidation-reductions, phosphorylations and an irreversible decarboxylation." And he goes on from there.

You can see what fun Davis can be, if you go in for that sort of thing. Having to talk to growers and winemakers, the professors have learned to state things simply — in this case — "Don't let the pot get hot."

They're freezing the wines in California, said Europeans, just as they used to say Burgundians boiled the wines in those days when some of the juice was warmed to get the ferment started. Cooling coils were put in the vats to keep down the temperature so that reactions producing unwanted volatile acidity would not take place. Fermentation was smooth, even, and complete, the yeast thus producing "more esters and other aromatic bodies," said Amerine.

Winemakers were delighted, having a great need for aromatic bodies — anything that would give taste and bouquet to the wine.

Yeast action, for instance. Various yeasts act at different stages of alcoholic concentration during fermentation, producing esters. Special strains of yeast aid the action; so-called wild yeasts on the skin of the grapes add more aromatic bodies. In short, the action could be controlled, and during the sixties, a collection of minute discoveries was put into practice to make good wines, first in California and gradually in other places around the world. One thousand years of winemaking research was compressed into ten years, it might be said. Just so, one thousand years of vine culture research was compressed into the same decade, to be put into practice during the seventies.

With the mysteries of winemaking under control, the mastery of vine tending remains. Vine management, as it is called, has much to do with pruning, trellising, working the soil, combatting insect and fungal diseases, harvesting technique, and suiting the grape to the microclimate. This last is the local, seasonal, even weekly, change in a particular vineyard. Grapes develop differently in a cool Region One than they do in a warm Region One, for instance. Morning fog, afternoon breezes, rainfall, exposure to sun — everything makes for differences in the wine. And what if noble vines could be brought to good bearing in the hot interior valleys?

There are 15,000 acres of quality vines in Napa and Sonoma, and suppose that could be increased to 25,000 with replantings? Consumption has stayed at a gallon per capita for years, nothing compared to the thirty gallons drunk each year by the French. Suppose it increased? We will have 300,000,000 Americans by the end of the century, and we'll need 75,000 acres of grapes, says Lloyd Lider, former professor of viticulture at Davis. He starts ticking off gallons on his fingers.

The total Napa Valley production is roughly 30,000 tons, to be increased by 7,000 tons by shifting to better varieties, a task that will be completed before the end of the decade. "Another five or six thousand tons will come by shifting out of prunes," says Lider.

"Maybe we can open new areas in Napa, get as much as another thousand acres in the hills to the east. That's three thousand more tons by the end of the decade. But we are still not sure of quality, so we are moving slowly." The price of Cabernet hit $600 in 1970.

To the north is the Russian River country of Mendocino, to the south is the Salinas Valley of San Benito county, and if these areas added another 10,000 acres to the total, there would be scarcely half of what is needed. Of all the 220,000 acres of vineyard in California, some two-thirds lie in the Great Central Valley and in the San Joaquin, south of Sacramento, and west of Los Angeles, around San Bernardino. New vines must go in the old vineyards. Driving along in the heat on Route 99, or swinging east on Route 66, there are vineyards everywhere, among the peach orchards and citrus groves, but most of them are for raisins or table grapes, more than 300,000 acres of them. The price of Cabernet hit $1,000 in 1972.

You can taste the problem at Davis. Talk of vinification and acreage and grape varieties suddenly takes on meaning as we all become explorers in the new world of wines.

Here is a Barbera, from the grape of the Italian Piedmont, not much bouquet, but full and fruity, with a good sharpness. Here is a Carignan, not distinctive, but sound, and here is Carignan crossed with Cabernet and called Ruby Cabernet, with some fruitiness and roundness. You have to taste the differences.

It takes time to get things right.

PART TWO

*Wines
and
Winemakers
of America*

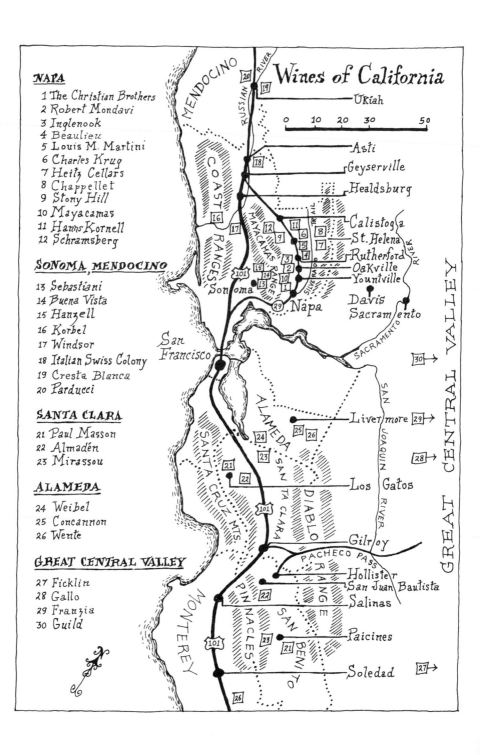

Wines of California

NAPA

1 The Christian Brothers
2 Robert Mondavi
3 Inglenook
4 Beaulieu
5 Louis M. Martini
6 Charles Krug
7 Heitz Cellars
8 Chappellet
9 Stony Hill
10 Mayacamas
11 Hanns Kornell
12 Schramsberg

SONOMA, MENDOCINO

13 Sebastiani
14 Buena Vista
15 Hanzell
16 Korbel
17 Windsor
18 Italian Swiss Colony
19 Cresta Blanca
20 Parducci

SANTA CLARA

21 Paul Masson
22 Almadén
23 Mirassou

ALAMEDA

24 Weibel
25 Concannon
26 Wente

GREAT CENTRAL VALLEY

27 Ficklin
28 Gallo
29 Franzia
30 Guild

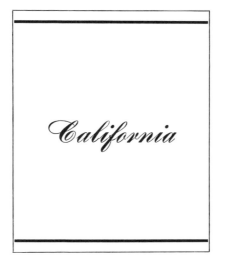

California

San Francisco is a great place for a wine buff to live. The city drinks ten times as much wine as the rest of the state, which consumes three times the national average and more European wines than any other. The city drinks all but a trickle of the best vintages from the North Coast counties. For the same reasons, an Easterner who has to go home after a few sips finds San Francisco a terrible place to visit.

From a distance, the wine center of America looks like a midden of oyster shells, a chalky mound bright in the sun or looming in its fogs. The northern thrust of a coastal range flanked by ocean and bay, the city is linked to eastern valleys by the Oakland Bridge and to those of the redwood country farther north by the long loop of the Golden Gate. Wine valleys lie an hour away, across the bridge or down the peninsula. At Christmas natives jaunt out to buy their trees, hauling them home atop their cars. In other seasons, expeditions are for wines, in much the way a New Yorker drives up to

Westchester for a jug of cider or a bushel of apples. Visitors fresh from the East know little of this.

An Eastern wine buff, perhaps one who drinks no more than a bottle or so a week and buys the odd case during spring and fall sales, may have his mind made up about California wines. Maybe he buys Mountain Red or Mountain White for everyday drinking. He may have tasted other California wines over the years and found them bland and light in body — lacking in acid, lacking in bouquet, somehow short in the tasting, without lingering overtones. Price for price, he's apt to choose a European regional over a California varietal. No reason to expect a San Francisco trip to change him.

Wines are something you buy in a shop, and a curious Easterner may poke his nose into Esquin's or The City of Paris to see what's there. All the big producers, of course — Gallo and Guild, Roma and Cresta Blanca, Petri and Italian Swiss — but mostly their table wines, plus a dozen other names in the same price range that he's never heard of.

He may be used to seeing a bottle or two on the shelves from producers known for varietals, but here is the whole line from Almadén and Paul Masson, from Inglenook and Beaulieu, from Charles Krug and Buena Vista, from Martini and Wente. There must be a dozen from the Christian Brothers, and a flock more whose names ring a bell because they have been mentioned in articles or books.

Bemused, a visitor may decide to try a bottle with dinner in Ernie's or Doro's, or maybe Trader Vic's. The Trader is noted for his rum drinks but he is also a wine enthusiast and his list has a dozen pages of North Coast vintages. All the famous ones are there, but so are Hanzell and Heitz, Stony Hill and Souverain, Mondavi and Korbel, Mayacamas and Freemark, Concannon, and Mirassou. The Trader is apt to go overboard, being an enthusiast, so a visitor may dismiss the matter. But the next day, in Chinatown — at the Imperial Palace, perhaps — he will be startled to see that the list has a dozen sparkling wines, half a dozen rosés from different grapes, a dozen white varietals, nine reds — and all up front, not buried in the back the way California wines are in Eastern wine lists. Over in Berkeley, at the Pot Luck, they have more than seventy different

Cabernets going back to 1940, thirty Pinot Noirs, and scores of others. There is not a decent restaurant in the Bay area that does not have a dozen of California's best.

There is no doubt the wines were lousy for generations, but there have been a few good ones getting better for a quarter of a century now, and the last decade has produced some marvels that are beginning to be shipped out of the state. People now notice the elegance that has come into North Coast wines, a light balance that comes from complete control of vinification. They have begun to seek them out. Visitors are welcomed at more than one hundred California wineries today, the winemakers carrying on a tradition that goes back to Roman days when the vintner stuck up a vine on a pole to signify that his wine was ready. The winemaker may have a dozen acres or a thousand, a few hundred dollars' worth of equipment or a few million. No matter. His reputation rises or falls on what is in the bottles. Everything is judged by this.

The best winemakers are worth a special trip. A month would scarcely be time enough to cover all of the best, and there are other things to see, from the redwoods to the sierras. What's needed is a list, and by tasting a wine or two from a producer, you get some idea of what the rest are like. There are difficulties. A winemaker may offer a selection of varietals, some good wines in short supply, several good blends. I have selected from major wineries a few of their best varietals — wines not to be missed. There are no generics listed, although one or another may be mentioned in the text, because such blends may vary. There's only one rule to keep in mind.

Good winemakers make good wines.

The Napa Valley

The way to Napa lies over the Golden Gate, north on 101, over a roadway tangle that snarls around a dock and warehouse clutter and strings up to stilted bungalows on sugarloaf hills, mostly ever-brown but tufted with evergreen of live oak and eucalyptus. San Francisco billows beyond the waterfront, across the Bay, then the highway swings into countryside, past the wide-arched galleries built by Frank Lloyd Wright for Marin County bureaucracy. Hardtops branch off around marshes at the top of the Bay, and one of them leads over foothills of the Mayacamas range to Napa, an Indian word for plenty.

Napa used to be the mouth of the cornucopia that is its valley. Fruits and vegetables came down by train; now the produce is mostly wine, hauled by truck, but Napa is still a market town, with business streets leading out past shaded houses into the broad valley, where a highway cuts up to the vineyard towns — Yountville, Oakville, Rutherford, St. Helena, Calistoga — a distance of fifteen miles. Napa now serves the needs of people escaping the city, who build houses in the hills. There is a large country club complex over east where visitors are put up, called the Silverado because it is near the Silverado Trail, the old stagecoach route. Now mostly repaved, the trail runs along the edge of the valley and leads to a string of mountain vineyards. On the west are the Redwood Hills leading up to the Mayacamas Mountains, with more mountain vineyards. These mountain vineyards are considered to be in Region One.

The Carneros area, south and west of Napa, was early planted in grapes, but came to be considered too cool for them. There is a tempering influence from the northern round of bay, San Pablo, a receptacle for rivers — the Sacramento and San Joaquin, the Petaluma and Napa — and many creeks. Cool air currents sweep down from the mountain and in from the ocean, bringing fog. It is a cool Region One, where clonal selections of Pinot Noir and White Riesling,* stocks propagated from hardy buds, are coming into bearing. Louis Martini has replanted one of the original vineyards; Beaulieu Vineyards and the Christian Brothers have more. Harold Berg can hardly wait. Trained as a chemist, he has been experimenting at Davis for over twenty years, watching as particularly fruitful vines were tagged in the vineyards, then propagated in the nurseries. One of his jobs has been to find optimum conditions for various varieties — to match selected stocks to the microclimates. Varieties adapt well

---

* The true Riesling of the Rhine is called White Riesling by Davis viticulturists, to distinguish it from other varieties that are legally allowed the regal name. Producers bottle the wines with Johannisberg Riesling on the label. Eventually, when the law is put in order, such wines may be called simply and properly Riesling.

when the soil drains well, and exposure to sun is good, but the range is narrow.

Grapes start growing when the average temperature rises above 50°, says Berg, but in "little climates" one vineyard may have a daily average of 65, which is not at all the same as another vineyard averaging 75. Early bearers may ripen in ninety days; late bearers can take more than twice as long, and these must be matched to climates in the vineyards.

Morning sun is fine for vines, drying up the dew, but grapes suffer from sunburn when temperatures get over 100°. A canopy of leaves will protect the bunches, making the shade as much as 20° cooler. By trellising, a vineyard can be shifted down an entire region. Screening the vines or spraying them with water can cause a similar drop. Water spraying can also be used to fight frost. When ice forms, a couple of calories of heat are given up, which is enough to keep the vines from freezing. The leaves may be coated with ice, but this acts as a shield. Smudge pots and giant fans are used when the expensive spraying systems are not installed. Combinations of these methods are used to ward off heat and cold. Add clonal selection of vines to the array, and Berg and friends get excited about Carneros.

Farther up the valley, vineyards all the way to Oakville are in Region One, with temperatures like those of the Rhine or Burgundy's Chablis. From Oakville to St. Helena the vineyards are in Region Two and this middle section is the heart of the Napa Valley, with temperatures like Burgundy or Bordeaux—but with a difference.

The noble vines found their natural abodes in Europe, after centuries of tasting. There is probably not a foot of arable land in France that has not been tried for growing grapes. Generations of vignerons tasted vintage after vintage, matching vine care to each swerve of soil, making wines to bring out a bit more color, a more elegant bouquet, a greater subtlety or depth of taste. After centuries of drinking and talking, the slightest of distinctions was isolated. They were preserved, even heightened, during the intricate process that led from vine to glass. Chambertin was noted for its rich color and depth of taste, Musigny for elegance, the Romanées for breed and balance. So it went, and goes, in the outstanding vineyards of

Burgundy, of Bordeaux, of the Rhine. Such precision is being sought in Napa.

Grapes develop a collection of yeasts, many desirable, that cling to the powdery film on the skins. These are called wild yeasts, which can live in the soil as well as on the grapes. Most of them work, during ferment, when the alcohol converted from sugar in the juice is about 5 percent or less. Yeast cultures that give a complete fermentation are now generally used, hopefully not so much that they totally inhibit the action of wild yeast, many of which impart overtones of taste to the wine. The action of the wild yeasts and of other trace elements produces other sorts of microclimate — in the vineyards and during the winemaking process. Such infinitesimals produce distinctions in the wine.

The workings of these yeasts have been pretty well mastered, certainly when it comes to grape varieties and little climates, and this is why the general quality of wines all over the world is improving. All of it is quite complicated, and the microclimate of yeast action is still elusive, so fine wines remain a product of art as well as craft, and may always remain so. In the Napa Valley, as in all of California, superior strains of noble vines are planted under amenable conditions, but noble varieties are planted together in blocks so that any homogeneity of wild yeasts is never developed. Better yeast colonies may develop because Pinot and Cabernet and Riesling are grown as neighbors, but nobody knows this for sure.

Napa winemakers are forever discussing their wines in terms of complexity of taste, a subtlety they seek because this is a characteristic of great wines. It is enough for most that the wines be good in all respects, living long enough to develop a range of secondary characteristics. But there is a third realm of wonder, and many winemakers seek it. It is there, somewhere in the processes of the microclimates. You can taste it in many of the wines of California, particularly in Napa.

Subtleties may simply involve good care and following the rules of custom, of the laboratory, and of common sense. There are many who are almost convinced that it is a matter of following what has been learned about techniques of oak storage, of time in bottle, of attention to detail — and not in the actions of wild yeasts or the effects of certain soils or other minutiae.

They are almost convinced. An old saw in the vineyards is that the wine makes itself, and man only guards it. No matter. The scientists will continue unraveling what mysteries they can. Meanwhile, there are some splendid guardians of wines to seek out in the Napa Valley.

THE CHRISTIAN BROTHERS

Tasting hasn't changed. You start with the young wines and then work back. You can start in the cellar with last year's vintage, standing in the damp gloom as the cellarmaster draws off from the cask wine that may still be working. It's cold — about 50° winter and summer. Not much light — even electric light is bad for wine — just a bulb here and there, so you won't stumble over hoses or the pumps and filters that are trundled about, and so you can hold your glass up against the light to see if the wine is clear and bright. It's wet — there's always something being washed down because winemaking uses lots of water to keep things clean, but it never gets into the wine — and there's a trickle here and there, maybe a gurgle from the wine.

You swirl the glass, holding it by the base, not the stem, to get a better swing. The inch of wine rolls around in a whirlpool. You stick your nose into the glass — mostly chimney so the vapors won't escape — inhale deeply to note what the wine is like, to detect anything unpleasant. You sip a teaspoonful, then suck in air around it so that it bounces all over your mouth. Then you spew it into the gutter and wait, as the taste changes, disappears. You taste another, then another.

You may start with bottled wines, a row of them set out on a table, glasses before each. You start at the left and go along the row in the order set for you, sniffing first, whistling in a mouthful, spitting each into a sink or bucket, noting the colors and the clarity as you go. Nobody speaks to you, except to answer questions or to tell you which vineyard the wine came from, how long it stayed in wood or has been in bottle, what the degree of alcohol is, some detail of its fermentation. Nobody asks you what you think — it's not polite — no one tries to sneak a look at your notes. Sometimes the bottles are laid out on the kitchen table or in a little tasting room, but these days more and more of the tasting is done in the laboratory, just beyond the winemaker's office, where all the technical notes are handy. At the Christian Brothers it is done in the lab, at Mont La Salle.

The Christian Brothers have been offering their wines for tasting ever since they first came to California a century ago. Usually someone conducts a tour of the winery, sketchy or extensive, and then guides you to a tasting room for sampling, where you can buy a few bottles if you want. More people come today, and many wineries have teams of guides. The Christian Brothers offer tours and samplings at their Greystone Cellars in St. Helena, where wines are aged and sparkling wines are made in one of the largest buildings in the world. There are occasional tours in the storehouses south of town and up on Mont La Salle.

The Redwood Road winds up into the Mayacamas Mountains, eight miles north and west of Napa, coming out near the tops at a low stone administration building, with the square bulk of the winery nudging into the side of the hill just behind. There are vineyards all around, two hundred acres of the thousand planted in varietals that are owned by the order in the Napa Valley. On a ridge to the east is the novitiate, a great, long building at anchor among the rolling vines, where men study to become Brothers of the Christian schools. The order was founded in 1680 by Jean Baptiste de la Salle in Reims, the cathedral city of the Champagne country. Its purpose was to educate the poor, and the teaching order now has headquarters in Rome. The brothers are not Catholic priests, but laymen who have taken vows of poverty, chastity, and obedience. They maintain nearly nine score schools in the United States, among them Manhattan College in New York and La Salle Military Academy on Long Island, mostly maintained by the sale of wines.

Brother Timothy arrived in 1935 to oversee the vintages at a time when America was mostly interested in fortified wines, sweet and strong, produced at the Mount Tivy winery and vineyards in the San Joaquin Valley. For the first twenty years, much of Brother

Timothy's concern was with such production, and with that of sacramental wines, bottled at Mont La Salle. With the fifties came a growing demand for table wines, and a range of generics was placed on the market. He did not like their names.

After the blight of Prohibition, during which so many noble vines were replaced by more productive grapes that could be used for the table, raisins, or distilling, the bulk of table wines were marketed simply as Burgundy, Rhine Wine, and so on. The Christian Brothers were lucky, having been able to keep their noble vines for their sacramental wines, but they continued the practice of generic labeling.

"Nobody really has any business using such names," says Brother Tim, "but it is a matter of the sins of the fathers being visited on the sons. We have vastly extended our varietal plantings over the last couple of decades, and now what we market as Chablis gets its taste mostly from Chenin Blanc. But the market is so large for our blend called Chablis that we would lose much of it by changing the name." Generic names are a poor tradition; there are many such in the world of wines, and they want to get rid of them one day. In any case, they now market Chenin Blanc under its grape name. The Christian Brothers are developing their own names for blends of wines, like the flowery sweet white wines called Chateau La Salle, and varietal wines from grapes grown in their vineyards called "estate bottled." They even include the number of the particular lot it comes from, the *cuvée,* or vat number, so people know precisely what they are getting. There is, for instance, a sprightly red wine from a variety dubbed Pinot Saint George; it is called Red Pinot by some, although it has no relation at all to any Pinot. Someday it may be called simply Saint George. A back label carefully explains what the wine is. This and other wines of the Christian Brothers consistently win gold medals at statewide wine judgings, and the Saint George earned four in four years. The significance of this is reduced by the fact that all top growers have drawers full of such awards for their best wines, but of late the brothers do seem to be winning a substantial share of the honors.

Much more significant is the tasting of the wines, particularly the Cabernet Sauvignon, Pinot Noir, and Zinfandel among the reds; the Chardonnay and Johannisberg Riesling among the whites. There was extensive planting of Chardonnay and Pinot Noir in 1968 to augment other acreage, and these vines came into full bearing by 1972, greatly increasing the availability of what the brothers call their Limited Editions.

Brother Tim particularly liked the Chardonnay that winemaker Brother John was producing and began sneaking it into the tastings held every few weeks by the Napa vintners.

Chardonnay is usually bottled after sixteen months or so. It has a tendency to get heavy and too big, and the brothers like to keep it light and round and clean, with some freshness — a green-stick freshness, you might call it — with a softness in it. Other winemakers are giving it top marks.

When Brother Tim became cellarmaster only a few of the brothers were concerned with the wines but now more than 200 people are involved in managing some 1,400 acres of Napa Valley vineyards, and another 1,000 acres in San Joaquin whose grapes are used for brandy and the fortified wines. There are long-term contracts with other growers and one of the tasks of Brother Tim's staff is constant checking of the vine management and deciding when to pick each block of grapes. Any delay between picking and crushing is bad for the wine. To simplify matters an unusual crushing and fermenting complex has been installed next to some vast new storage houses, down in the valley near Louis Martini.

The complex is in the shape of a wheel, with rows of stainless steel tanks arranged like spokes, getting shorter and smaller around toward the center. At the hub is a glass roundhouse, with a console hooked into a computer that switches the crushers on and off and controls the flow of grape juice to the various tanks. In the pilot house one can see everything that is going on and control everything from the console. There was talk about providing the console with a microphone so its operator could direct workers manning the crushers and the hoses, but with the trucks dumping grapes and the crushers pulling off stems, and the juice flowing through the hoses, nobody could hear what came from the pilot house. Bell signals are used, more or less audible above the grind, gurgle, and gush.

It's quite a system, remarkably simple, motors making it possible to handle the grapes more gently and quickly than men with hand tools. Less air and fewer bacteria come in contact with the juice to contaminate the fermentation, temperatures being controlled so that the tumultuous action does not develop unwanted qualities in the resulting wine.

The winemaking staff must come to agreement about the varying details of making the wines. Cabernets form a stringy cluster, loose on the vine; they are very hardy and dry out quickly after a rain. Pinot Noir and Chardonnay form a tight cluster no bigger than a fist — so do Sauvignon Blanc and Chenin Blanc — and wetness is a problem. Each must be vinified differently. Then there is the matter of residual sugar. Some producers of generics leave as much as 5 percent of the sugar in the fermenting must, so that the final wine will have a trace of sweetness. The brothers question this practice, as do most producers of fine varietals, and are not following the practice, even for generics produced in substantial volume for a wide market. The general feeling is that what is made can be sold readily, and while "mellowed" or softened wines may appeal to a wider market of inexperienced buyers, the wines fermented completely dry are preferable; flaws in winemaking can be hidden under sweetness.

As for Cabernets, the classic Bordeaux taste is strong of wood, from the small oak cooperage in which the wine rounds out. Here, the taste of the grape is preferred and allowed to dominate. The Cabernets spend at least three and sometimes as much as four years in wood, but the taste from the grape is preserved. Then there is the matter of Merlot and Malbec, part of the planting in many a Bordeaux vineyard. Merlot is like the Cabernet, but softer and quicker to mature, while Malbec is prompt to start its secondary fermentation. This is the malolactic fermentation that commences after the initial tumultuous fermentation has finished, and it may continue for months. An "early malic" serves to lower the acidity of the wine, and when some of it is part of a Cabernet fermentation, the whole is softened. Some such action is desirable, but the brothers tread cautiously.

The Christian Brothers do not market wines until they have rested in the bottle, where they pick up subtle secondary characteristics and compose themselves into a unity. Consequently, Cabernets are not marketed until five years after the vintage, and Chardonnays are marketed after two years. The Christian Brothers do not use vintage years to identify their wines, which is certainly a mistake when it comes to their best red varietals; vintages like 1964 and 1966 were superior in the Napa Valley, and the Christian Brothers made outstanding wines. Consumers argue that vintages on white wines are also desirable, helping them find such outstanding wines as the 1968 Chardonnay. The brothers acknowledge that there are arguments to be made for vintage dating, but one gets the feeling that they think wines are quite complicated enough for most consumers, and everything should be done to make wine drinking simple.

The winery staff are trained scientists but they are also artists, with a will to decision that is so much more than a knack or an instinct, knowing just how and when to plant or till or cultivate, the perfect moment for picking or for ending fermentation or for drawing the wine for bottling. They make their own luck. More than one grower has even suggested they get help from more remote sources, a feeling that has persisted in vineyard country ever since the Cistercians began tending vines in the Middle Ages. No matter, so long as the wine continues to be good.

The brothers are vastly helped in getting their bottles around the country by Fromm & Sichel, a distributing company that is a subsidiary of Seagram. The partners came from families with long histories on the Rhine, and had no hesitation at introducing wines in foreign markets or in encouraging the development of an expensive pot-distilled brandy to compete with French Cognacs. Wines are now in several dozen countries and as much XO Rare Reserve is sold as can be made. For years, the partners and members of the order gathered treasures to go with winemaking — goblets, pictures, drawings, books, tools — touring an exhibit to various museums each year. Now they are on display, along with a collection of more than a thousand corkscrews gathered by Brother Tim, in a handsome museum near Fisherman's Wharf. The largest producer in the Napa Valley is doing the industry proud.

A SELECTION
Pineau de la Loire
Château La Salle

Pinot Chardonnay
Cabernet Sauvignon
Gamay Noir
Pinot St. George

LLORDS & ELWOOD

Wine merchants often get carried away by enthusiasm for what they sell, but few have gone so far as Mike Elwood. Heartily encouraged by his wife and son, he sold his shops in Beverly Hills and began making fortified wines and blends, which began winning prizes at the state fairs. Further inspired, he opened three bonded wineries in San Jose and began planting 125 acres of Chardonnay and Pinot Noir up near Yountville, next to a vineyard called Oak Knoll, which is owned by a Kaiser executive who may follow Elwood's example and open a winery.

Elwood is concentrating his efforts on the vineyards, determined to make exceptional wines of the Burgundy grapes; he has equally great expectations for his Cabernet Sauvignon and White Riesling.

A SELECTION
Pinot Noir
White Riesling

OAKVILLE VINEYARDS

Californians come to wine naturally, but the prime mover behind Oakville Vineyards takes it almost as a birthright, for much of his growing up took place in Vina at the Stanford Winery, which was part of the lands managed by his father. Bud van Löben Sels, called that because his first name is Wilfred, had a banking grandfather who was Dutch consul in San Francisco. A degree in agricultural economics and an acquaintance with Louis Benoist while he was developing Almadén led to some amateur winemaking with friends, and this led to the group that in 1969 bought an old winery and some 280 acres of vineyards in Oakville. Peter Becker, the winemaker who was involved with the early Almadén expansion, had joined the group, others among the limited partners had some 600 acres, and with the 1970s the first wines began to be marketed. Then the home vineyards and the big house belonging to John Daniel's family at Inglenook came on the market and van Löben Sels formed Oakville Associates to buy that, the grapes going to Oakville Vineyards. Managed vineyards now consist of more than a thousand acres and production is projected to reach 100,000 cases in 1975. Becker has been joined by an old friend and former winemaker at Schloss Vollrads in the Rheingau, Karl Werner, who is responsible for a lightly dry Sauvignon Blanc.

The various associates in the limited partnership enjoy their relationship, taking part in the vintage and drinking their own wines. The van Löben Sels now live in the handsome old gingerbread mansion built by Gustav Niebaum, who established the Inglenook ranch, and associates are entertained on the fifteen hundred acres of gardens, groves, and mountainside trails. More importantly, however, one of the partners has observed that at a time when eastern corporations and capital were investing in the valley, Californians have taken part in the venture with the intention of preserving the California tradition.

Becker and Werner are excellent winemakers and their responsibility is to make the best wines possible, not to compete in the marketplace with larger firms, an activity which can lead to focusing on price and quantity at the expense of quality. They may be winning a part of the market almost in spite of themselves, however, because Bud and his friends expressed a desire for a dry but inexpensive wine that could be served casually. It had to be dry, fresh, fruity — just a nice wine to drink. It should come in both white and red.

The wine had to go with a sandwich. Bud and his family like picnics and over the years have worked out a sandwich that even the children like. It consists of a small square of dark bread, spread with cream cheese topped with two or three thin slices of cucumber and a good round of salami. The wine had to go with simple things like that.

It is called Our House Wine. Everybody who drinks it asks for more, particularly with that sandwich, and it costs two dollars and change. At a time when most low-priced wines are sweetish and sort of empty in taste, Oakville Vineyards is having trouble keeping up with the demand. Becker and Werner and everybody else are pleased, of course, but they wish you'd try their Zinfandel, their Gewürztraminer, their Gamay Rosé. Not to mention their Cabernet Sauvignon.

A SELECTION
Our House Wine, white and red
Sauvignon Blanc
Chenin Blanc

ROBERT MONDAVI WINERY

Suppose you had grown up in the family winery, uprooting old vines and planting new, helping with every vintage, tasting in every wine region, organizing distribution. Suppose, after thirty years, you had the chance to start from scratch, with new plantings in the best grapes, the latest equipment, a new winery laid out just so — why, it would take five years to get started, and maybe a million dollars every year. You would need long-term contracts with the best growers and technical help from expert researchers so busy they scarcely have time to answer the phone. You would have to borrow from competitors to start — everything from bottles to bins. There wouldn't be enough hours in the day. Still. . . .

Suppose you had a conviction that the curse of the California wine trade was a line of wines. The tradition was to have table wines, both varietals and generics, dessert wines like sweet Sherry and sweeter Port, appetizer wines, even Vermouth and Brandy. This made the vintage a nightmare, with maybe a score of fermentations, each requiring separate handling and all sorts of extra equipment. And suppose you were convinced that the market had become big enough and mature enough for you to concentrate all your attention and energy on perhaps a dozen of the best wines so that you could make enough of each to provide national distribution. You would need more than a fairy godmother; you would need a whole family — and a little help from your friends.

And you would need a list. It is repetitive here but worth repeating, because it shows what a master Napa Valley winemaker would do, given ideal conditions. Cabernet Sauvignon and Pinot Noir to top the reds, Chardonnay and Johannisberg Riesling to top the whites. Zinfandel and Napa Gamay for wines that would be ready to drink in three years, with some Gamay reserved for rosé. Then Sauvignon Blanc for a lightly sweet and fruity white, but as the grape can also produce a round dry white, as it does in the Loire, that would be called Fumé Blanc. Chenin Blanc for a fresh and aromatic wine; the Traminer for a spicy wine hard to handle but worth the effort. For a wine to be produced in quantity, a good blend of whites — call it Riesling, as a bow to tradition.

Pure wishful thinking, of course, to plan a new winery from scratch, but this is what Bob Mondavi has done.

Driving north from Napa on the highway that runs up the valley, the first big installation you come to after passing through Oakville, is the Robert Mondavi Winery, on the left, surrounded by vines. A tall, square tower with a red tile cap rises above a low-pitched roof that crowns a semicircle arch. Wings angle off to both sides, winery on the right, tasting rooms on the left, chalky adobe walls shaded by the tile roofs, designed by Cliff May with elements from early California mission buildings. The complex is the essence of style in modern techniques, as Bob Mondavi's wines are the essences of what traditional vines can produce using today's methods. He made his first Cabernet in 1966, 7,000 cases. There are now 300 acres in bearing, up behind the winery, another 500 coming in, near Yountville. The fairy godmother for the winery was a company that produces Rainier Beer, popular in the Northwest.

The winery is a United Nations of the wine world. The grapes are brought to a Swiss drum with an auger that pulls the stems off, then the pulp and juice are pumped into horizontal tanks from Austria, which are sealed and topped with nitrogen so that no air will come in contact. These revolve about once a minute for twenty-four hours, while the skins give color to the juice, which is kept cool so that fermentation does not begin. The mixture, called the must, then goes to a cylindrical German press, and from there to fermenting tanks built in France and the United States. White wines go directly to the press, and then to the fermenters, where temperatures are kept near 50 degrees and fermentation may last as long as a month. Red wines are now generally fermented in less than a week. From the fermenters wines pass to holding tanks to settle down. All this equipment is stainless steel, which imparts no contaminants to the wine.

The wines then pass to large oak vats, made in Germany or central Europe, and finally, for aging, to small cooperage made mostly of French oak. Corks are Spanish; bottling machines, French; labeling machines, American. Bob Mondavi makes a special point of small cooperage. This allows maximum contact between wine and wood, he says, so that one can expect an even development of complexities of bouquet and flavor. He uses Burgundy casks bound with willow for Pinot Noir and Chardonnay, German ovals for the Rieslings, the traditional casks are of Nevers oak for Cabernet. Dense-grained Yugoslavian oak is used for other wines and American oak from the Ozarks when that seems best, for each oak has its special effect on the wines.

The white wines were on the market as the decade turned, and the red wines were beginning to come in, with distribution extending gradually beyond the state. The wines disappear as fast as they appear, confirming the belief that a line is not necessary, just a few good wines.

All the Mondavi wines indicate the vintage year, so that one can tell how old the wine is.

The white wines are ready to drink as soon as they are marketed, and should be drunk before they are five years old. The same is true of the Gamays and Zinfandel. Pinot Noir really comes into its own five years after the vintage, although it can be drunk after three. Mondavi hopes that people will wait at least eight years for the Cabernet, and will begin the practice of buying a case each year, so that eventually they will be able to save a bottle or two until fifteen years after the vintage. People are beginning to do this, he insists, and when he turns the winery over to his son in a decade or so, he hopes to travel around the country and taste his first wines with his first customers. His son Michael says there won't be any left to drink. Bob says there will be. That is wishful thinking, of course, but Bob Mondavi has always been one for daydreaming.

A SELECTION
Cabernet Sauvignon
Pinot Noir
Fumé Blanc

INGLENOOK VINEYARDS

Driving north from the crossroad scatter of houses that is Oakville, the highway edged now and then by tall eucalyptus and spreading sycamore, one begins to get the feel of the valley, five miles across at its widest. Vineyards stretch from rim to rim, running up to the wooded slopes of the Mayacamas Range on the west, half a mile high in places, and pushing into the lower mounds of hills to the east. An old railroad line, still used from time to time, swings over to the road as it nears Rutherford, and just as you approach the station, a private road cuts west through the vines, marked by a stucco gate and an arching sign — Inglenook.

Back a thousand yards, before a knoll of trees, is the long stone front of the winery, with a pedimented central pavilion crowned with a cupola. The stone face is thick with ivy, as if vines could not stop growing. The greenery closes over a row of white-painted arched doors and leaded windows and runs up to the white cornice of the red tile roof and its string of white-trimmed dormers. Hollywood can scarcely make a movie about wine country without filming scenes at Inglenook.

The founder was Gustav Niebaum, a Finnish lad who earned his master's papers at nineteen, sailed his own command into Alaskan waters at twenty-one and brought his cargo of sealskins through the Golden Gate right after the Alaska purchase in 1867. It was worth half a million. Gustav was twenty-six.

It took him a dozen years to find the place, a cozy corner given its name by a Scot because it caught the first rays of the morning sun, and another dozen years roving Europe to find the vines he wanted.

Droves of coolies cleared the land and planted vines, carved a skein of roads through the soft and sandy stone that hardened when exposed to air, dug a dozen tunnels deep into the mountain side. They built the winery with the stone, paving all with cinders to give a trim and shipshape look. Atop the knoll, they built a Victorian fancy of a house, painted mustard with white trim, a confection of gingerbread and wide porches festooned with wisteria. Captain Niebaum lived until 1908, and inspected his domain each day, wearing white gloves.

The gentler hand of a relative by marriage guided the winery through its early fame, and after Prohibition the reins were taken over by his son John Daniel, Jr. Under his guidance the vineyards prospered. Inglenook was the first to offer wines bearing the names of the grapes from which they were made, and the first to make a rosé that was given a local name, Navalle, after a stream that winds down from Mount Saint John, the highest peak of the Mayacamas. Young John Daniel was a leader in experimenting with new varieties, offering wines from the Charbono, a grape probably related to the Barbera of the Italian Piedmont, and from a California grape called Red Pinot at Inglenook and Pinot Saint George elsewhere, although not a true Pinot — which produces a sharp, light red wine.

Wines from Inglenook helped set a standard for fine wines of California, generally soft and light and perfumed. Under the deft hand of a German winemaker, many of the wines were aged in an array of stout oval casks of German oak brought over by Captain Niebaum, but John Daniel introduced much smaller French cooperage. Many of the wines matured for a time in great redwood vats, a California tradition. Visitors took to identifying the soft, light, quick taste as a redwood taste, the berrylike, fruity quality being unlike European counterparts. The redwood is gone now, replaced by oak, although many wineries keep the redwood vats and casks to store the wines for a period, before racking them off to small oak cooperage.

Racking is one of the vital steps in good winemaking, the wine being drawn off the lees, those dregs that settle out of a wine after fermentation. Wine evaporates in the casks, and a constant task in the winery is ullaging, topping off each cask with wine to replace what has evaporated so that there is no surface on the wine exposed to air. The casks are filled to the bunghole, then stoppered, and each cask is inspected every few days to be sure it stays full to the bung. Racking is carried out every few weeks at first, and continues less frequently all the time the wine is in cask. When life in oak is over, the wines are filtered, allowed to rest for a time, and then bottled, to begin their life in glass.

Some 1,000 acres provide the wines that are bottled from the estate, all of which carry the date of the vintage. Casks from special vintages of Cabernet Sauvignon are frequently handled separately, such wines carrying the cask number to identify them. The Pinot Noirs and Chardonnays may receive special handling as well, but cask numbers are not used.

Production from members of Allied Grape Growers enables Inglenook to offer a line of generics that are called District Wines, all being made from grapes grown in the North Coast counties. This is a new development since 1964, when John Daniel sold the vineyards, after thirty years of directing its operation, to Allied Grape Growers, a cooperative of 1,800 vineyard owners that accounts for a quarter of all California wine production; the two main labels are Italian Swiss Colony and Petri. The marketing arm for all these wines is United Vintners, which in 1969 was acquired by Heublein, an international company that imports, produces, and markets a number of wines, spirits, and specialty foods.

A young group of graduates from Davis and other wine colleges around the world, with researchers and other specialists, now manages Inglenook and guards its fame. There is much experiment with new varieties and new blends, especially for the line of wines marketed in half-gallons. These are vintage bottlings from North Coast Counties and estate-bottlings of varietals from the original Inglenook blocks and from some 1,500 acres in the valley that belong to members of Allied Grape Growers, part of the United Vintners-Heublein complex. There has been considerable speculation as to what might happen under Heublein control, but the major change has been that of making much more wine of good quality widely available. The answer is in the wines.

Reporters are ushered into the small tasting room just inside the main door of the winery, where Captain Gustav Niebaum and then the Daniel men (father and son) met with cellarmaster and vineyard

manager to decide policy. It is a small room with carved oak panel-
ing, stained glass above a counter at one end, shelves and cabinets
built in around the walls; most of the space is taken up by a giant
oak table. A '67 Pinot Noir may be opened. It is a big wine, clean
and fruity and round, with a sustained aftertaste. Then a '57 may be
poured, from a lot that has been "put away as being representative
of Napa, and particularly, Inglenook," says the cellarmaster. The
wine is still bright red, with no hint of brown, with a light nose, the
taster's slangy way of referring to bouquet. The taste is soft, clean,
and light, a little short in the aftertaste, but good and characteristic
of the grape. But the '67 is far better, and not just because the earlier
wine is getting past its prime.

In the two wines could be tasted the wonders ten years had
wrought — all those little improvements in fermentation, in vine
stocks, in vineyard management, in aging in small cooperage and
continuing, anxious care. There is Cabernet to taste, the '64 and later
vintages, seeming to get better with the years. Then there is the soft
and rounded Chardonnay of 1967, the other whites, then Navalle
Rosé and the soft, bright red from Gamay. Still light, the wines have
a roundness to them, which means a depth of taste, a certain elegance
of balance. Even Captain Niebaum might have smiled. Inglenook
seems to be in good hands. In fact, looking at the young guard
hustling about the place, it bears watching.

A SELECTION
Charbono
White Pinot
Traminer

BEAULIEU VINEYARD

Napa has a magnetic effect on people from the wine lands of
Europe, and it was a great day for the valley when Georges de Latour
arrived at the turn of the century and decided to follow Noah's example. He tended his vineyards for forty years, making some of the
finest wines California has known, which was to be expected because
his family roots were in Burgundy and Bordeaux. There are now

more than 750 acres in vines; three large blocks border the road north and south of town, another block across the valley to the east, and a fifth section down in Carneros near the Bay, west of Napa. The property passed to his daughter, then his granddaughter, and their mates, but for a third of a century, the making of the wine was the province of Andre Tchelistcheff.

Andre's parents were Russian, settling after the revolution in France, where he learned the craft of wines and became an artist in that realm. He was called to Beaulieu in 1938 by Georges de Latour, who was considered an expert taster, meaning that he was accurate, consistent, able to describe the complexities of a wine and remember them. So was Andre, who was also able to taste a wine and decide how it should be handled.

Tasting takes place in the morning. At Beaulieu the bottles are set up in the tasting room of the winery, which is a cluster of stone buildings just beyond the crossroads that is Rutherford. There may be a sample from a wine that is still fermenting, and ones from other vintages that have just been racked off into wood, have been in wood a few months, or have been recently bottled — each progressively more composed and complex. The newer the wine, the more recognizable are its various elements.

Most important is the acid-sugar balance. Acid builds up early in the grapes, and a good European vintage in northern vineyards occurs when there is plenty of sun to build up the sugar and balance the high acidity. As sugar increases, acid declines, and a good American vintage in North Coast counties occurs when there is not too much sun to overwhelm the fruit acid. The situations are reversed, Europeans tasting for sugar, Americans tasting for acid. Tannin comes mainly from the skins, a great deal making the wine slow to mature; very little resulting in a wine that will fall apart. Long fermentation with the skins builds up tannin, and some European vintners are returning to the old way of letting red wines remain with the skins for as long as three weeks, while some follow modern practices that may be as short as three days. A week of fermentation seems about right for many reds, generally long enough to impart enough tannin so that a wine can develop well; whites are fermented off the skins, so their lives are short, usually less than five years. The tealike taste of tannin, somewhat bitter, is noticeable in young wines and must be in balance with the natural acids and sugars. No one of the trio should overwhelm the others although one or another may dominate pleasingly in a good wine. With time, tannin content diminishes in the wine, changing to a brown sediment, which can be a sign of a well-matured wine, but calls for careful pouring. And so it goes.

Uncontrolled bacterial action in a wine, or contamination during fermentation or aging, produce unpleasant qualities, which is a sign that something is wrong. A master winemaker must anticipate what may happen, and take steps to prevent it.

Georges de Latour had Andre to help him in this task, and through the years Andre has trained a number of men who have gone off to become vineyardists or cellarmasters elsewhere, or set up their own wineries. Andre retired in 1973, but continued to act as a consultant, officially or not, to all of them, including his son, who is in charge of a vast vineyard development in Mexico.

Heublein purchased BV in 1969, the new Beaulieu owners sticking to the traditional Old World winemaking practices that have always distinguished the house. Few innovations have been allowed. Years ago, for instance, when it was felt that the company name was hard for American tongues, the wines came to be called BV, and the initials appear prominently on every label. The same went for the varietal wines that are marketed as Beaumont (Pinot Noir), Beaufort (Pinot Chardonnay), and Beauclair (Johannisberg Riesling). Cabernet Sauvignon is called just that, although specially selected Cabernet grapes are separately produced and given extra aging and are marketed as Private Reserve. There is Beaurosé among the blends, but others carry traditional names. Beaulieu pioneered the designation of vintage years on its bottles, not just to indicate the age of the wine, but because there are differences.

What may be advantageous to white wines in one year may impart very different qualities to the reds. Accordingly, the well-known and best regarded vintage years for red and white wines do not necessarily coincide. That gives the student of vintage years something to fuss over.

September was hot in '69; the crop of Johannisberg Riesling was short, but the wine was fine. In '68 there was an early bloom, a fairly cool summer, and a late vintage, which produces full wines. The '68 Beaulieu Cabernet is like the '64 and '58, resembling the outstanding '51, while the '67 is lighter. Pinot Noir and Chardonnay, planted in '63, grow unusually well down in Carneros, and both the '70 and '71 Pinot Noir vintages are expected to be outstanding. The Chardonnay was Andre's pet, strong in character and clean. Andre said its taste was reminiscent of white sage, which may be the true taste of the grape, something that nobody has tasted, perhaps, because of virus infections in vines all over the world. Virus-free vines may reveal a lot of subtle new secondary characteristics never before known.

Innovations are the result of research that shows ways of improving the old winemaking practice. Beaulieu is installing stainless steel fermenters, for example, which provide simplified methods for positive control of fermentation temperatures. Experiments include field crushing grapes and transporting in closed vessels so air is kept away. Other tests involve studies of fermentation under CO_2 pressure. It took over a decade of study prior to the sixties to isolate each enzyme step during fermentation. Fermentation curves for each grape have been worked out and refined.

The second great development has been in clonal selection. This enables the vintner to choose particular grape strains that will produce specific desirable qualities and characteristics. These may then be grafted on certified virus-free root stock. They must be planted in specific microclimates so they reach field maturity at the proper time. Carneros is a cool Region One. Around Yountville, it is about one and a half — you can often see the fog line in the morning that marks the difference. Near Oakville, it is a cool Region Two, where Beaulieu grows its Johannisberg Riesling, up behind Bob Mondavi. Rutherford is a solid Region Two but it is warmer in Vineyard No. 3, to the east, because it gets the late sun. Up around Calistoga, it is Region Three. Designations of ten years ago are no longer precise enough for today. The winemakers must marry the proper varieties to proper soil types as well as to microclimates and as this matching goes on, the certified vines will be producing a bewilderment of astonishing wines during the seventies.

Rutherford is tops for Cabernet, says Dr. Peterson, and the BV reputation was founded on its red wines. But even during its first decade, Beaulieu was successful in making a Napa Valley Cuvée reminiscent of the Sauternes of France — a blend of sweet wines from Sauvignon Blanc and Sémillon, with a little Muscadelle du Bordelais — as well as a dry one without the latter. But the whites of a decade ago had a dead character and an oxidized taste. No more. The whites are fresher, fruitier, less woody. Care must be taken with the wood, which gives a taste opposed to fruitiness. When wine is in oak for just the right amount of time, there is a tremendous improvement, not just a change of character. When it is in too long, you can get something really bad. Beaulieu expects to become known for its Chardonnay, because of the Carneros vineyard and the Limousin oak casks, which are just right for it.

There has been long experimentation with other grapes. There is some Colombard in the blend called Chablis, lending flintiness to the basic Chenin Blanc. There is some Gamay Beaujolais planted in Carneros, where microclimate and soil seem to be as perfectly suited to this grape as Rutherford is to Cabernet. There are great expectations, following old ways in new places. With an eye cocked on experiment, BV will continue to lead the way. Georges de Latour saw to that.

A SELECTION
Cabernet Sauvignon Private Reserve
Beaumont Pinot Noir
Beauclair Johannisberg Riesling

LOUIS M. MARTINI

Louis Martini was born on the Italian Riviera; his family brought him to San Francisco when he was entering his teens, and sent him back to study enology at the University of Genoa when he was in his twenties, after carefree boyhood years helping out in his father's fish business. That was the year of the earthquake, 1906, and after a second adolescence in the wine trade, including stints in the Italian Piedmont and the Cucamonga district at Guasti, outside Los Angeles, he opened his own winery in the southern San Joaquin in 1922, making brandy and sweet wines. His true interest was in the

Napa region, though, with dry table wines, and he went there in 1933. The winery is a couple of country miles above Rutherford, on the right, surrounded by vines, just before the town of St. Helena.

The winery is a great block with a low-pitched roof, enclosing nearly an acre. Built in bays, the walls are hollow tile, lined with eight inches of redwood bark and cork, equal to stone walls a good ten feet thick. There's a tasting room and office in one corner and a door leading into the winery proper, where there's a bottling line and some case storage, but never enough. Behind that are holding tanks, filter equipment, storage tanks, casks, fermenters, and so on through the building, to the pressing area where the grapes come in. Below it all are cellars, where special reserves are stored, small lots of wines that are released now and then, to the joy of 21 Brands, Martini's Eastern distributor. Ranked behind them are rows and rows of small cooperage containing the varietals that made Louis Martini famous, and that are now produced by his son Louis P. Martini, who labored in the vineyards until he was in his thirties before his father admitted that maybe the lad knew a thing or two. The change came in the fifties when Louis P. began replanning the cold fermentation of white wines, one of the first to do so. It got so that whenever a technical question came up, Louis M. would say, "Go ask young Louis. He knows all about that." He did, too.

The vineyards number close to 1,000 acres, 300 of them up in the red volcanic soil atop the Mayacamas Range, across the county line in Sonoma; another section lies on the slope near St. Helena, where the earth is fine gravel and drains fast. Another section is down in cool Carneros, where the gravel is coarser and underlain with clay. Louis M. likes the cool mountain air, and so do the grapes, from noble vines whose planting was supervised by Louis P. Vineyards are frequently called ranches in California, a remnant from mission days, and the Martinis have one near the Russian River in Sonoma, near Healdsburg, and another in Chiles Valley, east of St. Helena, at an elevation of 900 feet. This is fine for Pinot Noir and Johannisberg Riesling, but it is lower than the Martinis like to go, by one hundred feet; most of their mountain vineyards are above one thousand. Bacchus loves the hillsides, said Livy. The Martinis go for mountains. Many of their wines go to market with the word on the label. The Mountain Zinfandel is pretty widely considered the best wine ever made from that grape. There are staunch supporters of his Mountain Gewürztraminer and the other varietals, red and white, but on these you can get arguments. Louis P. even argues against himself, claiming he is not happy with his Chardonnay. Most of the varietals are labeled with vintage years, not merely to indicate age. In exceptional years, lots of Special Selections and Private Reserves are made, some in magnums.

Martini offers a range of generics — too many, some say — and even Sherries and a Tawny Port. The most appealing of these may be the jug wines, Mountain Red and Mountain White, sold by the half-gallon. All of the wines are fermented out completely, says Louis P., because that is the best way to make them. There are those who say that a little sweetness will widen the market, but he is not going to lower the quality of his wines just to sell a few more cases, or even a lot more. By stopping the fermentation, some residual sugar from the grapes is left in the wine, the sweetness hiding imperfections. Louis P. feels that people will discover his wines, sooner or later, appreciating their dryness and natural taste. Even if they don't, he intends to go on making the wines the way he knows best. Like father, like son. There are grandsons Michael and Peter coming along to carry on the tradition. Honoring their ancestry, the Martinis also make a Mountain Barbera, a full, dark, rough red from a grape that does better in Napa and Sonoma than it does in its home vineyards of the Italian Piedmont. It is by far the best wine from Italian grapes made in California. Another unusual wine is a Moscato Amabile. It is fermented at very low temperatures, sometimes for as long as a year; it is lightly bubbly and is fruity and sweet. It cannot be shipped because it must be kept chilled, deteriorating rapidly if it warms up.

Louis P. is known throughout the world of wines as a master winemaker, and no tasting of California vintages is complete without his Cabernet Sauvignon or his Pinot Noir, his Zinfandel or his Sylvaner or his Chenin Blanc. And there are those who will automatically include his wines in any comparative tasting of California wines, just to make sure they are not missing any good bets. And that includes the Chardonnay, which should make all the Martinis happy.

A SELECTION
Cabernet Sauvignon Special Reserve
Mountain Pinot Noir
Folle Blanche

CHARLES KRUG WINERY

Just above St. Helena the surrounding hills begin to squeeze the valley and the road bends west beneath them, presenting on the right a sweeping view of the Charles Krug Winery and some of its vineyards. Krug came from Germany as a young man, returned to take part in the populist revolution of 1848, and when that failed, he took off for California and eventually went to work for Ágoston Haraszthy at Buena Vista. By 1858 he had learned enough to make more than a thousand gallons of wines from a Napa grower's grapes in a cider press. This was the first commercial wine made in the Napa Valley, and it was so successful that he began building his own cellars in 1861 and marketing his own wines soon after this. He was one of the first to sell California wines in the East, in Mexico, and back in Germany and England, following Haraszthy's lead. The Krug Ranch was a showplace and later pioneers like Carl Wente and Jacob Beringer got their first California experience there. The family continued operations until Prohibition.

Cesare Mondavi came to the Minnesota iron mines from Italy in 1906, and in 1922 his fellow workers sent him to California to buy some grapes so they could make some wines. He enjoyed the chore and moved his family out to Lodi, where he set up a fruit shipping business. This included grapes and after Repeal he began to concentrate on wines and bought the Krug Ranch in 1943. Both his sons grew up in the winery, coming back to work there after graduating from Stanford and doing graduate work at Davis. His wife assumed the head of C. Mondavi & Sons after his death, with Peter in charge of production and Robert as general manager.

If Louis Martini is not the outstanding long-time, large-scale independent winery in the Napa Valley, then Charles Krug is. Both Inglenook and Beaulieu are units of large companies, the Christian Brothers are a large order, and Bob Mondavi is just starting out, having left the family business to build his own. Charles Krug made the first commercial wines in the valley, but it was Bob and Pete Mondavi who made the first good dry whites. They began experimenting over twenty years ago, when most attention in Napa was focused on red wines, and whites were considered little more than something to fill out a line.

The Mondavi brothers started with Chenin Blanc, Johannisberg Riesling, Chardonnay, and half a dozen others, comparing wines with Andre Tchelistcheff at Beaulieu, Louis Martini, and various small growers who had experimental plots. Techniques of harvesting when there was proper acid in the grape and of getting a smooth fermentation were developed. Special yeast strains were used for the long, slow, cold fermentation to develop the bouquet; time in wood was carefully matched to each variety to round out the taste. There were filtration problems. But the biggest problem of all seemed to have to do with air.

Air causes a wine to rust, or oxidize, turning it brown, an action called maderization because the taste is sought in the wines of Madeira, in Sherry, and in the *vins de paille,* or straw wines, of France. Care is needed along the way, but an account of the bottling process at Charles Krug, now followed by many, gives an idea of the meticulousness.

After its time in oak, a white wine needs at least six months in the bottle. The wines are racked — that is, drawn off — into stainless steel or glass-lined storage tanks called Pfaudler tanks, after filtering. Wines are sometimes left in these oversized glass bottles for a year, during which time acids react with the alcohols to form esters, which have flowery or fruity qualities.

When time for bottling has come, nitrogen is forced into the tanks under pressure. The nitrogen is inert and does not affect the wine; it is used instead of pumps because pumping would rouse the wine. The wine is forced into the bottling line, where the bottles have been blown out with nitrogen. After filling, the bottle goes to the corking machine, where a slight vacuum is created in the neck of the bottle before the cork is plunged in. Some white wines are cooled before bottling, down to a temperature only a little above freezing, so that tartrates in the wine will crystallize and settle out.

Some rosés are handled like the white wines, but more often they are handled like red wines, left with the skins to pick up color, then quickly fermented. Sulphur is used in all stages of winemaking as defense against bacteria and oxidation, but such handling reduces the amounts needed, a great advantage because sulphur imparts its taste to the wine. The taste is like the smell of a flaring match. To get rid of bacteria, wines were once pasteurized, meaning that they were held at high temperatures for some time until the bacteria were killed. Unfortunately, the process killed good bacteria as well as bad, arresting the development of the wine, and leaving it bland and insipid to the taste. Seitz filters developed on the Rhine have all but eliminated pasteurization. There are microscopic filters available that can leave the wine absolutely sterile — and almost tasteless. Most filters used are fine enough to abstract dead yeast cells, but not so fine as to eliminate taste. Filtering is carefully controlled, and the minimum is used only when necessary. Many winemakers prefer the old method called fining, which is letting a liquid net of egg white, or some other agent like Bentonite, fall through the wine, catching any particles in suspension.

Wines are hardy, within limits, and while all the care sounds fussy, the execution is relatively straightforward. Disaster only comes when one of the little steps is handled sloppily or passed over as not worth the effort. Racking of wine, for instance, is a nuisance. There is a little less sediment each time the wine is transferred to a new container, but there always seems to be some, and there is a tendency to put on a fine filter and be done with the job, once and for all. This takes the life out of the wine. Most home winemakers get poor wines because they do not rack enough times or with enough care. Care is what makes Pete Mondavi a fine winemaker.

The Charles Krug Winery has some 1,400 acres of vineyard in fine grape varieties, a continuous program of experimentation and contracts with other growers, whose vine management must be supervised. In addition to varietals and generics, they also produce a group of fortified wines. Then there is the series of jug wines marketed under the CK label, and other lines called Napa Vista and Mondavi Vintage.

There are frequent tastings on the lawn at the winery, plus

August Moon concerts of chamber music in the oak-shaded picnic grove beside an old stone building that survived an ancient fire. A quarterly newsletter called *Bottles and Bins* is edited by Francis Gould, an enophile who has long been a mainstay of the Wine & Food Society and a close friend to its founder, Andre Simon. An avid collector of recipes, he has published a book of them with the same title as the newsletter and a biography, *My Life with Wine.* You can get copies at the tasting rooms, then wander over to a pinic table and read about the delights of Chicken Vurpillat or Venison Diable. On the way, don't miss the old cider press. You might give it an affectionate pat. That's what started it all, just a few vintages ago.

A SELECTION
Gamay Beaujolais
Gewürztraminer
Chenin Blanc

STERLING VINEYARDS

The most noticeable new winery is on the prow of a hill jutting out into the valley above St. Helena, its 400 acres of vineyard stretching before it. A road winds up the hill but visitors come by a tramway to the lofty building whose arches and tower give it a monastery look. The hill is at the base of Mount St. Helena, which marks the end of the valley and the farthest reach of the Pacific colonies of Imperial Russia. The mountain was named after the daughter of the czar of all the Russians, and on its slopes Robert Louis Stevenson spent his honeymoon and wrote *Silverado Squatters.*

The vineyard was planned in the early sixties by the three partners of a San Francisco paper products company; a former London newspaperman named Peter Newton heads the venture with Michael Stone and Martin Waterfield. They know just what wines they want to produce. There are 90 acres of Cabernet and half as much Merlot, their featured wine being a blend of the two. The rest of the acreage is Chardonnay and Chenin Blanc, Sauvignon Blanc and Gamay Beaujolais, plus some experimental plantings. Small casks of European oak are used for maturing the reds. Sterling is the first vineyard with sufficient quantities of Merlot to make a blend with Cabernet Sauvignon in the old tradition of the best Bordeaux châteaux, and the success of the wine may influence others to make similar wines.

BERINGER/LOS HERMANOS

The Beringer Brothers came from the Rhineland in the middle of the last century, building a replica of the family home that they called Rhine House, today a tasting and visitor center. The winery behind the house was built by ship's carpenters and has floors like decks, so tightly laid that it can be flooded a couple of inches deep when it is swabbed down. A thousand feet of tunnel, cut into the side of the hill by Chinese labor, has a stone façade backed by a room containing some of the old German casks. The heads are carved with vineyard scenes and they continue to be used for wine.

The grounds of the estate run along the hill at the north end of St. Helena, which lies along the western edge of the valley. There are some 1,200 acres of vineyards down in the valley, many of them replanted in top varietals since Nestlé bought the company in 1970. Grapes are bought on long-term contract, and the wine is made by Myron Nightingale, a classmate at Davis of Louis P. Martini. Nightingale is a legendary winemaker, having pioneered in the use of the submerged-*flor* process of making wines like Sherry, whereby that special yeast is stirred with the wine.

Nightingale is always experimenting. He had an idea he could produce a wine from grapes on which the noble rot had been induced, an action caused by the mold, *botrytis cynerea*. The resultant shriveling of the grapes occurs naturally in Sauternes, where it is called *pourriture noble,* and along the Rhine, where it is called *edelfaule.* The result is a sweet wine of great lusciousness. To get it, Nightingale dusted the grapes with the mold and then wrapped bags around the bunches.

He is almost too busy for such experiment now, for he is perfecting techniques that will make the Beringer grapes produce the best of traditional wines, in quantities large enough to support national distribution. Some of the most successful are marketed in half-gallons. The wines he is making are just beginning to appear on the market and should be looked for.

OTHER WINERIES

St. Helena is right in the middle of the Napa Valley vineyards, and it is a good place to stop and see what has been missed. The local library has a collection of wine books, and may be the only library in the world that conducts tastings — a winter series for enthusiasts and a weekend session for students at vintage time. There are also a number of art galleries and antique shops. One of these is the Hatchery, on Railroad Avenue, and while the railroad does not take passengers any more, its depot down in Yountville continues in use as a shop. So does an old winery nearby, a craft center called Vintage 1870. Among other things, they sell antique wine bottles. In one of the buildings is the Compleat Winemaker, Bob Ellsworth, where you can buy everything needed to make wine, including a five-dollar kit with grape concentrate and other necessaries to make a gallon of your own at home. During the vintage, Bob airfreights boxes of fresh varietals, complete with yeasts and all other essentials; he also lets amateurs rent his full-scale equipment, and he runs a winemaking workshop.

A couple of blocks south of St. Helena's main street is the Napa Valley Olive Oil Manufactory, where you can see the press that squeezes out the virgin oil and stock up on various delicacies for a picnic. Restaurants are rare in the valley. There are a couple in town, and there is another near the crossroads at Rutherford, the Colonial Dining Room, which has good Mexican food, but the preferred place is the Grapevine, on the highway near Oakville, with a good selection of local bottlings. There are many more wineries in the valley, whose national distribution is small. Exceptions are the sparkling wine producers, who deserve a separate chapter for themselves, and two large cooperatives that sell their wines to proprietors of national brands. Small producers of quality wines who offer vintages now and then to a mailing list will be found in a later chapter. Those whose offerings are restricted mainly to California or who are just beginning some distribution outside the state are discussed below.

Near St. Helena, Michael Robbins is starting with a few wines from his Spring Mountain Vineyards. He expects to add some

Pinot Noir and market perhaps 10,000 cases by mid-decade. At that time the present 24 acres will have been doubled. Robbins directs things, more or less as a hobby, from a handsomely refurbished Victorian house whenever he can steal time from his business in San Francisco.

Spring Mountain is well on its way to becoming a separate district in its own right, much like Carneros, or the vineyards around Oakville. A century ago most of it was La Perla vineyard, now partly replanted by Jerome Draper, whose son is planning to reopen the old stone winery when the vines reach maturity, perhaps in time for the country's bicentennial. Another 100-acre section owned by Fritz Maytag, a brewery executive, is now called York Creek Vineyard and sends its grapes down to the big Napa Valley Cooperative Winery in St. Helena, whose production eventually winds up with Gallo. Nearby is the Victorian house and old stone winery of Château Chevalier, where two San Franciscans wild about wines, Gregory Bissonette and James Fruhe, are now replanting some 100 acres in Riesling, Chardonnay, Pinot Noir, and Cabernet, the wines to appear on the market in that order. Further uphill is a similar reconstitution at Yverdon Vineyards, the winery built stone by stone by Fred Aves and his son, Russell. Not far away is the less extensive Lyncrest Vineyards, owned by a group headed by Richard Lynn. There are more to come.

Perhaps the most intriguing will be the wines from the rural retreat of art collector Rene di Rosa, down in Carneros at Winery Lakes. The land is embellished with peacocks, ducks, swans, and assorted greenery, with flocks of artists as far as the eye can see, who seem to drink up most of the wines. On well over 100 acres are now being nurtured a setting of Gamay Beaujolais and plantings of Chardonnay and Pinot Noir.

The wine with the oddest name comes from the St. Helena winery of Davis Bynum, who has a shop in San Francisco and aging cellars in the town of Albany, near Berkeley. Barefoot Bynum comes from his 26 acres of vineyard, a wine so popular that he must buy grapes to meet the demand. He makes a range of wines, among them something called Camelot Mead.

A new star in the firmament may prove to be Franciscan Vineyards, with a winery in the old California style, complete with bell tower and reflecting pool, on the road near Beaulieu.

A popular old establishment is the Sutter Home Winery, across the street from Louis Martini, once in the family of the man on whose land gold was discovered in 1849. The winery was first built on the eastern hills, then moved into the shadow of the Napa Valley Cooperative, whose members supply Gallo. Now the property of the Trinchero family, Sutter's best wine is Zinfandel, from old vines in the Sierra foothills.

The most important of these small wineries with vineyards in the valley is Freemark Abbey, on the north side of St. Helena — a handsome winery that had so many ups and downs it was turned into a candle factory and epicure's shop by an enterprising family called Hurd. An equally enterprising group of growers with some vineyards down in the Rutherford area decided the cellars would be a fine central place for their wines, and now Freemark Abbey is back in business to stay.

There are 200 acres now bearing, with additional acres coming in by 1976. The first vintage of Pinot Chardonnay and Cabernet Sauvignon was 1967. The wines were made by one of the seven partners, Brad Webb, who was the winemaker for a famous mountain vineyard, Hanzell, which he continues to watch. Frank Wood and Chuck Carpy formed the group, Webb agreed to advise on winemaking, Bill Jaeger, Jim Warren, John Bryan, and Dick Heggie joined. The chummy group plans to be marketing perhaps 25,000 cases a year by 1975, including Pinot Noir and Johannisberg Riesling. By the end of the decade they expect to have 300 acres bearing grapes, many of them in the Rutherford area.

The Silverado Trail and Mayacamas Range

Back in the hills on both sides of the Napa Valley are a handful of wineries, not as small as one might think, producing outstanding wines. They are known to wine buffs, mostly by hearsay outside of California. A few cases may get across the Rockies to people lucky enough to be on the mailing lists and willing to struggle with the complications of getting the wines. Knowledgeable New Yorkers flying out West have taken to traveling with spare suitcases, lugging them back full of bottles, which they tuck carefully under their seats and scarcely let out of their sight. But it is not easy, for a case of wine weighs nearly forty pounds.

When these wines show up on a wine list or in a shop, they are usually ignored, for even a wine buff will know about them only generally, or will have forgotten the names. No store east of the Rockies will have anything like a representative selection, nor even much of a choice among the larger premium producers. This is changing now, as even the small producers begin to reserve lots for Eastern distributors. The decade will see more and more wines leaving the state, as the number of small producers increases, and as they grow more sophisticated about the national market. And the prices will rise too.

The trouble is that premium producers have lost their inferiority complexes. They have taken to thinking that their wines are as good as almost any that are made, better than most, and cheap at twice the price. What's more, they are unique, because of the use of certified vines and advanced winemaking techniques. A grower tastes a white wine that has rounded out after a year in bottle, or tastes a red wine three years after bottling, and revels at what is there. No matter that nobody much beyond the valley knows about them. Enough come to buy at the winery, so it is scarcely worthwhile to worry about distribution. It is a heady daydream, and comfortable — and false. Certification and technique will not be limited for long to California, and then the fight will begin for an American public suddenly gone wild about wines.

It's peaceful now.

The Silverado Trail rambles up the eastern side of the valley, side roads leading up into the hills and canyons. Similar roads wind up into the Mayacamas Range on the west, from the main road that runs up the valley floor called the St. Helena Highway, Route 29. Many of the vineyards are owned by large producers down in the valley; some are owned by growers who sell their grapes, and others are owned by growers who market their own wines. These independent wineries produce some of the best wines of California, and in small compass present a picture of what the future will hold.

HEITZ CELLARS

Joe Heitz was a G.I. stationed in California when he became interested in wines, and when he got out of the army he enrolled in the enology course at Davis. For ten years after graduation he was in demand at various wineries around the state, ending up as assistant to Andre Tchelistcheff at Beaulieu. In 1961 he began taking stock.

"I happen to believe that America is ready for individual enterprise again," he said at a surprise birthday party celebrating his fiftieth year. The remark was no surprise because he had suited his action to his words when he bought the Brendel Winery, right next to Louis Martini.

Brendel came from a family of distinguished wine growers in Alsace and had served as a chemist and wine consultant in Switzerland and Mexico before doing the same in California. He bought his winery in 1949, having strong faith in the Grignolino, a grape from the Italian Piedmont that produces there a light red wine and a distinctive rosé. He must have had a special stock, for the grape performed well. Brendel called his winery Only One, and Grignolino was the only wine he made until the day he died. Joe continues to produce the wine, hesitating to disagree with that large number of Californians who think it is the dandiest wine they have ever tasted. In any event, it is the best Grignolino in California.

So Joe became a full-fledged member of the fraternity along Vintner's Row, with 8 acres of Grignolino. Joe is a superb winemaker — of a sort, one suspects, that comes along once or twice in a generation. Various growers, accustomed to selling their fine varietals to large wineries where their grapes would get lost in the vats, encouraged Joe to take their tonnage and make special lots of wines. This is precisely what he had in mind. In 1964, he bought the Spring Valley ranch, a winery with 160 acres that had been out of production but well maintained. A grower supplied him with enough Pinot Noir to make a couple of hundred gallons. Five years later, he had half a dozen stainless steel fermenters, each holding 3,000 gallons, a spanking new Willmes Press, and a rack three casks high for his sixty-gallon butts of Limousin oak — plus assorted cooperage, holding tanks, filters, and a pump.

A pump to handle the must sends the grapes and their juice from the crusher to the fermenters, and is designed to handle thirty tons an hour. Joe has one of these simply because it is the best made. His production, though, was just three tons an hour. It was embarrassing. The pump emptied the crusher in one quick slurp. When it was about to be turned on, everybody gathered around to watch.

With the seventies, vines planted by many of the smaller growers who had come to the valley began to reach maturity. Some 20 acres of Grignolino that Joe had planted were beginning to bear. The old stone winery was scarcely big enough to hold his Chardonnay and White Riesling and his blends. Joe had started by borrowing five thousand dollars, then spent two decades putting everything he had into his wines. After years of trying, the banks finally let him increase the debt a hundred times. In 1972 he built a new winery, an octagon of block, beam, and tile to hold 600 casks for his reds, plus vats and storage. There's even an office. Fermenters are on a pad outside. He says he is going to need another octagon like it, maybe bigger, by the time the bicentennial rolls around.

Joe now has a happy group of growers who would not think of having anybody else handle their grapes. A party at Joe's can be mostly growers, this one with 40 acres of Cabernet, that one with 20 acres of Pinot Noir, another with 30 acres of Johannisberg Riesling. Altogether, this may add up to the equivalent of a producer with national distribution, something over 200 acres. When it makes a difference, wines are marketed with vintage years. Grapes from a particularly good ranch may be so identified on the wine label, a sort of estate-bottling. This can make things difficult, because some of his best Chardonnay comes from Zinfandel Associates, so named because the holding is on Zinfandel Lane, a road near his tasting room down on the highway. Joe thinks this could be confusing. Like many producers, he is continually tasting his own wines against European wines he considers similar. He is now tasting his Chardonnay vintages against those of the First Growths of Puligny-Montrachet and Chassagne-Montrachet.

Ever hopeful, Heitz makes full use of his skill at winemaking. Too full a use, some people think, for he makes more than a dozen wines just because he can, his particular tours de force being a dry Sherry and a Tawny Port. He buys special lots of these wines and gives them special care. Another such is Angelica. Joe agrees that maybe he should concentrate more, but a fine lot of grapes puts a glint in his eye. Now the most despised wine of California is probably Angelica, perhaps named after Los Angeles and made by blending sweet wine with brandy. It was invented to make bad wine taste good, heavily sweetened to mask off-tastes, and heavily dosed with brandy so that you would not mind what was wrong, in case you noticed. But suppose you started with good materials? You could make something remarkable, a dessert wine uniquely Californian. Just like Joe, to make something silken out of a sour tradition. That is a winemaker's job, and that is why he makes small batches of such wines — to show what can be done. He does not consider his Angelica a waste of time.

"What we are continually trying to do is to sell outstanding wines of whatever they may be," he says. He once produced some bottles that said Alicia on the labels, named after his wife. Alice is one of the best cooks in the valley. She does some of it on an old wood-burning stove because it gives such good control of the heat. She has an electric stove, which she uses mostly for warming plates. Her cooking is not why the wine is named Alicia.

"This was made from Chardonnay, from one of the experimental vineyards," says Joe. "*Botrytis,* that is, the noble rot, had struck a few of the grapes and I noticed them as I was driving by. The vineyard had been picked, and the next time I saw Keith Bower, the manager, I asked him about them. He said I could have them if I wanted, and that night my son David and I went out to get them — enough for eighty-five gallons. David and I decided to make some and call our version Alicia."

Winemakers are forever handing out things to taste, after you have already tasted perhaps a dozen wines in the cellar or tasting room. If lunch or dinner is involved, there are sure to be two or three wines with each course, and then a prized bottle with the cheese. If things have gone well thus far, maybe another bottle will come out, and another. The winemaker will describe some detail of each, usually in a couple of different ways, to make sure you understand something like Alicia.

Well and good, but there are many who feel that Heitz is such a master of traditional table wines that he ought to concentrate on those, taking as little time as possible for such things like Chardonnays with noble rot. *Botrytis cynerea* is a mold that attacks overripe grapes, causing the water in the juice to evaporate. Wines made from them are exceptionally sweet. The sweetness is like that of extremely ripe fruit and a famous example is the Trockenbeerenauslesen (dried berry selections) made from Riesling on the Rhine; another is the Sauternes of Bordeaux, made from Sauvignon Blanc and Sémillon.

Alicia was nicely fruity and pleasingly sweet, with a prolonged and subtle taste, a treat, an experience. Drinking it was an event, a unique one that comes rarely in a lifetime. A man ought to be free enough to make a masterpiece if he wants to, taking time to go beyond excellence. Why Alicia? "It sounded nice," says Joe, "and anyway, Alice lets us do such things without fussing too much. Besides, we're sentimentalists around here." How in the world could anybody have guessed that?

A SELECTION
Cabernet Sauvignon
Pinot Noir
Johannisberg Riesling
Grignolino Rosé

CHAPPELLET VINEYARDS

A road cuts east off the Silverado Trail and over the hills to Conn Lake, which is a dammed ravine with two arms in the midst of a recreation area with a big swimming pool near its spillway. Past this, another road winds up to Pritchard Hill, where you can look down on the lake and across it into Napa Valley, 100 acres of vineyard on its flanks.

The Hill was bought in 1967 by Donn Chappellet, who had

started out with a partner and a coffee-vending machine in the forties and wound up twenty years later running a multimillion-dollar firm dedicated to what is delicately called mass feeding. His dedication having worn thin, he installed his wife and six youngsters in a rambling ranch house overlooking the vineyards and started replanting — 35 acres of Cabernet, half as much Chardonnay, about a dozen each of Merlot and Johannisberg Riesling, and a couple of dozen Chenin Blanc. Then he built his winery, from a design sketched by an artist friend.

It may be the best-looking winery built in this century. It is certainly the most inconspicuous, tucked into a stretch of live oaks between two sloping vineyards, and it looks like a rusty pyramid. The winery is laid out in a triangle, nearly a hundred feet on a side. Buttressed concrete walls eight feet above ground level and four below support three great triangles of ribbed steel that is supposed to rust, becoming a dull orange-red against the olive drab of the trees as it is weathered by mists and winter rain. The three-sided roof is separated at the corners, allowing for wide doorways at ground level and forming a six-sided room at the peak, which is reached by a single long flight of cantilevered steps; there are a couple of wide slabs on the way up, so you can catch your breath and look down into the winery.

Cooperage is ranged along one side, stainless steel fermenters along another. A raised rack jutting in from one door holds the presses and filtering equipment; it can also be used for a loading ramp. Light filters in from the glass-walled room in the peak. Up there, you can look out all the way to the Mayacamas Range or look down into the winery and see each of the steps involved in handling a vintage. The original idea was to cover the roof with sod so that the winery would not be seen at all. Nobody could figure the loads and stresses though, so earth was piled against the walls to the roof line, and these banks were sodded.

From a little bottle cellar built under the terrace of the ranch house, the winery looks like a tent made from one of the children's sheets of orange construction paper. To make them feel part of it all, Donn had the youngsters put their handprints at one of the entrances when the floor slab was poured. The prints get progressively smaller — there's Lycia, then Cyril Scott, Jon Mark, Carissa, Alexa. Dominic is at the end, but there's his footprint because his hand was too small.

The first Chappellet vintage was in 1968, of Chenin Blanc. With no equipment in his winery, Chappellet had to call on friends. Joe Heitz made the wine, and when it was done, it was loaded into one of the new fermenters that had not been installed as yet, and this was hauled down to Bob Mondavi, who bottled it. Then it was hauled up to Schramsberg for bottle aging in the deep tunnels. Whenever Chappellet wants a case, he has to hop in his jeep and run over to Schramsberg. The winery was finished in time to take in his first Cabernet, and there was a party for all when the butts were set in place.

There will be some 25,000 cases in distribution by 1976, the first of them in New York. "The days of peddling wines from the winery are passing," says Chappellet, "and we are going to start nationally, but slowly. We want to make good wines for the whole country, not just for Californians who seek us out. It's a big country and it wants a lot of good wines. We will supply some of that." Chappellet is over six feet and weighs over two hundred pounds. He wears a round of beard and work clothes and a steady look that takes in whatever is around. Winery capacity is twice what is needed. His winemaker is an Englishman trained in Bordeaux, who learned all about the old wines and decided he wanted to make some new ones. Chappellet manages the vineyards and makes the wines from some adjoining vineyards owned by a friend, so maybe he'll have more wine by decade's end. When you ask him how he and his family like the change from hectic Los Angeles, he looks at you quietly for a moment, then grins. "We like it fine," he says. "Would you like to taste some wine?"

Somehow, one gets the idea it will be good. It is.

BURGESS CELLARS
(formerly Souverain Cellars)

Halfway up Howell Mountain, just before you get to the hairpin turn in Deer Park Road, which goes to the summit, is the stone winery, aging cellar, greenhouse, and home built by J. Leland Stewart, who got sidetracked on his way to Mendocino one day in 1943 and bought himself a winery. He could not resist the view from the hillside vineyards, first planted in 1871 by a Swiss named Rossini, then operated as a winery by Peter Stark. It was a chicken farm when Stewart first saw it, but looking down to the Silverado Trail and across the valley to the Mayacamas, he saw what it could be.

Today there are 30 acres of vineyard on the mountain flanks, mostly in Zinfandel and Cabernet, with some Grenache for rosé, some Petite Sirah, and some Flora, a Davis hybrid based on Traminer. There is also some Green Hungarian, a wine Stewart pioneered in the state.

The winery also offers Sherry and Port types under the Los Amigos label. The name was made famous by a small winery run by Rob Mayock down in Mission San Jose, but it is now overrun by houses.

Production is something like 12,000 cases a year, and there is no intention to expand much. The reason is the greenhouse, which is full of orchids. Stewart found he was spending more and more time with the orchids, which began to fascinate him more than the wines. After all, he made his point — that making a few wines superbly and offering them to a small list can be a productive and satisfying way of life. But so can raising orchids. He sold Souverain Cellars and the name was moved to the large development project down the road. Now the vineyard is owned by a retired pilot from Poughkeepsie and his wife, Tom and Linda Burgess, who are carrying the tradition set by Stewart, but without the orchids.

A SELECTION
Mountain Zinfandel
Chenin Blanc
Green Hungarian

STONY HILL

It just may be paradise on earth, although a little hard to get to, which is probably what a paradise should be. It is straight across the valley from Burgess on Howell Mountain, seven hundred feet up in the Mayacamas Range, between Diamond Mountain on the north and Spring Mountain on the south, just above St. Helena. Stony Hill pokes up between the mountains, vineyards rolling up and down and edging up to forest, where mist swirls on rainy days. The owner's house rambles along the brow of a hill, walled terraces on every side so that you can look down in the valley and across, or to the lower swale, where a curving walk leads you past the angled deck of a swimming pool to the stone winery, framed in laurel and backing into a rising vineyard. The laurel is pungent when wet, and Fred McCrea may give you a few leaves to put in a stew.

He found the place in 1943, the same year Stewart bought Souverain, and he built his winery in 1951, retiring from the advertising business in the process, in time to make his first vintage in his new winery. There are 29 acres in all: about 12 in Chardonnay, another 10 in Johannisberg Riesling, 5 in Traminer, slightly more in Pinot Blanc, and a little in Sémillon. McCrea makes perhaps 1,000 cases of wine a year, sending a notice to a mailing list during the winter, then handling the hustle until the wine is gone — a matter of days. He first marketed only two wines, Chardonnay and Riesling, but now he offers some three hundred cases of Traminer. He drinks most of the Sémillon. His wines are among the hardest to find, but he lets Trader Vic have a little for his San Francisco restaurant, and Richard Wing gets some for his Imperial Dynasty, Hanford. There are those who insist that Stony Hill Chardonnay is the best in California; others hold out for Hanzell's, over in Sonoma. It is difficult to say, because it is so hard to get a taste of either.

There is no point in making selections, for Stony Hill offers only three wines, all of them impeccable, to be tasted whenever you find a bottle.

MAYACAMAS VINEYARDS

The Redwood Road wriggles into the Mayacamas Range from the highway intersection at the north end of Napa, topping out after nearly ten miles near a sweep of terraced vineyards that step south and slightly east. There were some 35 acres in bearing at Mayacamas Vineyards when the decade began. The highest of them reach to 2,300 feet, occasionally sprinkled with snow when the valley is deluged with winter rains. They are the highest vineyards in the district, with perhaps the lowest yield, and Robert Travers hopes they will produce the best wines.

His goal to have 20 acres of Cabernet Sauvignon by 1972 was met, producing a ton and a half of grapes per acre, maybe one hundred cases of wine from each. He aims at only half as many grapes from 30 acres of Chardonnay.

Travers was a stockbroker in San Francisco for eight years, until he said to hell with it in 1967 and went to work for Joe Heitz. There was only so much to be learned from tasting and textbooks, and he sought practical tutelage with a master winemaker. Whenever Heitz could spare him, Travers would rush off to look at properties, more than one hundred in the course of a long year. He finally settled on Mayacamas. The old stone winery had been Mount Veeder Vineyards before the turn of the century and was restored and renamed in the forties by Jack and Mary Taylor, who ran it as a family corporation. Stockholder friends would jounce up at vintage time to help with the picking, then come up again after the winter rains to pick up their wines. A few cases got past the stockholders in the fifties, and by the sixties some even went East, attracting visitors who would toil up the mountain to talk the Taylors out of a few bottles. Some even brought sleeping bags, camping out in the vineyards, watching the night glow from San Francisco and being guarded from marauding jackrabbits by disapproving winery dogs.

When Travers took over, he set up a system of allocations for old friends of Mayacamas, leaving room for new ones who might be interested in his production of 4,000 cases. The capacity of his winery allowed him to produce some 7,000 cases by 1972; now he buys some grapes, including Gamay Beaujolais for a red wine, some Zinfandel for a red and a rosé, some Chenin Blanc, and some Cabernet and Chardonnay to augment his own supply of his two main grapes. Twenty percent of the Cabernet is now reserved so that he can offer an increasing number of bottles from older vintages.

Travers holds to traditional techniques, fermenting his wines in oak, the reds for as long as eight days, and the whites longer. The whites go into large oak casks for fining, then into small casks of Burgundian oak. Like many California winemakers, Travers seeks to avoid long contact with oak for white wines so that they taste of the grape, not of the wood. His Chardonnay is the exception, the grape needing contact with wood almost as much as do wines from red wine grapes.

There are some sixty kinds of oak used in winemaking, Travers points out, and while strong traditions may be accidents of geography or supply, they should not be lightly set aside. He intends to preserve the classic character of his wines, yet follow the modern methods of vinification that permit the character of the grape to come out, at the same time seeing to it that this character is not lost by long holding in wood. With such nice balances are the best wines of California being made. A tasting of various Chardonnays from such meticulous winemakers can demonstrate how subtly the wines can vary. Travers suggests that one of the nicest ways to do this is to serve cracked crab, cold, with a light mayonnaise and plenty of good California sourdough. For Easterners who can't get the crab from Pacific waters, Maine lobsters might do and good French bread.

OTHER WINERIES

The rises on the east side of the valley above the Silverado Trail have attracted San Franciscans who want to get away from the city. To keep the valley from becoming a summer resort it was denominated an agricultural district in 1970, with new holdings limited to 40 acres or more. Up near St. Helena, two scientifically minded men, physicist Thomas Cottrell and engineer Thomas Parkhill, combined talents and bought a vineyard planted in Gamay and Pinot Noir, building a winery they call Cuvaison Cellar. Part of the Beringer clan, Roy Raymond and his family, have set out 90 acres of vines and built a small winery. Vineyard owner Charles Wagner has set up Caymus Vineyard with the intent of doing some estate bottling. An old hotel built in the 1880s and called Stag's Leap has been remodeled by Carl Doumani and 50 acres of an old vineyard have been replanted, its wines to be marketed as the vines come into bearing. Like Stewart and McCrea and others that have gone before them, these enthusiasts may make a name for themselves before the end of the decade.

An Oakville vineyard owner expanded on the idea. Fred Holmes and some associates bought a tract of land above the Silverado Trail and built a big new winery they call Souverain Cellars. They purchased Lee Stewart's Howell Mountain vineyard to get the name, and then in association with Pillsbury, the flour company, they planned a series of vineyard estates — plots sold to individuals. Souverain manages the vineyards and takes the grapes. There are bridle paths between the vines, a small French restaurant near the winery, and well-kept roads for the entire community to enjoy. Leland Stewart's place was sold to an airline pilot from Poughkeepsie, and is now called Burgess Cellars.

To solve marketing problems, vineyard owners may band together as they have at Freemark, or sell their grapes to people like Joe Heitz, who may estate bottle them under his label, or be content to sell to friends and visitors as is the fashion at Stony Hill or Mayacamas. Many of the wines will remain distinct, and buyers will get used to reading back labels describing where the wine comes from and what it is, scrambling to get on the mailing lists and struggling to keep track of release dates. New names will be appearing all through the coming decade as vineyards go in to the east, in Chiles Valley, and to the north, in Pope Valley and Alexander Valley.

Enthusiasts and amateur winemakers have come to the valley in a steady stream for decades, reviving old wineries and replanting old vineyards or starting new ones. Some set out new vines and sell the grapes, like Wendell Mackey, whose 40 acres of Cabernet Sauvignon go to Joe Heitz. Others start out like Lee Pashich, who replanted an old Calistoga vineyard to guarantee a good supply of grapes for making wines at home. This wasn't enough, so Pashich and a couple of other enthusiasts bought an old installation above Calistoga called Château Montelena, reconstituted 90 acres of vineyard with Chardonnay and Cabernet, and have begun marketing the wines. Château Montelena is a fascinating place built in the 1880s by an old San Francisco family called Tubbs. The stone buildings are said to be modeled after Château Lafite. A Chinese engineer bought it after the second world war and developed an oriental garden around a 5-acre lake, complete with arched bridges, islands, and a Chinese junk. The small new wineries are as varied as their patrons.

Another winery is Nichelini Vineyard. Anton Nichelini was born in Switzerland, studied winemaking in France, worked in a California winery to learn the business and founded his own winery in 1890. It remains a family concern, over the eastern hills in the Chiles Valley. The winery is at the head of the canyon in an oak grove, built into the hill under a house. There is a wide terrace at the entrance to the cellars, dominated by a massive old Roman press that is probably still workable, although it has not been used for a decade or so. Several varietals are made, and some blends, as well as a rosé from Zinfandel. These are mostly available at the winery and a few shops in California.

All these activities, like those of the Heitz Cellars, are watched closely by other growers, because there is constant talk about forming a market cooperative to handle small lots of premium wines, perhaps 10,000 cases or so of each of the top varietals. This has always worked well for big grower cooperatives like Italian Swiss Colony or Guild, which market mostly blends, but small growers with top wines have never been able to get together. With so much business acumen involved in ventures like Freemark and Heitz, the time is near. The development is enthusiastically supported by out-of-state wine buffs, who are getting tired of dragging home bottles in their luggage.

Sonoma and Mendocino

Sonoma, like ancient Gaul or modern Burgundy, is divided into three parts. The southern Valley of the Moons section attracted Ágoston Haraszthy; the middle section where the Russian River rages west attracted Luther Burbank; the northern section attracted a lot of Italians. All of it is reached by driving north across the Golden Gate on 101, which ought to be called the wine highway because it skirts or runs right through the wine valleys. It even does so south of San Francisco, following through Santa Clara, San Benito and Monterey, the old mission route of El Camino Real. In Sonoma it is called the Redwood Highway, perhaps in memory of the old glories that have been mostly chopped down. As you drive along it, you are never much more than ten minutes away from a tasting room, that California phenomenon that has influenced its citizens to consume wines at more than thrice the national average.

The town of Sonoma was the site of the northernmost mission of the Franciscan fathers and the seat of the last governor of Mexico, Mariano Vallejo, whose wines competed with Haraszthy's under a label named after the estate, Lachryma Montis. The tears came from a spring on the estate, which has been restored, as has the mission. The mountains were the Mayacamas, which come between Sonoma and Napa. The way the moon comes over them — out from behind one peak, hidden behind another, out again — chasing shadows across the dale, moved the Indians to call it the Valley of the Moons. Sonoma also marked the southernmost push of the Russian occupation, at nearby Fort Ross. What is left of that presence is little more than some architectural touches, best seen at the Korbel winery, on the Russian River. A few other names remain, intermingled with Spanish ones, in what has become a resort area.

Jack London settled north of the town, in Glen Ellen, where he tried to raise, not vines, but eucalyptus trees. The trees flourished but the business died. Luther Burbank raised all sorts of things at Santa Rosa, crossing and breeding just about everything — even wine grapes although he was a teetotaler — and the orchards along the way bear testimony to his labors. On hills too steep for trees or vines, ranchers graze their sheep. The lamb is delicious with the country wines from vineyards scattered for a score of miles along the road. Foppiano and Cambiaso are south of Healdsburg and Simi is above; Nervo is below Geyserville, with Pedroncelli above. In Asti is the home of Italian Swiss Colony, which takes in the production of dozens of other local growers. Over east is the Alexander Valley.

The big news in the Alexander Valley in 1969 was that Widmer's of New York had bought 500 acres of prune orchard and was replanting it in Pinot Noir and Cabernet Sauvignon, the first modern wine company to have premium vineyards on both coasts. With the two big Windsor Winery blocks, Russ Green's vineyards for Simi, and smaller blocks owned by others, it was the largest concentration of noble vines in the county. It became even larger when Moët & Chandon, the great Champagne house that is part of the international firm that also includes Hennessy Cognac and Christian Dior, planted a large vineyard from which to make sparkling wines.

The old firms that had happily sold their grapes or their wines in bulk began to get busy. Among the first of these was Pedroncelli, west of Geyserville. John and James took over some 60 acres from their father in 1955 and began bottling a few of their own wines. They were encouraged by Henry Vandervoort, one of San Francisco's leading wine merchants, who took a cask of their Cabernet and made a special bottling of it. By 1970 they had doubled the size of the vineyard with noble vines and were offering such things as Zinfandel Rosé, the wine that had won a prize at the State Fair and had started all the activity in the first place. Nervo, south of town, offers some varietals at the winery. Seghesio has replanted half of their 300 acres in noble vines, but like most of the others, still sells in bulk. But there will be new wineries to reckon with before the end of the decade.

Of these small wineries, Pedroncelli may be the most admired, with something less than 100 acres in bearing as the decade began, and a sale of something more than 10,000 cases. Both will double during the decade. Foppiano and Cambiaso are admired for their traditional way of handling country wines. Simi is singled out as the only known bottler of Carignane. Nervo is always singled out because there is a stock of old Zinfandel that is a curiosity. The winery is a small version of the traditional Sonoma building style — a square fieldstone structure with a pitched roof, capped with a dormer that is a miniature of the larger mass.

The county line crosses the road above Cloverdale, past some noisy lumber mills that are smoking up their little hollow. Mendocino begins just before you get to Squaw Leap, a promontory above a gorge, where the customary lovelorn maiden is said to have leaped. It is tight, rolling country so full of sheep that ranchers' wives took to calling themselves Bo-Beeps and published a book, Mountain Lamb Cookery. It is ring-bound, with covers donated by the local hardboard producer, and includes instructions on how to smoke

lamb and make mutton jerky, the story of a shepherd dog and various notes and comment. The book looks as folksy as a church supper,
and it is. The labor was one of love, and the recipes reflect the world-
wide backgrounds of the valley — Europe, Asia, Africa, South America — all given a California twist. There must be two hundred of
them, many of them marvelous, and like the country wines, they express the simple abundance of the valley — not to be ignored, not to
be missed, worth a special trip.

Just north of the border in Mendocino is Hopland, where an experimental vineyard is testing new varieties for replanting and for
new vineyards being planned. The coming decade will produce some
remarkable new wines to join with the few outstanding ones now
available. But most encouraging of all will be the flood of good wines
coming. "At last we're getting out of prunes," said an orchardist,
spreading out his vineyard plans. It is none too soon.

BUENA VISTA

Ágoston Haraszthy said it might take a hundred years before
California wines became what they should be, and it has. Just before
the Civil War, his wines of Buena Vista were sold not only in San
Francisco but also through offices in Chicago, Philadelphia, New
York and London. He dwelt in a Pompeian mansion fronted by an
arc of pillars, and two of his sons married two of General Vallejo's
daughters. It was here that he wrote the report on his European
vineyard tour, addressed "To the Honorable, the Senate and Assembly of the State of California," who did not honor his bill for $12,000.

He came on strong. "California can produce as noble and generous a wine as any in Europe; more in quantity to the acre, and
without repeated failures through frosts, summer rains, hailstorms,
or other causes." Such strident chauvinism proclaimed so much and
so often led to indifference, and he remained a prophet without
honor in his adopted country, which he deserted at the end. But it
was those "other causes" that did him in.

He was an autocrat suspected of Confederate sympathies in a
state that backed the Union. There was a scandal, probably trumped
up, concerning his management of smelting for the San Francisco

mint. He lost money in a market crash, a ruinous brandy tax caught him short, there was a disastrous fire at the winery, and phylloxera attacked the vineyards.

His two sons, Arpad and Attila, stayed on after Haraszthy left for Nicaragua, the first becoming famous for his "Eclipse Champagne," the second for attacking the phylloxera. But everything came tumbling down in the earthquake of 1906, and that was the end of Buena Vista — until 1943.

In 1943 Frank Bartholomew, the chairman of United Press International, bought some of the acreage and replanted it in noble vines, restored the two winery buildings, and generally tidied things up. The wines came to be known, not only the well-known varietals, but such specialties as Green Hungarian, Vine Brook, made from Sylvaner, and Rose Brook, pressed from Cabernet Sauvignon. There is a Zinfandel, said to be from Haraszthy's own vines, and another called Sparkling Sonoma.

It is a lovely place, at the end of a lane outside the town of Sonoma. Past some hundred acres of vineyard, in a grove of eucalyptus bounded by a tumbling brook on one side and the stone winery buildings on the other, is the old domain of Ágoston, now a historical monument. Nearby is the tallest eucalyptus in the state and a sign that proclaims this fact; recently a well was dug, and it was discovered that the tree stood above an artesian spring, which may account for its size. When it rains, the trees give off their spicy scent, filling the air outside in aromatic contrast to the fruity smell inside the winery. In the open court a mossy column supports a spurt of water, its sound lost in the trickle of the brook. There are picnic tables all around.

In 1968, Bartholomew sold the winery to the Young brothers of Los Angeles, operators of a chain of supermarkets. A corporation was formed to build a winery on 700 acres of land, up in the Mayacamas on the Napa-Sonoma line. There is some speculation about just where the line is, but nobody worries about it and the winemakers joke about a new name — Sonapa, perhaps, or Napoma. When the new corporation was set up, Bartholomew retained most of the home vineyards, agreeing to give the new group first call on the grapes, and continued as president. He also retained control over an organization he started called the Friends of Ágoston Haraszthy. It is a century late, of course, but nobody deserves recognition more. There are the good wines, 50,000 cases of them by 1975, to make Haraszthy's prophecy come true.

A SELECTION
Pinot Noir
Gewürz Traminer
Rose Brook
Zinfandel

SEBASTIANI VINEYARDS

Shortly before the turn of the century, at the age of fourteen, Samuele Sebastiani ran away from his home in the hills of Tuscany and came to Sonoma to make cobblestones. When he had saved enough money, he bought a redwood tank, some other equipment, and some grapes, and soon after, began selling his first Zinfandel. In a few years he had a small stone winery on the edge of Sonoma and a son who grew up working in the winery. For the first fifty years, the wines were sold to other wineries, but as the grandsons came into the business, a desire grew to offer wines under the name of the founder. Today there are a score of table wines, more than half of them varietals; one of the most distinguished is Barbera. There are 550 acres in vines, being added to at the rate of 50 acres a year, but Sebastiani still gets most of its grapes from other growers.

The pattern is typical of many wineries in California, and it seems to be much like that established by vintners who supplied Caesar's armies or by the traders of the Hanseatic League. A good winemaker establishes a reputation, which expands through succeeding generations. Today the family wineries are being swallowed up by conglomerates, which can afford the large development costs, and only a few will continue as separate entities.

Sebastiani plans to be one of them, having refused enormous offers. For one thing Auguste Sebastiani would hate to see anything happen to the vineyard irrigation pond set up as a bird refuge, or to his aviary, which includes hundreds of birds from all over the world. His son, namesake of the founder, works with him in directing winery operations. They make the wine from Cabernet Sauvignons planted in the old Vallejo vineyards, owned and named for the last of the Mexican governors. One day a retired sign painter named Earle Brown showed up at the winery and asked to try his hand at carving the ends of one of the casks; now there are dozens of examples of his revival of an old art. The nearby Swiss Hotel captures the flavor of old California. There is a good new restaurant in town, Au Relais, and the Lazy D Cafe for morning coffee, where the Sebastianis can catch up on the latest vineyard gossip. There are always new wines to try, like their Nouveau, made of Gamay Beaujolais, vinified quickly and offered within weeks of the vintage, in the fashion of the Beaujolais Nouveau of France. The winery is a way of life, and through their wines the Sebastianis can share it. Who would want to give that up?

A SELECTION
Pinot Noir
Barbera
Zinfandel
Green Hungarian

HANZELL VINEYARD

Most men who fall in love with wines are content with drinking them, but some seek total involvement. One such was James D. Zellerbach, who doted on Burgundy, and set out a model vineyard on a hillside above Sonoma to grow Pinot Noir and Chardonnay. The winery he built was a replica of part of Clos Vougeot, that Côte d'Or vineyard held in such esteem that French troops are expected to salute when they pass by. The winery was planned so that the amount of grapes crushed in a day would fill a single fermenting tank, while storage casks, bottling facilities, even the vineyard acreage, were scaled to suit. The first vintage was 1956, and soon after, winemaker Brad Webb discovered that the expected yield from the 6 acres was too small to produce the hoped-for yield of a thousand cases a year. There was only six inches of soil under the vines in some places, and yield was sometimes only a quarter-ton, so acreage was increased to 16. When Zellerbach died in 1963, nobody appeared to carry on the operation, so Joe Heitz bought the inventory of wine and the casks were sold off. There were those who thought that Hanzell produced the best wines ever made in Sonoma, and one of these was Douglas Day, who bought the winery in 1965, quickly getting it back in shape. Brad Webb had joined Freemark Abbey, but found a young winemaker named Kim Giles to take over. Webb still runs up every now and then to see how things are coming. Production is so small, few people get a chance to taste the wines, but reports are that they are just what Zellerbach wanted them to be — wines to be drunk whenever they can be found.

WINDSOR VINEYARDS AND TIBURON VINTNERS

One way into the world of wines is to have a grandfather who owns a vineyard and another is to lead a dance troupe through Europe. Still another is to note that the present generation has a greater interest in wines than prunes and a fourth is to be a good letter writer. Put these four together and you have the beginning of Windsor Vineyards. In the end, it is a matter of taste.

As the decade of the sixties began, Rodney Strong started bottling wines in an old building in Tiburon, across the bay from San Francisco. Strong made blends of stocks he'd tasted in countless trips north, through the cellars of Sonoma and Napa, a skill he'd learned while touring his Dance Quartet through Europe. Between engagements, he'd work at his grandfather's vineyard, study at wine schools, taste in the wine regions, and strengthen his resolve to make his own wines when he got too old to dance. He stopped dancing in 1960 and by 1964, many San Franciscans had come to like the wines from Tiburon Vintners.

A friend from New York observed that people liked to see their names on the labels of wines bottled expressly for them. Suiting the action to his words, Peter Friedman drew up a letter offering such bottlings to Californians. Wines by direct mail seemed like a fine idea to Strong and the two leased a winery and its vineyards up in Windsor, near where the Russian River swings west to the ocean. Soon Windsor Vineyards was sending wines all over the West. Strong needed more wines, but he wanted grapes from vines adapted exactly to the varying soils and climates, with each variety in separate blocks, not in a hodgepodge with a few rows of one variety next to a few rows of another. Tiburon Vintners needed its own vineyards.

Strong began developing the vineyards and now there are a dozen plots of almost 5,000 acres, half of them in full bearing. Many of them were once prune orchards. It is the largest vineyard holding in the North Coast counties. Chardonnay comes from a cool zone around Windsor and toward the ocean at Iron Horse, where there is also a block of Pinot Noir. Cabernets grow in the slightly warmer Alexander Valley, in the Dry Creek area around Healdsburg, and along the Russian River. Rieslings and others are on the lower Russian River and on the Santa Rosa plains. Cost is enormous — up to $4,000 plus land cost per acre before the vines produce mature grapes — so the developing vineyards are sold to investors, with Tiburon Vintners signing a management agreement and reserving the grapes for Windsor Vineyards.

A new winery was needed, so Windsor Vineyards went public, selling shares of stock to raise capital and building a spectacular structure in the shape of a cross. Each arm is a sort of giant ramp leading to a central block where a tasting room and office overlook the great stainless steel fermenting columns and pressing equipment. Smaller ramps and bridges between two of the arms lead over a reflecting pool with water jets, from a tree-lined parking area to the tasting room. A flight of wide steps between adjoining arms leads from the tasting room down to a walled lawn where garden parties are held and a buffet can be served. At other times, visitors sit on the steps to watch a concert or ballet; sometimes string quartets or a theatrical group will perform on the steps with the audience seated in the garden. There's a staffed kitchen that caters both small and large parties, with tables set up in the tasting room or in the garden or in the storage bays where red wines age in small oak casks. Space between the other arms are for receiving grapes or for loading trucks. The roof of the central square is a terrace overlooking a square mile of surrounding vineyards.

A modern California winery is a new kind of recreation center, where the making of wine is joined with other pleasures of the table and the performing arts, an outgrowth of the beer halls and wine gardens and theatrical restaurants of the turn of the century. Windsor Vineyards is a delightful example of such a winery. A little cookbook from the French chef in residence, Yvonne Boulleray, enables you to make some of the dishes that flatter the taste of Rod Strong's wines. Another booklet offers some good recipes from the winemaker's wife, Charlotte.

There are a score of table wines from Windsor, plus some fruit wines, sparkling wines, and fortified wines. An appealing trio is labeled Bonded Winery #999, extremely low-priced, a red, a white, and a rosé expertly made and blended to preserve fruit and freshness. There are some special reserves to be offered under a "Sonoma Vineyards" label and sold in wine shops across the country, among them a Pinot Noir, a Zinfandel, and a Petite Sirah; whites include a Sauvignon Blanc, a French Colombard, a Gray Riesling.

An appeal beyond a splendid winery and well-made wines is needed for success. Somehow, the wines must express a certain grace, a flair, panache — the sort of thing expressed by a fine actor or musician or dancer. It has to do with a sense of timing and a sense of rightness. Rod Strong learned it, maybe, in his grandfather's vineyard or while touring Europe, or by tasting and making hundreds of wines. No matter. There is something about the wines of Windsor — all of which comes together in the glass.

A SELECTION
Cabernet Sauvignon
Johannisberg Reisling
French Colombard

SIMI WINERY

Russian River country is a great place for children, so an oil engineer named Russ Green bought an old ranch on a tributary, Hoot Owl Creek, where his family could spend the summer far away from hectic Los Angeles. There were 50 acres in the Alexander Valley near Geyser Peak, just above where the valleys of Sonoma and Napa almost come together, too much land to remain unproductive. Green wasn't interested in sheep, which had been there before, or prunes, or orchards, which were all around, so he began a vineyard.

That was in 1958, and after he enlisted the aid of a Davis viticulturist named Dale Goode, he added a few more acres — Zinfandel and Johannisberg Riesling and Cabernet. Then in 1970, Green bought Simi.

Simi Winery is down on the highway, near Healdsburg. It was founded a century ago by a couple of brothers from Montepulciano, a wine town in the hills of Tuscany. At first they named the winery after the town, but Simi was easier for American tongues and that was the name that stuck, although some of its best-known bottlings were labeled Hotel Del Monte. Some of the old bottles were found in the cellars when Green took over. The last of the Simis had been content to sell a few bottles to passersby and there were hundreds of cases of wines from the 1930s and earlier, many of them subsequently sold at auction.

The winery is a fine old stone building, now completely refitted with steel fermenters and the rest of the modern equipment set up by Bob Stemmler, the winemaker who was trained in Germany and worked for a decade down in Napa at Krug and Inglenook. The winery now draws on some 500 acres of vines, including those from the neighboring Wetzel vineyards. That addition provides Simi with the largest production of Cabernet Sauvignon in Sonoma County, part of which is an ingredient of a full, dry Cabernet Rosé.

Green is particularly proud of his white wines, one he calls Gewürz Traminer, a fruity Chenin Blanc, and a flowery Riesling. His most novel red is perhaps the Carignane, which is rarely bottled as a varietal. He also produces an unusually fruity Zinfandel rather light in body that is a nice contrast to the fuller ones more often found. And you shouldn't miss the Cabernet Sauvignon, which sells for less than four dollars, a remarkable price when you know it comes from well-matured vines. Might even call it Hoot Owl Cabernet.

A SELECTION
Rosé of Cabernet Sauvignon
Cabernet Sauvignon
Carignane
Johannisberger Riesling

KORBEL

The Russian River churns down around a bulge in the coast range snaking west before it reaches Santa Rosa and chuting past Guerneville as it hurries to the sea, picking up creeks along the way. The heights were all redwoods once, and are now back in scrubby ground cover on the steep northern sides, among which are some of the Korbel vineyards, 340 acres of them, still full of stumps. The south side of the river forms a series of benches planted in vineyard and orchard, where 400 more acres are planted, somewhat less stumpy, and 1,000 more acres are being sought, to be brought into bearing by mid-decade, to augment the goodly supply of grapes bought each year under long-term contracts.

There were three Korbel brothers, Czech machinists turned loggers, who cleared the land and began planting it in vines a century ago. Three Heck brothers, descended from an Alsatian wine-maker, took over the establishment in 1954, having learned about making sparkling wines from their father, who had managed the Cook's Imperial Champagne Company of Ohio. Oldest brother Dolph manages the sparkling wine operation, Paul manages the vine-yards and the varietal wines, and Ben manages sales, through Jack Daniel. This link with the makers of Tennessee Sour Mash has turned backwoods mountaineers and Nashville country music stompers into lovers of the bubbly, and made that state into a prime market, where you can be sure to find Korbel Cabernets, Chardonnays, and other wines.

Varietals and other table wines are a relatively new venture, for the firm's reputation has been built on sparkling wines: *Nature,* which is completely dry; *Brut,* which is almost completely dry; *Extra Dry,* which is dry; and *Sec,* which is not quite so dry. There are also a *Rouge,* which is somewhat dry, and a *Rosé,* which is fruity. These are among the most popular of American sparkling wines, fermented in bottle. Their production is a delight.

When fermented in bottle, sparkling wines develop a sediment, which has to be removed by riddling. The wines rest on their sides, and the sediment is gotten to the neck of the bottle by shaking and tipping it up on its neck over a period of days. This is a tedious job traditionally done by hand. The Hecks decided to automate it.

Great racks were built with cradles for each bottle. The racks were hooked up to a vibrator that gives the bottle a gentle shake, or riddle, and are so geared that the bottle is tipped up on its neck slightly, a little more each time. In the racks, thousands of bottles can be riddled simultaneously. The first models rattled, making a mammoth tinkling. Later designs riddled so lightly that the tinkle became a low rumble. But the sediment thus formed was a light and cloudy mass in the neck. It needed to be compacted, and this was accomplished by making the bottles flop. This occurs just before the winery opens in the morning, during the lunch break, just after the winery closes for the day, and in the middle of the night.

The sound is like the breakup of an iceberg, or the final yawn of the San Andreas fault. One unwary visitor thought it was the crack of doom, bounded from the winery in giant leaps, and was discovered some minutes later sitting on a redwood stump on the banks of the river, staring vaguely at an eddy. People have traveled clear across the country just to hear the flop of some ten thousand bottles. Breakage is less than a tenth of 1 percent.

The Hecks' secret weapon is a man named Ben Randrep, who is kept out of sight. He is the mechanical genius who took the rattle out of the riddling and who has also automated a complete bottling line. The traditional way to finish sparkling wines is to freeze the neck of the bottle, pull out the cork, let the pressure of carbon dioxide force out the frozen plug of sediment, refill the bottle with more of the same wine and a dosage of sugar, recork the bottle, label it, put the foil on it, wrap it in tissue paper, and deposit it in a shipping case. Ben Randrep has made this into a single continuous operation — untouched by human hands.

Racks of upended bottles are set on a belt, where they are carried through a bath of freezing brine; then each bottle is held by grippers, uncorked, and so on, separate machines and variously shaped grippers placed along the belt performing one task after another. Workers stand around, watching, giving this bottle a wipe, that one a twist, as they jiggle along to the packing cases, the trucks, the world. Visitors can watch the line for hours.

The winery itself is a handsome stone building with a square stone tower, overlooking the river. Tasting takes place in an old depot of the Northwest Pacific Railroad, which was bought for five dollars and decked out with old wine posters and odd bits of winery accoutrements, including a giant glass with a pump in its base, big enough to hold a girl in a bath of bubbling wine. Occasionally, it still does. Visitors are taken down past Guerneville for lunch, to a handsome restaurant in a redwood grove. Most seasons of the year there is time for a ramble up and down the hilly vineyards, with long views down the river or up into the hills.

Nobody visiting the wine country should miss the flopping of the bottles. One may even get a glimpse of Ben Randrep. Failing both, there are the wines to console you, 2,000,000 bottles of sparkling wine in 1970, and 200,000 cases of table wines by 1972. Not all of them go to Tennessee.

A SELECTION
Pinot Noir
Cabernet Sauvignon
Chardonnay

ITALIAN SWISS COLONY

People going to a new land find places just like home. The English found New England hills and Virginia tidelands; the Dutch found Jersey flats and York state rivers; Scandinavians found pine forest around the Great Lakes; the Spanish found the Southwest. Italians found the North Coast counties around San Francisco Bay — a new Piedmont, a new Tuscany, a new Rome. The Gold Rush yanked people out of Middle Europe and the Middle East, and the hills and sun and soil drew millions — many of whom were miserable in San Francisco fog and winter rain. In 1881 a successful grocer, who became a banker and builder, decided to do something to make them happy.

Andrea Sbarboro set up an Italian Swiss agricultural colony for misplaced Alpinists yearning for the vineyards of home. He found 1,500 acres in north Sonoma, far from the scurry and babel of tongues that made up San Francisco. He called it Asti to console the homesick, and provided room and board and wages, part of which was to go for building up a share in the homestead. Vineyardists who had heard tell of such schemes since Caesar's day decided to settle for wages, suspicious of benefactors who always seemed to end up owning everything when hard times hit.

There were plenty of hard times. Nobody wanted the grapes when the vines began to bear. A winemaker turned druggist was hired to revert to his old trade. Nobody wanted the wines. The Colony decided to market its own — to Italians in New York, and in the new factories of New England and the South, in the cities sprouting on the plains. This worked fine.

Sbarboro built a castle modeled after Hellbrun in Salzburg, full of whimsies to amuse himself, if not his guests — wobbly boards, doors that would not open and others that sprang back at a touch, air jets to send skirts on high. The fun house even had hidden sprinklers to douse visitors, but nothing could dampen the parties. The nights were loud with yodeling and the groans of accordions. One merry time after another, it would seem. And then came Prohibition, the biggest joke of all.

The Rossi twins, who took over the management from their father, turned to selling grapes and making grape juice. Sbarboro retired, still protesting loudly. The firm prospered again after Repeal, was bought by National Distillers during World War II, then sold to the Petri family, which made it a part of Allied Grape Growers, the big cooperative of more than 1,800 growers. The group controls almost one-third of California wine production and is the second largest entity in the state. Marketing is handled by United Vintners, now part of Heublein.

Italian Swiss Colony believes in visitors, and 300,000 are greeted annually by dirndl-skirted maids or red-jacketed guides who conduct tours and tastings. Taste tests are conducted to see what people think of new blends.

There are a lot of wines, all in lines — and a dozen of them might be set out to give you an idea. The top line is Private Stock and there is a low-priced range called Gold Medal. There is the line of Lejon — Vermouths and sparkling wines. There is a group called the "vino" type, the long-time favorite being Tipo Red, in a Chianti bottle. There is a pair called Chablis — one Gold, one Pink. There is an undercurrent of feeling that there may be too many wines — at least, members of the public think so — and many glances are being cast in the direction of the growing market for varietals. Twenty thousand tons of grapes are crushed each year at Asti; and of the 400 grape growers in the North Coast counties, 150 are members of the Italian Swiss Colony cooperative.

The area between Dry Creek and Dutcher Creek is a lot like Burgundy, says Joe Vercelli, one of the plant managers, in that there are dozens of vineyards, each of which could make a distinctive wine, sometimes good, sometimes not so good. They all might do so one day. Right now, the job is to keep all the owners happy, and to provide wines to the public that have continuity from one year to the next. But Italian Swiss is always experimenting.

One direction is into potables based on wines, latter-day relations of the aperitifs so popular in Europe. One of these is Swiss Up, described as having just a whisper of lemon and lime. This is no more startling to a wine buff than Silver Satin, a light, bright imitation of Gallo Thunderbird; there is also a Silver Satin with bitter lemon and Vin Kafe, which contains both coffee and cocoa. Most startling of all is Bali Hai, billed as tropical magic in a bottle, a light pink wine with natural tropical fruit flavors of Guava, Pineapple, Lemon, Orange, and Passion Fruit. A new one is Annie Green Springs.

After rolling these over on your tongue, a rather exuberant view of what the future may bring dances before the mind's eye. A country bored with cocktails might easily develop a raving thirst for a wine-based drink. As drinking water gets loaded with chlorine and whatnot, something is needed. Something without soda-pop sweetness. Something like nothing you ever tasted before.

One such is Cold Duck. A sparkling wine with a pronounced flavor of Concord grapes, it became the rage around the Great Lakes and has begun to flow into other parts of the country. It tastes like a punch one might remember from children's parties, grown up a little. Some people think that it makes an excellent highball when spiked with brandy or gin. This and other possibilities that can be imagined can give a senior member of a wine society the fits. Youngsters on campuses across the country are not so hidebound, and the various exotics, even the more traditional blends, are finding an unprejudiced audience.

Another creation is a softened red wine of a type called Vino, Vino Rosso or Mellow. This is a blend in which the fermentation has been stopped so that some of the sweetness from the grape remains in the wine. Italian Swiss markets two of them, Vino Primo and Cappella, the latter being the mellower, and both being fruity and bland.

Italian Swiss Colony has an enormous responsibility to its growers and an equally immense concern for its customers, so it must produce wines in large volume. This would seem to leave little time or space for experiment, but because the marketing firm is a separate unit busying itself in a widening market, invention can become a rich resource by which to gain new customers. There is sure to be an effort to become involved in premium wines made from good varietals, marketed under grape names or brand names, and these will be wines to look for.

A SELECTION
Tipo Red
Private Stock Grenache Rosé
Lejon Extra Dry Vermouth

MENDOCINO VINEYARDS

There are many vines in Mendocino, and there are due to be more, as orchards are ripped out and vineyards are put in. A Davis experimental planting at Hopland, whose name echoes a former crop, is developing various grapes that are expected to do well in a district that has areas in Region Three. Mendocino is somewhat warmer than Sonoma, where the bay provides a tempering effect, although hillside vineyards produce some remarkable wines from shy bearers. The land around Hopland was mostly pear country at the beginning of the decade, with vineyards on slopes farther north, mostly around Ukiah. The close hills and many lakes make it a haven for campers and hikers; because it is two hours away from San Francisco, it may be saved from developers for a time.

Cresta Blanca is a grand old name in California, that of a Livermore vineyard planted from European cuttings almost a century ago by Charles Wetmore. The grapes from Château d'Yquem and Château Margaux did well enough in the new soil to win a Grand Prix at the Paris Exhibition in 1889. It's also the name used in one of the first singing commercials a generation ago, spelled out in a rising crescendo then diminuendo unhappily difficult to forget. The firm also had its ups and downs as a branch of Schenley's until 1970, when it was purchased by Guild and set up as an independent corporation to market wines from cooperative members in the North Coast counties, some fifty growers with some 2,000 acres of top varieties. The winemaker to launch the new wines was Roy Mineau, who had been making those of Cresta Blanca for thirty years. Cresta Blanca is on the edge of Ukiah, a small tasting lodge backed by a massive stone winery full of small European oak casks where the red wines age for as much as three years. In addition to those from the original Livermore vineyard, there was a chance to introduce some new wines from Mendocino varietals, including Zinfandel, French Colombard, and Green Hungarian. And there was the opportuity to revive two famous special wines. Sauvignon Blanc and Sémillon. They were first offered to Californians by letter, pairs of six varietals in a compartmented wooden case, but distribution is being extended slowly along the eastern seaboard and around the Great Lakes. Cresta Blanca is again a name to be heard from.

A SELECTION
Gamay Beaujolais
Petite Sirah
French Colombard
Sauvignon Blanc

PARDUCCI WINE CELLARS

A visitor rambling around the wine country does not know which way to turn. Napa is not so difficult, or even the Valley of the Moons or the Russian River, because he will have heard of some of the producers, but as he goes up the Redwood Highway, the wineries with Italian names become a jumble. By the time he gets to the pear orchards of Mendocino, he may begin thinking of the two-hour drive back to Fisherman's Wharf for dinner and call it a day. This will be a mistake — there is still Parducci.

Guidebooks say that Parducci is one of the northernmost wineries in California, in business for half a century, offering the expected varietals and blends, plus some oddities like Petite Sirah or Flora, this last being the Davis hybrid of Traminer. Adolph, the founder, was born in Santa Clara, went back to Italy to learn winemaking and eventually settled down three miles north of Ukiah among what was to become 225 acres of vineyards. Two of his four sons wanted to go into varietals, and in 1964 they bought out the other sons, who did not want to pursue such a career. John is winemaker, George is business manager.

John is too busy to do much more than present the highlights when he talks about his wines — a few words and lots of running back and forth with a handful of glasses between vats and casks and storage tanks and fifty-gallon butts of French oak. A flash flood tore off part of the winery roof in 1969, and things are shipshape now, but not apple-pie, and while the third and fourth generations help out, there is still too much to do.

The place looks like a jumble, but it is not. The grapes come to the top side, John explains, leading the visitor up some stairs to show him the crushers on a platform against the uphill wall. Then the red wines come into the winery and the vats, of redwood so old it does not impart any taste. The whites go into the fermenters along the downhill wall for two or three weeks. The reds finish in a week, go into these old, closed redwood storage uprights and then into Limousin oak cooperage. The time depends on the wine. Try this Chardonnay. Now the Sémillon. Now the Sylvaner. You shouldn't miss the Chenin Blanc. Don't let me forget the French Colombard. Practically nobody else bottles it. And there are four '69 Cabernets from different areas.

"We make high quality or we forget it," says John. "If the wines don't come up to our standards, we won't bottle, we'll bulk. We're not blending anything now. You want to taste the Petite Sirah? Some say a wine like that is good for twenty years. I bet it could go for fifty."

It's for all the world like being in Burgundy, the winemaker intent on your tasting the wines in the various stages before bottling, so you can get an idea of what's coming — next year, two years from now, ten years. There's really no time for such tasting, and John is eager to have visitors know what is already in bottle, leading the way to the tasting room down the drive, near the road. It's as cluttered as a gift shop, with a rack of monographs from the local historical society on local lore and the mythology of the Pomo Indians, strange and subtle. Corks are pulled at a counter in the back.

Parducci has 120 acres in varietals on the home ranch, with another 275 on new ranches just south of Ukiah planted in Pinot Noir, Chardonnay, and Johannisberg Riesling. The '69 whites are big and full, the '68 Pinot Noir is enormous, the '67 Cabernet is also full, the '67 Zinfandel has a big nose and great balance, the '65 Petite Sirah has a fabulous nose and measures 13.7 in alcohol. Incautiously, because a taster is traditionally deadpan and secretive, you say the wines are certainly full, with fine bouquet. We like them big, John always says. A new winery to make them was built in 1972.

Driving home late, a visitor keeps an eye out for the vineyard south of Ukiah, replanted from a pear orchard. This one, maybe, or that one — all those pears — must be lovely in spring. They will be in vines before the decade is out, a lot of them. There are now 6,000 acres, half that of Napa or Sonoma, but more to come.

There is only one Parducci. How many more like him will there be in ten years' time?

A SELECTION
Chardonnay
Pinot Noir
Zinfandel
Sylvaner

OTHER WINERIES

Like the Napa Valley, Sonoma, Mendocino, and adjoining counties are blessed with an influx of enthusiastic amateur winemakers turning professional, corporate groups, and expanding wine firms who are rebuilding vineyards and establishing new ones. All of them are racing city people who are seeking country living and developers who cater to the escapism; there's no agricultural districting or green belt zoning of the sort that gives some protection to adjoining Napa Valley. A descendant of the Bundschus who established the Rhinefarm near Sonoma is rebuilding that vineyard. Robert and Fred Kunde have replanted their grandfather's Wildwood Vineyard. Gino Zepponi is doing the same with his family's vineyard with the help of Norman de Leuze, renaming it the ZD Winery in the process. Another pair, Allen Ferrara and Robert Magnani, have revived an old installation and call it Grand Cru Vineyard.

Up the valley around Healdsburg, Leo Trentadue took advantage of the Italian meaning of his name and is now offering varietals with a big 32 on the label. David Stare, whose father conducts nutrition research at Harvard, graduated from there, took courses at Davis to round out the experience gained making wines at home, bought 80 acres, and began planting them in noble vines at his Dry Creek Vineyard.

Further north above Geyserville, an old winery has been renamed Viña Vista by its new owner, Keith Nelson, because it overlooks the Russian River. Overlooking the highway is extensive Geyser Peak Winery, once known for its vinegar, now taken over by the Schlitz beer people, who are expanding the hundred-odd acres of vineyard. This is the merest beginning, for breweries have elaborate distribution systems that could handle wines, especially so now that some states are beginning to permit the sale of wines in supermarkets.

Perhaps the most important of the new installations is up in Mendocino in Redwood Valley, where Bernard Fetzer bought a ranch in the late fifties and began building a winery complex with the help of his wife and their eleven children. The first grapes went to amateur wine makers across the country, but with 90 acres bearing and more coming in, Fetzer Vineyards has begun to market its wines. Their success has led others to put in top varietals, greatly extending the range of vineyards northward. Toward the Pacific, in Anderson Valley, Husch vineyards has begun to offer its wines, starting with Chardonnay and Gewürztraminer. Up in Lake County there are perhaps a thousand acres of new vines, many of them Cabernet

Sauvignon, and a group of growers has made plans to open a winery and market jointly. In between are a score of others, some day to be heard from. Vineyards may extend all the way to Oregon before the decade ends.

Santa Clara, San Benito, and Monterey

There are some who think San Francisco looks more than anything else like the hump of a great white whale whose backbone is the Santa Cruz Mountains, running down the peninsula. A drive called the Skyline runs along the spine, cresting the wintergreen hills and sweeping past evergreen side ridges and lengths of dammed ravine. It is a lovely drive, with glimpses of the bay on one side and rarer ones of ocean on the other, but those in a hurry to reach the wine country around Saratoga, Los Gatos, and San Jose are more inclined to take the Bayshore Freeway, which is Highway 101, or the new Junípero Serra Freeway, which runs along the bayside flank of the range and through Stanford University campus, where the founder planted immense vineyards — now long gone. (The original winery is now a muddle of shops and restaurants; Leland Stanford loved wine but his wife did not, and she outlived him.) Whichever way you go, your first stop will probably be Paul Masson or Almadén. They are the two largest producers of fine wines in the country.

The indecisive may prefer to go first to the Novitiate in Los Gatos; the town has a restoration section of old buildings that are worth a ramble. Wine buffs might first seek out California's smallest winery, Woodside Vineyards, 24 feet square, run by Robert and Polly Mullen. They have some acres of Cabernet Sauvignon in part of what was once La Questa, a vineyard that commanded the highset prices of all California growths in the 1880s. Much more modest today, there is some Traminer and some Riesling, and even smaller amounts of Pinot Noir, Chardonnay, and Chenin Blanc. You have to make an appointment, just to taste the wines.

Not at all modest is Martin Ray, whose wines are the most expensive in the hemisphere. His vineyards crown Mount Eden, and his wines carry names like Mount Cabernet and Mount Chardonnay.

From his vineyards 1,800 feet above the valley, you can see the problem; the Santa Clara valley was once farmland and is now suburb, ranchless houses sprouting where the orchards bloomed, pushing the vineyards up into the hills or out of the valley altogether. Martin Ray came from a Saratoga farming family, made a fortune as a young stockbroker, bought the mountain vineyard of Paul Masson in 1936, and began making classic wines in traditional ways from the noble vines of Burgundy and Bordeaux. By 1943, the world was pressing close, so he sold out and moved up on Mount Eden, where he now makes a few sparkling wines from the free run of juice (or light pressing), with such names as Sang de Pinot, Blanc de Noir, and Champagne de Chardonnay. He also makes three kinds of table wines, depending on racking the wines, using no filtering or fining, and making sure that the grapes ripen thoroughly on the vines. His Pinot Noir marketed as "La Meilleure Récolte" is made from over-ripe grapes. Paired with this "best vintage" is another called First Crush, made from a light pressing. He makes similar wines from Chardonnay, his Great Crush being identified as coming from "Le Fruit Mûr des Vignes Dorées," because the ripe fruit is picked when the vine leaves have turned to gold. His Cabernets are often held for a couple of decades before being released, and are sometimes labeled "Mariage," indicating a blend of vintages. He has little to do with the rest of the California wine world. Atop Mount Eden he is content to go his own way, leaving his wines long in small casks, releasing a few bottles to those willing to pay the price, and gradually turning operations over to his son, Dr. Peter Martin Ray, who is a plant physiologist. With the senior Ray's retirement, control of the vineyards passed to others.

Still higher, 2,300 feet up on Monte Bello Road, is Ridge Vineyards, a small clutch of vines once part of a larger holding, and now being extended gradually by a small group of enthusiasts. The wines are among the best varietals and bear the date of the vintage. The operation is similar to that of David Bruce, a San Jose physician who has some 40 acres in the peaks above Los Gatos. Prices of both are much lower than Martin Ray's, and wine buffs seek them out because the wines are as good as they are rare, carefully made with the guidance and advice of Davis and industry experts. Such small-scale endeavors are a rich and vital part of California's heritage.

The first vineyardists were mostly French, arriving in the wake of the Gold Rush, and their successes led to the establishment of many vineyards by California's early landed gentry. These, in turn, attracted Mediterranean immigrants, whose ancestors had tended orchards and vineyards in the wake of the Romans. Many of the early Italian families remain and still own wineries that offer various reds, whites, and rosés. They are in two general areas; around Morgan Hill and on the road that cuts west from Gilroy, through Hecker Pass. The first group includes Guglielmo and Pedrizzetti, the second such names as Pappani, Conrotto, Bertero, Cassa, Solis, Bonesio, and Giretti. These are country wines of little or no distinction, with the possible exception of Gemello, who is way up in Mountain View, and who offers some interesting varietals. A quick sampling of the general run available can be made at Richert & Sons, on the highway above Morgan Hill, which concentrates on sweet fortified wines, or the big San Martin tasting room, south of the town, which offers a trio of varietals from part of its 1,100 acres (plus such things as Blackberry, Loganberry, and Advent Wine, which is made in December for the holiday season).

The major wineries — Paul Masson, Almadén, and Mirassou — are transferring much of their vineyard operation down into San Benito County and Monterey County. Some bottling and storing and aging facilities are continued by these major firms in the area once famous for vineyards, but they are well worth following all the way to the Pinnacles country, where a revolution in California viticulture is taking place.

THE NOVITIATE OF LOS GATOS

A band of fourteen Jesuit novices established the vineyards of the novitiate on the flank of the Santa Cruz foothill that rises above Los Gatos. That was in 1888, and the brothers and fathers have continued ever since. Eighty percent of their wines are sacramental — altar wines available only to churches — but some 10,000 cases are offered commercially, including a few varietals like Cabernet, Pinot Blanc, and White Riesling. There are some blends of table wines and some Sherries, but the most famous are the sweet dessert wines, particularly the Black Muscat, Muscat Frontignan, and Angelica.

The winery runs up the hill, offices and quarters on a shelf, the valley and the vineyards below. In all, there are some 640 acres in vine, equivalent to a square mile, half of them located in Modesto, others in the hills behind Alma, some in Hollister, and only 120 acres around the novitiate itself. Some 400 acres were sold to become subdivisions, and these are gradually being replaced with plots planted in varietals. Vineyard management is in the hands of Father Henri Charvet, who was born in the middle of a vineyard, not in his ancestral France but in the state of Washington. The Black Muscat has been a secret wine, scarcely known even in California, and the varietals are even rarer, but the novitiate is in the process of expanding its production and widening its markets.

A SELECTION
Black Muscat
Grenache Rosé
White Riesling

ALMADÉN VINEYARDS

Winemakers seem to be forever taking to the hills. The Gold Rush brought Etienne Thée from Bordeaux, but he quickly became interested in and planted a vineyard around a knoll on land he bought from the old Rancho San Juan Bautista. The land stretched along a creek called the Guadelupe, a few miles south of San Jose, near Los Gatos. On the knoll he built a house, and named his domain Almadén, after a quicksilver mine nearby. His vines came from the great districts of France, and were planted with the help of a friend who arrived from the Parisan suburb of Passy. His name was Charles Lefranc, a tailor who dressed the vines and who eventually married his friend's daughter.

This history was to repeat itself, for when Lefranc inherited Almadén, he sent for a young man from Burgundy to help him out.

The young friend was Paul Masson, and he married Lefranc's daughter and eventually set up a vineyard of his own.

Both vineyards prospered until Prohibition, when Almadén became moribund, only to get a new lease on life in 1941. This came about when a San Francisco businessman named Louis Benoist met a travel writer turned wine importer named Frank Schoonmaker. Schoonmaker had written a book about European wines shortly after Repeal and became so interested in his subject that he began bringing the bottlings of small producers to the United States. The result was so successful that he was asked to do a book on American wines, and so he toured California. What he found confirmed findings from earlier tours — that some good wines were being made, but that many of them were being marketed under outlandish European names and that many of the best wine properties, and grapes, were being ignored. His idea was to play up a faltering California tradition, marketing wines under the names of the grapes or with local names, so that people would know what they were getting and could distinguish the wines of one locality from another. Benoist liked the idea, and bought Almadén on Schoonmaker's advice.

During the next twenty-five years, Almadén came back to life. Low-priced wines were marketed as Mountain Red and Mountain White, setting a new standard for good and simple table wines. A group of wines bearing grape names was marketed around the country. Schoonmaker believed that California could make outstanding pink wine, using the Grenache grape planted in the Rhone district of Tavel. Almadén Grenache Rosé was accepted so readily that the firm now has a larger planting than exists in the original district. Spanish grapes that produce Sherry should do well in California, Schoonmaker believed, so Palominos were planted and a *solera* system was set up to blend the wines; it now consists of 35,000 casks and covers an area the size of a football field. There was no reason at all why California could not produce fine sparkling wines and Almadén today offers half a dozen, including a Blanc de Blancs.

Benoist had the time of his life. The old Lefranc house on the knoll was refurbished, the tub in which Anna Held bathed in Champagne was installed in the guest suite to entice visitors, a dining room seating forty was decorated with chandeliers, and part of the cellar under the house was set up to look like a back alley in Paris. Terraces and gardens and pools were set around the house. A pheasantry was set up near one of the winery buildings, which were of soft sandy stone or were wood painted mustard with white trim, a color that is close to the monarchy yellow of the Austrian empire and popular among California vineyard owners. Schoonmaker came out every few months to taste the wines and admire the impeccable care given the vines and the winery. And he began to notice how surrounding vineyards and orchards were giving way to streets and bungalows.

The Santa Clara valley runs south into San Benito County, where there are upland valleys south of Hollister called the Paicines country, after Indians who once lived there. On the west are the Pinnacles, jagged peaks between the vales, which are now a national monument and were once a hideout for a local bandit. Beginning in 1955, Almandén purchased various vineyards in the area — the Sykes Ranch, Valliant Vineyards, and La Cienega vineyards with its old winery that lies astride the San Andreas fault. Here a new winery was built, plus the largest storehouse for table wines in the world, as big as four football fields. As the decade began, there was an additional plantation of about 245 acres, up in the Livermore Valley, near Pleasanton. There were only 45 left around the home vineyard at Los Gatos, where Champagne is made and much of the bottling is still done. All in all, there were 3,500 acres in bearing, the largest single holding of fine varietals in the world.

The acreage will be doubled by 1976, much of it in Monterey County to the west. The vineyards are on down Route 101 in the Salinas Valley, almost 1,000 acres near King City, another 1,400 at San Lucas, and almost 1,000 acres up near Livermore in Alameda County in a district called Sunol, named after an early winemaker. Another 8,000 acres planted and supervised by Almadén will provide grapes under long-term contract.

Some of the vineyards will cost as much as $4,000 an acre to bring to bearing, requiring a dozen small reservoirs to provide water for the sprinkling systems, and a small factory that makes the necessary plastic pipe. The sprinkling systems are underground, with standpipes every few feet, emitting a fine spray that cools the vineyard air or wards off frost, and also serves to water the vineyards in times of drought.

Even the tasting rooms have moved away from the home vineyard at Los Gatos. A restoration settlement in the old town of San Juan Bautista, near Hollister, contains a neat room in an old building, and there is an outdoor deck shaded by trees a few steps away, with a view of some vineyards. The main tasting room is on the fork that leads through Pacheco Pass into the San Joaquin valley and on to Yosemite. It is one of the loveliest passes in California, skirting an enormous lake full of bays that provides water brought from northern California to the great valley.

Dr. A. J. Winkler, professor emeritus of viticulture at Davis, was adviser on the vineyard installation. Louis Benoist realized that the necessary expansion was too much for one man, and sold Almadén to National Distillers in 1967. Frank Schoonmaker has always said that Americans would become wine drinkers once they knew what they were missing, and what they could get. Now they know. Even Frank is surprised that they have learned the lesson so well. The company markets almost two million cases of wine a year, expecting to increase this by half before the middle of the decade, continuing to ride the wave of revolution it began.

A SELECTION
Grenoir
Mountain Red
Sylvaner
Pinot Blanc

PAUL MASSON VINEYARDS

Paul Masson wanted to stand alone. He was pleased to come from Burgundy in the 1850s to help Charles Lefranc make wines at Almadén. He was charmed to marry Lefranc's daughter, if only to carry on a tradition. He was delighted to set up a separate company with Lefranc to concentrate on the making of sparkling wines. But he wanted to be master of his own vineyards, and in the 1880s he bought a hunk of mountain above Saratoga and set to work.

His wines made his reputation quickly and sustained it for half a century. The earthquake in 1906 knocked down his winery but he rebuilt it with stones from an old San Jose church that had been demolished, incorporating a Romanesque portal of the twelfth century that had been brought from Spain for the church. The old winery looks something like a shrine today, and in front of it, during the summer, chamber music concerts are held amid the vines. Tickets are booked far in advance. Listening to the sounds of a string quartet soaring over a leafy vineyard is a lovely way to pass a summer afternoon. There is a spreading ranch house on the brow of the vineyard hill, and from its terrace you can look down into the valley of the Santa Clara, to the modern sparkling wine cellars, bottling facilities, and valley vineyards of Paul Masson.

The valley winery is a structure of many arched bays entered by a circular covered ramp that winds up above a pool full of water jets, so that you circle up in a mist of splashing. A mosaic mural of vineyard scenes forms an outer rampart that circles up with you. It is covered with a disc roof and if you squint going up, it is possible to imagine you are a bubble in a glass of sparkling wine, which may have been what the designer had in mind. The ramp leads to a gallery that runs the length of the winery, past 800 feet of upright storage tanks and round casks and bottling lines.

Masson was as interested in the people who drank his wines as in the wines themselves — it was his sparkling wine that Anna Held bathed in — and at times it seemed that more wine was drunk at parties at the mountain vineyard than was grown there. Big and round as one of his butts, Masson was a joyous presence and much preferred those who drank his wines gladly to the solemn ones who sipped cautiously and jotted down punctilious notes. He was a fine taster, and once won the top prize in a national wine judging contest in Paris, which so confounded Parisians that the rules were changed so a foreigner would not win again. In his seventies, he began to lose his ability to make the fine distinctions, which is perhaps why he sold his firm to Martin Ray in 1936, in hope that Ray would carry on the tradition. Masson died four years later, a year before the winery was swept by fire. Ray rebuilt the winery, but sold it to Seagram's in 1943, when he decided he would rather have fewer vineyards still farther up in the mountains. After the war, the firm was managed by two members of old Rhineland families, Alfred Fromm, representing the fifth generation of his family, and Franz Sichel, representing the seventh of his. Another Rhinelander, Otto Meyer, took over the Sichel minority holding at the latter's death, until Seagram made the firm a subsidiary of Browne Vintners in 1971.

The postwar sprawling of suburbs turned the gaze of the partners south, first to a tract of half a square mile near Gilroy, and then to the Salinas valley, which runs down from Monterey Bay. Davis viticulturists had long considered the Pinnacles district of the Salinas valley to be prime vineyard area, but the problem was one of water. Vines like arid country, their roots can reach deep, but they need water before and after the flowering. There is an enormous underground river under Salinas, too deep even for vines, and yet the firm believed the market was growing fast enough to warrant the expense of drilling to this source. Running east of south, these valleys catch the early sun; cool ocean breezes shortly after noon serve to keep temperatures down, while the coastal ranges shade the vines from the westering sun. With water, it was perfect for the grape.

The grape is called a complete plant because it pollinates itself; the most difficult is the Chardonnay, but the breeze would help in this. The area south of Soledad, running for nearly twenty miles through Greenfield to King City, would be ideal for noble vines, a solid Region Two, the ranch managers say. More than 900 acres were set out around Greenfield, nearly twice that in the slightly cooler area of the Pinnacles vineyards up near Soledad. In all, Paul Masson now has some 4,000 acres of vineyard, with plans for more.

The new winery among the Pinnacles vineyards is a model, the gleaming columns of jacketed stainless steel fermenters flanked by stainless steel crushers forming a giant abstract behind the sand-color mass of the air-conditioned building. Within are great rooms full of tall oak holding tanks, racks of small oak cooperage, and large stainless steel storage tanks.

The firm shows a flair for anything entertaining and beguiling, and this is focused on widening the interest in California wines, not only in the United States but also in Europe and Asia. An active export division supplies British and German markets, beginnings are being made in Asian countries, several international airlines serve Paul Masson wines regularly, and there is an active trade with embassies around the world. The international background of many members of the firm makes this seem only natural, and they are only too glad to compete with European shippers for a share of the world market. At a time when many other firms are just considering venturing east of the Rockies, it is encouraging to know that Paul Masson is exploring possibilities in Hong Kong and Singapore.

Pioneering a new vineyard region presents special problems, and while Davis experts are near at hand, a trick or two may still come from old world know-how. Otto Meyer brought over a young graduate of the wine college in Trier, Ed Friedrich, to see if techniques developed on the Moselle would be helpful at Pinnacles. Guy Baldwin, who had been busy making wines in Canada, came down to take over the winemaking when Friedrich moved on to Arkansas to see what could be done there. Winemakers are as busy solving problems as vineyard managers. There is the problem, for instance, of the malolactic fermentation, the slow, secondary working of the wine that takes place when the tumultuous fermentation has subsided. This is inhibited in some white wines of the Rhine by keeping them at low temperatures, by using sulphur dioxide to kill unwanted bacteria, and by clarifying the wine and controlling its stability. There is a strong feeling that wood should contribute very little, if any, character to white wines, its presence masking bouquet and subtleties of taste. There are those in Germany who say that Rhine wines should never touch wood, and this seeming heresy is being tested at Pinnacles. Now others follow that lead.

The firm makes changes slowly, and thinks of the growing public for wines as a discerning and disparate aggregate that warrants careful wooing. Some tentative wine drinkers start out liking white wines, for instance, because they are served cold. Paul Masson introduced Rubion recently, a soft and light red wine with a flowery aroma that appeals to such drinkers and encourages them to try other reds. Similarly, there is a soft white wine called Emerald Dry and also a full, soft red called Baroque that may intrigue those seeking something beyond the tried and true. The aim of the firm is to have a number of different wines readily available all around the country, so that a bottle of Paul Masson is at hand whenever the spirit moves. Nearly a score of different table wines are offered, over a dozen fortified wines, and half a dozen sparkling wines, so that trying one will lead you to try another, and another. . . . To keep ahead, Paul Masson has taken to introducing one new wine a year, in only a few markets when supply is short, then gradually extending the availability. There is always some reserved for export. No reason why traditional Paul Masson exuberance should not be sent around the world, and the firm is now represented in some fifty countries.

A SELECTION
Cabernet Sauvignon
Baroque
Johannisberg Riesling

MIRASSOU

French winemakers who settled in the Santa Clara seem to have done well by their daughters. Whoever heard of Pierre Pellier, for instance, who — like Charles Lefranc and Etienne Thée — also had a daughter? He settled opposite his countrymen, over east, in the Evergreen section beneath Mount Hamilton, and began planting what eventually became half a square mile of grapes. A Mirassou married his daughter. You might never have heard of Mirassou, either, except that there is a heritage of sons, and two of them produced five more, who are now working in the vineyards, with nineteen offspring in the generation coming up. For a century and more, the vineyards produced exceptional grapes and superior wines — that were sold to other vintners. It was a sad day for those other vintners when the five boys of the present generation cornered their fathers in 1965 and told the pair that Mirassou was going to market its own wines. Amiably, Ed and Norbert agreed. It was almost as if they had planned it that way.

Winery life is not easy. The way you get sons to follow along is to tell them maybe they do not want any part of it. But you give them free run of the place — in the vineyards, around the crushers at vintage time, among the fermenters when the wine is making in the cellars. You do not worry about them too much. You let them pick grapes, along with the other pickers, and pay them the going rate per box. Then you let them be checkers, as the boxes are brought to the gondolas, and you let them prune and cultivate and bud new vines. They get to run the sprayers and drive the tractors. Then they make the wines, racking them off the lees, fining them, filtering them, tending the wines in casks, running them through the bottling line, manning the tasting room. You pay them the going rate for each job. And when college nears, you mention that Fresno has a good school where you learn all the practicalities of the business; why don't you run down and look it over? With luck, Ed and Norbert figured, you might get one or two. They never expected to get the whole lot.

Let's see. Steve and Daniel are in sales. Pete is setting up the new vineyards in Soledad. Jim is controller. Son-in-law Don makes the wines. They buy the grapes from their elders, and rent from them storage space for the wines. Ed and Norbert give advice when asked, which is often, because the boys figure the fathers are pretty shrewd. In every way, Mirassou is a family affair.

After the vintage in 1966, the first bottled wines went on sale at locations other than the winery. By the end of the decade, national sales had risen to 25,000 cases. They were expected to reach 200,000 by mid-decade, then double again by 1980. Distributors are on allocation. There are some wines offered as Limited Bottlings, which are sold without allocation, and there is a Petite Rosé made from Petite Sirah. This was first put on sale in 1969, and the year's supply was gone a month after release.

The Mirassous look to the south, and have been doing so since the late fifties, soon after Almadén began planting its first vineyards at Paicines, down in San Benito County. They looked everywhere at first — up in the Mother Lode country, in the foothills of the Sierras, north of Sacramento near Redding, north of Sonoma and into Mendocino, into southern California. In 1961 they found Monterey and its Salinas valley, particularly between Soledad and Greenfield. It was none too soon. When they started looking, the Mirassous were accustomed to buying 3,000 tons of grapes to augment their own, but the supply had dwindled to a tenth by 1969.

Today they have more than two square miles of vines in bearing. As the home vineyards are sold for building lots, more acreage will be planted in the Salinas valley. As the decade began, various firms had planted more than 6,000 acres of vines in Monterey — nearly ten square miles — with perhaps another 40,000 by mid-decade. Well before the end of the century, say the Mirassous, Monterey will be the leading area for grape growing of all the North Coast counties. Bare land had risen to $2,000 an acre at the beginning of the decade, and often cost as much again to bring into bearing.

The Mirassous like to talk about the advantages they see in Monterey, where they say there is little chance of rain during vintage, which begins late, about the first week of October, and may continue into November. Winds during the summer serve as natural air conditioning, down from Monterey Bay in the early afternoon. The Mirassous feel this is an advantage over the more closed-in vineyards to the east of the Gavilan Mountains. There is no danger of spring frosts, as in Napa. The soil has a high percentage of gravel. And so it goes — being the nature of vineyard owners to feel their own has advantages over all others.

Winemakers are always comparing, and as an example, Daniel Mirassou rated his vintages of Cabernet Sauvignon with those of Bordeaux. The first year of the 1960s was a toss-up; Bordeaux excelled in '61, '62 and '66, and showed a slight edge in '64. Mirassou excelled in the other five vintages; very good in '67, wonderful in '68, and even better in '69, according to Daniel. The comparison has a certain validity, because Bordeaux counts itself lucky if half the vintages are outstanding, while California thinks itself unlucky when half the vintages are short of wonderful. When Europe has an off-vintage, it is not illogical to suppose that the same California vintage may provide some remarkable wines. The telling is in the tasting. Mirassou and the other pioneers of California winemaking are investing hundreds of millions of dollars to see to it that there are enough wines available for people to make up their own minds.

The Mirassous now tend 1,250 acres of vineyard. They offer a dozen varietals, some of which are specially reserved stocks marketed as Harvest Wines. They offer a few generics and four sparkling wines. They are unhappy about their Sauvignon Blanc, acknowledged to be one of the best produced, because the variety is losing favor with the public. They are delighted with their Pinot Blanc, which the family considers to be on a par with the Chardonnay, at least in their own vineyards. And they are ecstatic about Zinfandel, which is admired because it can be drunk as a fresh and fruity young wine or one that has elegance and finesse after five years or so in bottle. For thirty years, bottles of Mirassou were secret wines, known only to wine buffs energetic enough to come to the winery for them. The fifth generation is seeing to it that they are secrets no longer. Ed and Norbert look at their nineteen grandchildren, certainly convinced that the family name will not be a notation in a wine book like that of the founder, who came from the Cognac district of France so long ago. Maybe you won't remember his name. You won't forget Mirassous.

A SELECTION
Petite Sirah
Zinfandel
Chenin Blanc
Gewürtztraminer

Livermore Valley and Alameda Neighbors

Livermore Valley is a gravelly basin behind a series of ridges that step back from the east side of San Francisco Bay. It is scarcely half an hour beyond the Bay Bridge and Alameda County's suburban scraggle, which sprawls from Berkeley down past Mission San Jose. Grapevines love the gravel, but even winemakers in remote sections keep an eye peeled for bulldozers.

Early pioneers were Louis Mel, whose El Mocho vineyard was acquired by the Wente family, and Charles Wetmore, who founded Cresta Blanca, naming it after a limestone streak that reared above the vineyard. Both planted cuttings from the great Sauternes vineyard of Château d'Yquem, and while red wine cuttings from Château

Margaux of the Médoc were also set out, the valley's reputation for white wines dominates. More is the pity, in a way, for the gravel produces noble reds, lost behind the white wine fame.

Such hidden wines are called intermediate wines, like a good vintage that comes between two great ones. California is full of such wines, like Zinfandel, planted in great quantities, with no known European antecedents, which make poor wines in hot vineyards and outstanding ones in cool regions. Another is the Petite Sirah, which is unrelated to the noble Petit Syrah of the Rhone, but may even be the Duriff, which is despised there. Yet it is a grape that produces remarkable wines in cool regions. So it is with wines bearing European regional names, shoved to market as imitations and therefore distrusted, although many may be blends that can stand out on their own. In dark moments, Californians feel that all their wines are intermediates, hidden from public taste by the glamor of the foreign. Hidden wines bring out the dour side of winemakers because they cannot command proper prices on the market. Wine buffs love them for the same reason.

Beyond a western ridge is Pleasanton, where a couple of wineries hide their wines. Ruby Hill sells most of their varietals in bulk, and Villa Armando ships theirs East in blends. Down south, on another ridge called Sunol, is the large vineyard of nearly 1,000 acres, being planted by Almadén. Its varietals, and those from a 245-acre vineyard in Pleasanton, will also be used for wines that will not carry the geographical name. Compared to Livermore, of course, Pleasanton and Sunol are intermediate names. The same might be said for Mission San Jose, where vineyards established by Leland Stanford were acquired by Weibel, whose name came to be associated with sparkling wines. As a result, Weibel red and white table wines are intermediates.

As for vintages in Livermore, which may vary somewhat from those in Napa and Sonoma, and will certainly be different from those of Santa Clara, San Benito, and Monterey, a quick judgment might be made. They seem to come in pairs, '64 and '65 being outstanding, '68 and '69 being splendid. This, of course, makes '66, '67, and '70 into intermediate years, sending all buffs scurrying to their price lists.

Alameda itself is an intermediate name, never having produced more than 2 percent or so of California's wines. You can be sure that Livermore is not, boasting two of the greatest names in California wine. One of these, however, is intermediate, and that is Concannon, which has never made much effort to sell beyond the state. This has never caused a problem for the Concannons; San Franciscans seem to race to their door to arrive before the rest of the state. It has disturbed wine buffs elsewhere, and now, reluctantly, Concannon is beginning to ship wines East. It is a nuisance, of course, all the paper work, but sooner or later everybody likes to see their lights shine forth.

WENTE BROS.

Some of the most distinguished white wines in the country come from Wente Bros., a firm founded by Carl Wente, who came from Germany and went to work for Charles Krug, up in the Napa Valley, to learn about wines on the local scene. That was in 1880, and three years later he set himself up in Livermore, planting grapes brought back by Charles Wetmore from Château d'Yquem. The present Marquis de Lur-Saluces, whose family has owned the great Sauternes vineyard since 1785, stops by Wente's whenever he gets to California to see how the Sauvignon Blanc and Sémillon are doing. He always tastes Château Wente, which is patterned after Yquem. Those who prefer dry whites seek out the Dry Sémillon, which stands alone, and the rounded Sauvignon Blanc, the two wines that established the firm's reputation.

The Wente Bros., as they insisted on truncating their name, were Carl's sons. Karl was the winemaker, perhaps the best of his generation. Ernest was the vineyard manager, although the running of the firm had been handed over to his son Karl, who also does the winemaking. The vines need plenty of managing, the 800 acres of the home vineyard constantly being replanted in certified vines so that 600 of them are always in full bearing. As a hedge against the expanding suburbs, a new vineyard of 300 acres has been brought into bearing down in Monterey in an area called Arroyo Seco, fifteen miles inland over the hills from Carmel. There will be about 2,500 acres in vines before the end of the decade, planted from foundation blocks maintained at both locations.

The new stocks are a revolution and a revelation, says Karl. The wines are going to be sensations, by any standard you choose to measure. Wente Bros. now have nursery stocks in excess of need, and people all over the world are trying to get them. If they were not using so many, they might make more money selling cuttings than making wines.

Wine growers with nursery stocks have a kind of gentlemen's agreement that California vineyards will be provided with the cuttings first. This is only proper, considering that the vines come from Davis or are supervised by them. Davis experts examine every vine in a mother block, and look over every one in a foundation block but inspect one in ten. They even keep an eye on the increase blocks from which vineyards are planted, and the vineyards themselves. It is called eyeballing. Viticulturists, as a class, are probably the world's scariest drivers, their eyes rarely on the road, but constantly roving the vineyards. They are always late because they are forever stopping to peer at a leaf, to study a graft, to test the tension in a trellis wire. It is even worse when grapes are on the vine.

The varieties planted are all the noble vines, including the reds, and there is a little Merlot and Malbec, those two grapes used in Bordeaux to soften the Cabernet Sauvignon; they may be used for the same purpose at Wente, although they are more apt to go into blends. There is an unusual white wine blend called Le Blanc de Blancs, of Ugni Blanc and Chenin Blanc; it is a fresh and fruity soft wine that is suggested for serving by itself at cocktail time, or with dishes that have a cream sauce, or with shrimp or lobster. Its success is encouraging other wineries to market blends under their own names, rather than those of European districts. The trend began with Château Wente, the original name for the wine patterned after Yquem, but this did not sound quite right, so the name was changed to Château Sémillon, which did sound suitable. The result was several similar wines from other producers with "château" in the name, a marked improvement over calling the sweet whites "sauterne," without the *s*. Nobody misses a circumflex.

Even the Wentes have not solved the problem of what to call their dry white blend, and they go along with the bad habit of calling it "Chablis," carefully pointing out that it is a blend of two "blancs," Pinot and Chenin. This is their second most popular wine, so like many others, they fear a name change would mean a market loss. Their most popular wine is Gray Riesling, originally planted by the founder. Wine experts look down on the grape, believing that it is the little-vaunted Chauché Gris, and that its wine is flabby and bland. This seems hardly fair, the wine having a soft and pleasing lightness but an odd bouquet. The taste complements fish like tuna or mackerel, or spicy shrimp dishes. It is a beautifully made wine, with a nice balance of qualities, and far superior, for instance, to heavy regionals with off-tastes from the oak, the soil, or careless vinification, and which are brought in under European regional or district or township names and sold at comparable prices.

Production is approaching 300,000 cases a year, including Pinot Noir and Gamay Beaujolais, and Wente enthusiasts are finally getting a chance to see what they can do with reds, whose quantities will increase during the decade. There is interest in any Wente wine because it is a model winery, closely surrounded by its wide sweep of vineyards. Carts about three feet on a side, and as deep, are rigged with small motors that can be throttled down to a creep. These haul the grapes to the jacketed fermenting tanks standing in ranks back of the winery, which are filled from the stainless stemmer-crushers; red wines ferment in vats inside the winery, passing down the ranks to holding tanks and small cooperage. The whites may or may not go into oak, for longer or shorter periods, depending on variety.

Modern wineries like Wente's have a strange air about them, men dwarfed by the thick columns and long ranks of tanks and casks, hooking up hoses to small pumps and filters, then attaching them to the great bulks above them, as if they were feeding some large sculpture. The solemnity disappears at Wente, when you watch vineyard workers bringing up the self-propelled, three-wheeled carts, nudging them to change direction as if they were robot oxen. There is a slosh and thumping as the crusher blades turn, tearing off the stems from the grapes tumbling into its maw, and the sound of gurgling as the pulp is piped into the gleaming columns. Some of the fermenters have frosty bands around their middles, where the cooling coils are icing up. There is a shipboard smoothness about the operation, something of the farm as well, something of a rocket launching as men hurry about the rearing columns. It is a long way from a group of happy peasants jogging in a vat, singing to an accordion's lilt. The wines are a long way from those of yesterday, too. And a great deal better. A lot of good things come together in a bottle of wine.

A SELECTION
Pinot Noir
Le Blanc de Blancs
Dry Sémillon
Chardonnay

CONCANNON VINEYARD

The Irish have always been drawn to wines, perhaps because none can be made on the sodden turf of Erin, which is, nevertheless, one of the finest places in the world for maturing wines in bottles because they develop so slowly. The Irish have been in the wine trade for centuries. It is said — probably without a word of truth — that the great Bordeaux vineyard of Château Haut-Brion, now owned by an American of Irish descent, started out with a Gaelic name. As is usual with the Irish, they get into things from odd angles. James Concannon got into wines by way of rubber stamps.

He came from the isles of Aran, made a fortune producing rubber stamps, and when the Archbishop of San Francisco suggested he tend a vineyard, he settled down in Livermore in 1883. Livermore is as good for sons as it is for grapes. James had five, all of whom busied themselves during Prohibition making sacramental wines, then turned the operation over to Captain Joe Concannon, who fought with Pershing against Pancho Villa, raised the largest flagpole in the valley and reared two sons. Young Joe presides over the corporation, and Jim makes the wines, with a small herd coming up to take over the 300 acres. Production is nearing 50,000 cases a year.

Part of the acreage is in a foundation block that provides virus-free cuttings for planting in the vineyards. One of the certified vines is from wood grown in Geisenheim from a single clone, or bud, that originally came from Schloss Johannisberg, in the Rheingau. Wine made from it has a special spicy taste, and all sorts of wonders are expected from the various varieties in the virus-free block. This matter of clonal selection, whereby a bud from a particularly desirable vine is propagated, bids fair to revolutionize the vineyards of the world, increasing quality and yield. The tedious job, from bud to vineyard, may take a dozen years, and there is great demand for such certified vines. Seedlings are never used, for a vine grown from seed will be vastly different from the parent. (Varieties like Zinfandel and Petite Sirah may well be seedlings.)

There is constant inspection by Davis experts of these vines, which are planted in fumigated soil. Yield declines in old vineyards, and when the vines are ripped up, the land is traditionally allowed to rest, sometimes for a decade. It is now known that the tiny worms called nematodes suck the roots, sickening the vines with virus. Chemicals put in the soil evaporate to form a gas, killing the nematodes to a depth of as much as eight feet. When a vine certified to be virus-free is planted in ground where the virus-imparting nematodes have been killed, there is a chance that there is no need for grafting. The process also kills phylloxera. Some planting is being done without grafting the stocks, with hopes that this will increase quality, as well as yield. Like others, the Concannons feel that such healthy vines cannot help but produce better grapes, although costs for such replanting can run well over $1,000 an acre.

At least partly to test the process, Concannon has leased a famous small vineyard down in Santa Cruz, Hallcrest, near the town of Felton. Johannisberg Rieslings and Cabernet Sauvignons from its 20-odd acres were remarkable. When they have to be replanted in new vines, they may be even more noteworthy.

The vineyards surround a homey compound of buildings with the flagpole high above, all with a family air. During the long hours at vintage time, the wives bring down bread and cheese and salami, some corks are pulled and everybody takes a break. The work can be exhausting, so every evening Joe Concannon doubles the wattage so that the brightness cheers up everybody and cuts down on accidents, mistakes, and cleanup time.

"Captain Joe never pushed us," says his son, "but we always wanted to be in the winery. At college I used to talk so much about wines that they called me purple toes. It takes all your time, but we generally manage to get off for duck-hunting and things like that. Want to know a marvelous marinade for duck? Equal parts of soy sauce, vermouth, and red wine. We use what we call Red Dinner Wine, or maybe Petite Sirah, and drink that with the roast duck."

Almost as much of a family affair as the vintage is a springtime event for thirty or so friends, neighbors, and longtime customers, one of whom is always a topflight surgeon. This event is a rabbit scoot, held as soon as twilight hours are longer, and it is bright enough to see well at six o'clock.

Texas jackrabbits like the young vine shoots, and the vineyards are full of both in spring. The shooting party surrounds the vineyard, working through top varietals first, beating along the rows. The scoot nets fifty or so rabbits and saves the vines for another year. The Concannons have some excellent recipes for jackrabbit stew.

The Concannons have some 60 acres of new vines coming into bearing, and they need plenty of water early in the season. Spring rains may be too light and often need to be augmented with sprinkling. This is done to a regular program, causing a passing neighbor to pull up one day when the sprinklers were operating during a shower. He watched for a while, muttered to Joe, "You Concannons are crazy," and drove off. Lots of things seem strange when you don't know, says Joe.

So customers will know, Concannon labels many of the wines with the date of bottling and the vintage, as well as the number bottled. There were 15,243 bottles of 1965 Cabernet Sauvignon, for instance, from a virgin clone originally planted in the Davis experimental vineyard in Oakville; bottling was done December 9, 1968. Such attention to detail, frankness, experiment, and general cheerfulness whets one's interest in the wines of Concannon. They made a special bottling of a single cask of Petite Sirah 1965 as another example. They saw that it needed no fining at all, so they could simply draw it off the lees, following this racking with the lightest of filtering when it came time for bottling. "This gave the wine more character," says Jim, "and we think it will live a long time, so we bottled it in magnums." Wines placed in such double bottles take much longer to mature, while wines in half-bottles mature more rapidly. When laying down several cases of a wine, it is a good idea to include one case of half-bottles; if you try the wine too soon, not much is lost, and when the half-bottles are well ready to drink, you know the time is near to begin on the full bottles. There is often a year's difference between the readiness of a wine in half-bottle and one in bottle, while a magnum may need two extra years, and more.

"Everybody likes the white wines," says Joe, "and now they're beginning to discover the reds. We're beginning to consider wider distribution out of state." It's about time.

A SELECTION
Petite Sirah
Cabernet Sauvignon
Red Dinner Wine
Zinfandel Rosé
Johannisberg Riesling
Château Concannon

WEIBEL CHAMPAGNE VINEYARDS

Fra Junípero Serra found the spot in 1797 near the foot of the bay, but the Indians had found it long before that and had made it sacred ground where men could come in peace to heal themselves in the warm springs. Leland Stanford found it the year after the earthquake of '68, bought a square mile against the eastern rise, and set up his brother there amid 350 acres of vines. Stanford wines became famous. A Champagne salesman of Swiss descent got tired of traveling Europe, and decided to come to America after Repeal, setting up as a wine importer. On a trip to San Francisco, Rudolf Weibel decided to make sparkling wines from native grapes, doing so for a decade. Then he found Mission San Jose. He bought the Stanford property in 1945, and the third generation of Weibels is now making wines there.

A tree-lined avenue leads back from the highway, silver-green eucalyptus right, dustier olive left and yellow-green of vineleaves beyond, marching to the far knolls. Low roofs of winery buildings run up the hill and the place holds the look of the Stanford days, hedged gardens with paved walks around the office-dwelling-tasting-room-compound.

Looking back toward the highway past 100 acres of vineyards you can see the twentieth century coming, an automobile assembly that claims to be the largest building under one roof, plus an industrial scattering of what Ludwig Bemelmans once dubbed "beautiful dreck." Encroachments have forced Weibel to look to further hills, up around Ukiah, where 500 acres are coming into bearing, and a new winery has been built. About 80 percent of the grapes are supplied by other growers, with production of table wines reaching perhaps 300,000 cases by 1975, an amount considered to be optimum production. By that time, sparkling wines produced will approach 150,000 bottles. Weibel was one of the first to send his wines east, a collection of nine sparkling wines that includes a Chardonnay Brut, ten varietals, almost as many blends, a trio of *flor* Sherries made from Palomino grapes, even an aperitif called Tangor, with a taste of tangerines. Weibel has done extensive experiments with wines flavored with natural essences and extracts, anticipating that happy moment when people will have loosened up enough to try new tastes.

Table wines have grown substantially, and Weibel now offers several vintage wines from their own vineyards, estate bottlings not easy to find but worth the seeking, particularly Pinot Noir and Chardonnay.

A SELECTION
Cabernet Sauvignon
Gamay Beaujolais
Johannisberg Riesling

The Great Valley

The Sacramento flows down from Mount Shasta, and the San Joaquin flows north to meet it, their waters merging to shape a delta that empties into San Francisco Bay. Their valleys join to form a great central basin four hundred miles long, where a scant two score wineries produce two-thirds of all the wines of California. The best of all is the smallest of all.

Vineyards share the land with orchards and giant squares of flowers and vegetables, beginning around Sacramento and its Gold Rush country, stretching on down through the counties that slice across the valley; San Joaquin, Stanislaus, Merced, Madera, Fresno.

Wine towns really name the districts along Highway 99, Lodi standing for all of Sacramento, followed by Modesto and Fresno. Vineyards extend south beyond Bakersfield. The wines, once heavy and sweet and fortified with brandy, are getting lighter because of new vines developed at Davis.

New plantings on high trellises are getting set for mechanical harvesters, but the ancient Italian style of long, bare trunks with canes arching high are still to be seen, as well as vineyards with vines close together, looking like dark corduroy or rough carpet from a distance. None of it would exist without the irrigation canals that track the land, the high dikes and overflow sloughs, with bare and tawny mounds here and there where the water cannot reach.

The best way to get there is over the Pacheco Pass, to Fresno from San Benito. At the fork from 101 is an Almadén tasting room to refresh you for your journey and just beyond is one of the stands of Casa de Fruta, where you can buy dried fruits and nuts and various farm produce. The main reason for stopping is the walnuts, which you are going to want to crack open when you pull the cork on a bottle of Ficklin Tinta Madeira. The reason for taking the Pacheco Pass is to get closest to Hanford without actually going into the valley, which is blazing hot most of the time or else soggy. Hanford is a little town some thirty miles south of Fresno, off the main road and out of the way of everything. The reason you want to get there is to dine at the Imperial Dynasty, where chef Richard Wing and more than a score of relatives run a restaurant that is the best in the west.

Some people go to California just to eat at the Imperial Dynasty. In San Francisco and Los Angeles planes are chartered to fly groups over for dinner and back after coffee. Richard has wit, imagination, and daring. The wine list developed by his late brother Ernie is an impeccable selection of the state's best, with some old bottles not available anywhere else. These are reserved for special occasions. Like his brother, Richard believes that a fine wine can be lost in the excitement of a grand dinner, and that it is often best to start off with a great bottle and some cheese by themselves, when appetites are sharp, so that the wine can be enjoyed completely. He even believes that it is not the best idea to build a dinner around a great bottle, because the light and delicate dish needed to show off such a wine may throw a meal out of balance; wines should complement the food, not necessarily the other way around. A selection of good wines, well matured and ascending in excellence as the meal progresses, can be much more satisfactory than a series of great bottles with each dish tamed down to suit them. It is with such cheerful attitudes that outworn traditions are blown away.

One such notion is that red wines should be opened well ahead of time to give the wine a chance to breathe and stretch. Fresh air may whisk away the traces of bouquet left in an old wine, and upset the fragile balance of the various elements — so goes the new argument. It is often better to open an old wine and pour at once, letting the drinker swirl his glass and note the changes, sipping to catch them, then drinking when the wine tastes best. Gaffers may grumble, but many an old wine has died on the sideboard, before anybody had a chance to taste it.

The Wings traipse all over California for the best raw materials. There is Maccagno Bakery nearby, some sheep ranchers in the hills, local quail hunters, certain farmers for vegetables, a special dairy, a couple of fishermen. Dinner will start, perhaps, with Richard's snails, with a bottle of Stony Hill Chardonnay, then a mushroom soup with chanterelles, served with flaky Armenian bread. With a bottle of Martini Cabernet '65 might be a roast quail on a crisply fried slice of eggplant, capped with a black Chinese mushroom. Then a rack of lamb with rice, the last of the Cabernet, and the first of a half-bottle of Mouton Rothschild '52; the full bottles are not ready to drink. Then some cheese with the rest of the wine. Perhaps fruit for dessert, maybe even mangoes with Chinese wild cranberries and some Premier Sémillon from Cresta Blanca.

Coming out in the cool of the evening, when the temperature can drop below ninety in summer, one is ready to tackle Fresno and the wineries. This is not nearly as cheerless a task as the old reputation for dreadful wines would seem to warrant. Many of the red and white wine blends have lost their off-tastes in the past few years, as have the sweet fortified wines. Still bland, still too sweet, still tasting odd to wine buffs accustomed to the dry, clean tastes of traditional table wines, the vast quantities from the Central Valley are weaning millions away from soda pop and beer, from synthetic cocktails and watery highballs. Davis experts are busily developing grapes that will stand up under the blasting summer suns. Two of these are Emerald Riesling and Ruby Cabernet, names that are unfortunate borrowings from nomenclature for noble vines, but containing enough of them in the crosses so that the names have validity. These grapes hold their acidity in hot vineyards, ferment cleanly, and make pleasant wines.

Dr. H. P. Olmo of Davis is in charge of developing new varieties, and a new one may take as long as fifteen years. The first cross of Ruby Cabernet, a hybrid of Carignane and Cabernet Sauvignon, was made in 1936, spent a year in the greenhouse, and then was planted closely in a vineyard the following year so that enough stock could be grown to plant a seedling block. The first fruit came in 1941, and by 1943 there was enough to make some wine, in batches of one-tenth of a gallon. There was a three-year wait to taste the wine. A trial block of selected vines was made, and after three years, lots of five gallons were made, to wait a similar period before tasting. The best vines of these went into experimental blocks in the wine districts. Then there were comparative tastings of these, the aim being to get wines from the Fresno station that would measure up to those from Oakville. Here are tasting notes of three samples:

28   Odd, baked quality. Distinctive, very fruity, full. Fine acid, good fullness.
33   Spice and fruit and heavy with gas. Some lightness.
56   Oldest nose, some secondary character. Clean, round, some pepper, long taste.

The first two samples were from Fresno, and the combined score of a dozen expert tasters following a meticulous score sheet rated the first sample 5.2 on a scale of 10, and the last sample 6.6. Number 28 was getting close.

A rating of 5 means that a good commercial standard wine can be produced. Ruby Cabernet was rated 6.2 in Fresno against 6.4 in Oakville. Tasters checked the wines according to the following list: watery, astringent, bitter, oxidized, overripe, off-odor, acetic, flat, plus others.

Once a satisfactory grape is found, there is a delay until it is accepted by the growers. The various European varieties are adapted to cool and rather wet climates, says Dr. Olmo, and the immigrants two generations ago wanted to make wines like those from home. Soil is important, and growers have been lucky in getting the Cabernets up to the best. White Riesling rates pretty high, although it is down below the Rheingau. But a new environment like the Central Valley demands a change to another variety. Dr. Olmo is only in the first round of crosses of Ruby Cabernet, but already it is making the best red wine in the valley.

Although *vinifera* grapes are probably the oldest cultivated fruit, hybridizing is recent, Dr. Olmo has noted. Mendel's efforts to cross garden peas were performed more than a century ago, but the genetic laws he formulated were ignored until 1900, and even then grape experimenters felt they did not apply. Only within the last couple of decades has this indifference been routed.

Crossing is as ticklish as it is lengthy. The flower cap and stamen must be removed from one variety before its flowers open. The pollen from another is then dusted on the pistil. There are many flowers in a cluster, and those not emasculated, as it is called, are plucked off. Then the cluster is bagged to prevent contamination. People with poor eyesight, lack of patience, or clumsy hands seldom are happy at this type of work, observes Dr. Olmo.

Seeds within the developing berries are finally extracted and eventually planted; the result is the hybrid. "Luck is a fine item," says Dr. Olmo. "The greatest gap in our knowledge is not knowing just what varieties best transmit superior qualities."

Even so, several are coming along, and the decade of the seventies will see new wines coming from the Central Valley. They will match a new spirit coming to the valley, which you can see in Fresno. Most people rush through to duck the heat, hurrying on to Yosemite and the sequoias. Wise ones pause, if only to eat at the Imperial Dynasty, which is thirty miles out of the way, down in Hanford. And don't forget the walnuts.

FRESNO

Fresno rises above the flatland, surrounded by grapes, producing with the adjoining counties half the wines of California, and perhaps more if you include the vineyards down around Bakersfield. A score of wineries produces the wines, the largest being Roma, with 4,300 acres spread over fifteen miles on its Delano ranches south of town and still more down around Bakersfield. The smallest is Ficklin, with 50 acres up in Madera.

Large firms like Gallo, Guild, United Vintners, and The Christian Brothers, growers groups like Del Rey and Sanger Winery Association maintain installations in town or nearby, as do Schenley (which maintains a distillery where its Dubonnet is made) and Vie Del (partially owned by Seagram) which makes brandy, concentrates, wine flavors for cooking, and blending sherries for distillers. There are some small wineries like Nonini (which makes wines only from its own grapes) and Landis (which labels its wines as coming from San Joaquin, rarely identified), but main interest is south and east, where thousands of acres are being planted in wine grapes suited to warm climates. Noble Land and Cattle has something like 5,000 acres coming along, bulk producers like California Growers have added 1,000 acres and are reviving brand names to sell their own wines. Cooperatives like Delano Growers, Sierra, and Bear Mountain (their brands include M. Lamont and Gold Peak) have also replanted several square miles and are reviving labels as well as continuing to supply regional bottlers. One of the most novel wines to try while waiting for the rest to come along is Perelli 101, half a mile of which is now bearing. The founder of Perelli-Minetti used to walk through the two miles of vineyards, taking cuttings or seedlings from vines that retained acidity in the grapes, patenting the first of several. Perelli-Minetti is the last member of the California Wine Association, a group that controlled much of the industry at one time. They owned such brand names as Greystone, Calwa, Ambassador, and Eleven Cellars, the last being the number of wineries involved in the organization. The other firms dropped out, leaving Perelli-Minetti with all those brands. Brandy labels include Aristocrat and A. R. Morrow.

Some of the growers have been carried away by the thirst for dry table wines and have even planted noble vines like Cabernet and Chardonnay in the hot regions, hoping that trellising and spraying will preserve enough acidity to make a palatable wine. If not, of course, they will have the names of the grapes for their labels, so buyers must continue to be tentative when the wines come on the market at what will seem like absurdly low prices.

The State University at Fresno is busy training young viticulturists and winemakers who may be able to influence any wayward elders to do things right.

FICKLIN VINEYARDS

It's not far. It's just up the road and west from Fresno, near the town of Madera and in that county, in a sea of lesser vines, are 50 acres of Tinta Madeira, Tinta Cão, Touriga, Alvarelhão, and Souzão. These are the best of the Portuguese grapes planted along the River Douro, and they were set out a quarter of a century ago by Walter Ficklin from cuttings grown at Davis. The first vintage was 1948, and Ficklin Port has ever since been recognized as the outstanding American version of that wine, on a par with many that come from the parent region.

The best techniques of the Douro are followed closely, the grapes fermenting in low open vats, the cap of pulp pushed down often into the seething juice, the fermentation stopped with brandy when enough color has been picked up from the skins. The wines are drawn off into small cooperage, racked frequently, topped often, and after four years in wood they are put in bottle and the bottles are binned. After another year, Ruby Port is put out for sale. There are occasional bottlings of Vintage Port made available. The Vintage Port is bottled after thirty months and released nine years after the vintage. Both Ruby and Vintage can be kept for twenty years before drinking and should live for another twenty. Total production is rising to a crushing of 100 tons of grapes each year, perhaps 6,000 cases.

Not many know the joys of Port, which is just as well, considering there is so little of it. It is best by itself, or with walnuts, although various fruits and mild cheeses are good companions. The classic marriage is Port with melon, a dollop poured in where the seeds were, but the Ficklins think that California melons are too strong in taste for their wine. A pear is fine, or a peach. Some people love Port with dryish cakes and cookies, others yearn for fruitcake, still others for rich mocha. Bread and various sorts of guava paste or jelly, with cream cheese, are popular in Oporto, the Portuguese town from which Port took its name. Nobody has the nerve these days to send the women from the dining table, leaving the men to sit with the Port, passing it clockwise around the table — that is the old English way.

Ficklin's sons are running the winery now, David having gone off to Davis to learn the winemaking, and Walter, Jr., tending the vineyards. The winery was built when the Portuguese vines were planted, out of adobe bricks made on the place. There are all sorts of casks in the winery, even including one of the long and thin kind called pipes, from the Douro. They are piled around and stacked on racks, wherever there is room, but the neat bins of bottles are what catch the eye, nestling together in stacks, twenty or so in a row and twice as high. The smallest bin is for the oldest wine, opened only on state occasions or family holidays, too expensive to be sold, but occasionally swapped or given away.

Ficklin put in the Portuguese grapes at the urging of Davis, and he has done the same with Ruby Cabernet and Emerald Riesling, bottles of which are occasionally available at the winery. They also maintain an experimental plot to test new varieties: If anybody can do something grand with them, the Ficklins are the ones to try.

Once opened, Port changes quickly, losing its rich fruitiness in a few hours, and while it is still good long after opening, the real joy comes right after the cork is pulled. Port lovers are rare in this day and age, generally unable to gather a group to drink up a bottle at a sitting, so half-bottles are much in demand. Wines mature more rapidly in half-bottles, moreover, and they can be an advantage to someone too impatient to wait a decade to drink his wines. People buying at the winery generally get an extra half-bottle to try as soon as they can find a nice place to stop. The trick is to find some shade in summer. In winter people have been known to pull up as soon as they get out of sight, down the road. You crack open the big, fresh, juicy walnuts you bought at Casa de Fruta and then you take a sip of the rich, fresh, fruity Port. . . .

MODESTO

The San Joaquin waters the country south of the county that bears its name. It names all the land as well, particularly when you speak in terms of what's called agribusiness, which is enormous. But when you speak in terms of wine, this midsection of the Central Valley is called Modesto. That's where Gallo is. It is also enormous, producing at least a third of all California wines. Most of the other wineries run north past Escalon; vineyards run south past Livingston. These are thought of as subdistricts in the upper valley. Gallo sets the style for all, each firm producing many wines of all sorts.

Franzia Brothers is one of the largest, maintaining more than 1,200 acres of vineyards in the valley and buying many grapes, claiming that roughly 40 percent of their wine comes from the Napa Valley. The firm has gone public, but is still managed by descendants of the founder who make the point that the firm produces wines amateurs can drink. The firm produces something like two million cases of wine a year, of which 75 percent are table wines. Most people do not like wines high in acid, it is claimed, and the majority would not drink wine at all if it were not softened. Wines low in acid are easier to drink and open the way to a liking for dry wines.

Smaller firms round about — Cadlolo, Pirronne, Bella Napoli, Delicato — share similar opinions. The last named is owned by the Indelicato family, who chose the positive approach in naming their cellars and who produce a specialty called Tingle. The other large firm in the area is Petri Wineries, up in Escalon. Louis Petri expanded the firm by buying Mission Bell, then Italian Swiss Colony; he sold the lot to Allied Grape Growers, the cooperative with 1,800 members. He retained marketing rights, which were consolidated as United Vintners. Along the way, Petri acquired such firms as Inglenook and Gambarelli & Davito, and devised such wines as Golden Spur and Silver Spur. Marketing all these brands is now the province of Heublein, who purchased United Vintners, altogether accounting for nearly a quarter of all California wines. Only Gallo is larger.

E. & J. GALLO WINERY

Gallo is biggest of all. Ernest and Julio got off to a running start when Repeal came in 1933, and they have not stopped since. They descended from a winemaking family of the Italian Piedmont, whose California operations had been cut short by Prohibition. But enough was kept going for the boys to learn the rudiments of the business, the most important aspect of which seemed to be that Americans were a thirsty lot willing to buy anything wet. They rented a warehouse in Modesto, crushed some grapes, peddled the wine, and by 1935 had built their first cellar near what was inaptly called Dry Creek. Today they produce more than a third of all the wines of California — some fifty kinds in assorted colors and tailored to what they think the public wants. Many of them are sweet.

Wine buffs get all excited when they talk about Gallo. Some are scornful of the cheap wines that taste watery and sugary and vaguely of the grape, mostly sold in pints, the cheapest alcohol you can buy. Some are admiring of their candid consumer approach, which seems to aim at being all things to all men, provided there are enough of them — an idea that is surely a first principle of much American enterprise. Some are respectful of the technical skill that can make a drinkable out of grapes better used for jelly or fruitcake, but contemptuous of an attitude that blandly panders to low elements of public taste. Gallo seems to consider such attitudes irrelevant and maybe even stupid. People growing up learn to like what they know.

Italians are used to rough wines without sweetness, ignoring any off-tastes or off-smells by serving them with hearty foods or sauces full of herbs and spices, sharp with accents like peppers and tomatoes and garlic. Gallo types are without roughness, with off-tastes masked by careful vinification and handling.

Ordinary French wines can also be rough, some of them quite full, others sharp and thin. Gallo types avoid such unpleasantnesses with blandness.

Americans are addicted to highballs and cocktails, beer and soda pop; they drink milk, coffee, or tea with meals, devour endless sandwiches and snacks, go to cocktail parties. Wines for such a public must be designed to fit such patterns, or be made for those larger amounts of time that come between meals. Gallo does so, just as the giant firms of Europe make wines to match their markets.

The fact of the matter is that most European wines are bad, or indifferent. Most Gallo wines are not bad at all, no matter how indifferent. Some of them are even pretty good. Considering the prices, some of them are among the best buys on the market. There is always something much better if you are willing to pay a little more, but many people won't.

Wine buffs would like Gallo to produce wines that would raise the standards of public drinking. But when Gallo burst forth, there was a century of bad practice behind it — an industry with a history of making wines from unsuitable grapes, of marketing wines under names borrowed or stolen, of passing off bad for good — and all of this presented to a public that voted for the inanity of Prohibition as a cure for social and cultural sickness. When the nation wants well-made wines of fine quality, and is willing to pay for them, Gallo will make them.

Gallo already buys the entire output of the two largest Napa Valley cooperatives, plus that of others in Sonoma, plus that from a host of independent growers in all the North Coast counties. What is more, Gallo is as interested in the noble vines as the next firm, but in proportion.

Gallo disdains even such defense, feeling no need at all to apologize, certainly not to wine buffs who make a thing of snobbery of wine drinking. By making ultrasimple suitable wines for large audiences, Gallo introduces them to the simple pleasures of wine drinking, opening the way for them to go on to the old and rare and subtle.

Gallo has perhaps the best technical and research staff in the world, certainly doing more testing and experimentation than any other private firm. No winery supervises production so carefully, and few have developed winery practices so capably. Independent research discovered that brown bottles protected wines better than green ones, so Gallo uses brownish bottles to guard most of their wines, and long ago set up their own bottling plant so they could have just what they needed.

Like Martin Ray, Gallo has little to do with press or public, letting the wines speak for themselves. Gallo has no tasting facilities and does not welcome visitors at its wineries in Modesto, Fresno, or Cucamonga. They are cheerful enough when encountered, Ernest and Julio, but are much too busy for social probings or psychological flights about the wine-drinking public. When they get an idea, they put it in a bottle. Over the years, they have introduced Ripple, Thunderbird, Gypsy Rose, Pink Chablis — wine drinks created to challenge the place of soda pop. None of these will replace Coke or Pepsi or even Dr Pepper, but who is to say they will not find something better than a Marguerita or a Mai Tai?

For traditionalists, there are wines called Burgundy, a soft red; and Hearty Burgundy, perhaps the best of the breed, as soft but fuller. In some of the wines, they stop fermentation before all the sugar in the grape has fermented into alcohol, making a wine that is lightly sweet. The change has caused a vast burgeoning of sales and a widening of the market, an excellent beginning for the timid who dread wines because they think they taste sour. Gallo makes Boone's Farm Apple Wine and Spañada for those whose tongues are still childlike, and there is Paisano for those who do not know what to order with spaghetti. The Gallos show great tolerance and understanding when it comes to people who do not know much about wine. These are the two classic virtues attributed to wine lovers. Ernest and Julio may be trying to tell us something.

A SELECTION
Barberone
Rhinegarten
Boone's Farm Strawberry Hill

LODI

When the Gold Rush hit California, the seekers brought their thirsts along, and wineries sprang up to slake the lucky. There are still a couple of wineries up around Sutter Creek, but frosts in the Sierra foothills keep production down. Similar troubles, like heat and dampness, did in others; the spread of Sacramento did in more.

What is left are a few in Lodi, in the wedge of land where the Sacramento and San Joaquin meet; the town name encompasses all. There is a festival the weekend after Labor Day each year to celebrate the local fortified wines and brandies, plus an increasing number of table wines that come from vines developed at Davis, over the hills, not far away. The main interest is in mosaics, and these are made of grapes, one of which is Flame Tokay, good for eating and not drinking, but lovely on the vine.

The wineries are an odd lot. The best of the smaller ones is Acampo, which is locally known as Barengo's, after the present owner. Barengo Cellars makes a long line of wines, the most widely distributed being their May Wine, but their most famous product is a splendid aged vinegar. Acampo was originally in the hands of Cesare Mondavi, who surrendered his interest when he moved to the Napa Valley and acquired Charles Krug. Not far away is Alexander's, operated by two sons of the Greek founder and still making a couple of wines flavored with pitch in the old Greek way, Retsina and Kokinelli, as well as a Sake type called Fuji. The firm is attempting to bring back to life the Coloma Wine Cellars, up in the Gold Rush country above Placerville. Another Greek winery below Fresno, Nicholas G. Verry, was founded by a Spartan and also produces Retsina, as well as an unresined wine called Philery, which means quick love.

Wine-Art started out as producers of kits for Canadian householders, complete with essence or concentrate, simple equipment, and the few chemicals needed, plus instructions. This proved so successful that an American company started a franchise operation, took over an old Lodi winery to produce concentrates, and by the early seventies had overexpanded, so the member stores are reorganizing.

Following another trend, a company called Pop Wines bought the winery of the Cherokee cooperative, changed its name to Montcalm Vintners, and set about marketing wines from the members' grapes. Defunct wineries are being revived throughout the valley, throughout California, all over the country, to cash in on the growing interest in wines.

A novel tasting room, a big vat, is maintained in Lodi by East-Side Winery, a cooperative of more than one hundred growers. It is famous for its brandy, much of which is sold in bulk to other firms that want a brandy to complete their lines. The company makes a lot of wines of the Sherry type, much of which is also sold in bulk, and a growing number of table wines, including a sweetish one called Gold, made from a Davis hybrid of that name.

The center of interest in Lodi is Guild, which maintains two wineries around the town, plus a tasting room at its central bottling and aging installation.

GUILD

By far the most important firm in Lodi, Guild Wineries & Distilleries is a cooperative of more than one thousand members, with vineyards extending from Ukiah down to Cucamonga and totaling more than 10,000 acres. The firm accounts for about 5 percent of all California wines, and was formed around a nucleus of Garrett & Company, makers of Virginia Dare, the Italian Vineyard Company founded by Guasti, Cribari and Sons, Bear Creek Winery Association, and several others. Most of the wines are bottled at Lodi.

The president of Guild is Robert M. Ivie, a marketing expert who tries his luck raising varietals in his backyard, and keeps an eye on the firm's test plantings at Lodi and up in Mendocino. Few people are as aware of the winds of change as he. New grapes will vastly increase the amount of table wines coming from the great Central Valley, and many of the large landholders of orchard and farming land are watching the grapes carefully. Techniques of climate control, such as sprays and fans for cooling, the training of vines to shade the grapes, field crushing of the vintage involving mechanical harvesters — such things will revolutionize vineyard management.

The purchase of Roma from Schenley and the establishing of Cresta Blanca as a separate company came just at the time when the vast installation at Lodi was being modernized. By 1973, the various activities were completed and visitors to Lodi will find the most modern case goods handling systems in the world — tracks overhead, slots for trucks, fork lifts scurrying about — a scene that looks more hectic than it is.

The handsome visitor center remains the same and so does the exhibition vineyard behind it, where some fifty top varieties are planted so that people can get an idea of what they look like. There is a kitchen at the center, supervised by Helen Sanguinetti, who sees to it that some of her best recipes are printed in the firm's monthly newsletter.

The intense interest in table wines spurred Guild to begin its varietal project in Mendocino toward the end of the sixties, but this, too, is a pilot project. There is scarcely an acre of Cabernet from Lodi to Sacramento, says Ivie, and with the study of microclimates, even this may change. Meanwhile, they focus attention on varieties in the North Coast counties.

What are called popular wines, like Roma or Guild's Cribari or Tavola (which has more North Coast in it, according to Ivie), are enormously successful on the market. Also called standard wines or bulk wines, twenty bottles are sold for each bottle of premium wine. The proportion will jump to forty to one by the end of the decade. Only half the wines drunk in America are now table wines, compared to 75 percent in France and 80 percent in Germany, says Ivie. This means that there will be an enormous increase in table wines to meet a surging demand. Guild is beginning to meet it; 60 percent of all their production is now table wines, only 14 percent is fortified wine. Eight percent is sparkling wine, 18 percent is brandy, both growing rapidly. Guild intends to be in the vanguard of the changes.

A SELECTION
Roma Country Red
Cribari Vino Rosso
Cribari Zinfandel

Southern California

The state's first grapes were planted in Southern California, beginning at the Franciscan missions, and soon there were vineyards in many of the valleys, producing wines that many people insisted they liked. They were made of hot-weather grapes, usually sweet to hide the taste. Despite the valiant efforts of men like Jean Louis Vignes, who planted on the site of the Los Angeles railroad station, most of the vineyards disappeared, except for those in a valley an hour out of town, in Cucamonga. Maybe the appeal was because of the name.

Encroaching suburbs and attendant smog threatened the remaining vineyards and in the sixties the search began for new locations. The largest Cucamonga producer is Brookside Vineyard Company, still run by the fifth generation of the founding Biane family, but owned by a Chicago conglomerate, Beatrice Foods. Brands like Assumption Abbey, Brookside Estate, and Vaché are sold through thirty tasting rooms, two of them in Arizona, where the Bianes have tried experimental plantings. The most promising site proves to be an hour away, on a Riverside County landmark, the old Vail Ranch at Temecula. Half of 125 square miles is being developed into country estates called Rancho California, where the Bianes have planted almost 1,000 acres in top varietals. Other vineyards of 20 acres and up are being planted by homeowners, and when the number reaches 5,000 acres in mid-decade, the Bianes will have a winery in operation. The ranch community, which includes avocado and citrus groves, kennels and stables, is the project of Kaiser Industries and Aetna Insurance in a joint land development. The other half will be developed when the first is done. More are planned.

Cool breezes on the high mesa are claimed to keep the climate in Region Three. Up in Santa Barbara on the foothills of the coastal ranges, inland from Santa Maria, breezes are said to cool things down to Region Two. Ranchers watched a test plot of 120 acres of top varieties with interest. When the wines were tasted at the end of the sixties, and yield of varieties like Cabernet Sauvignon reached 4.5 tons, neighboring ranchers and developers began planting. The vines are planted directly into the soil, ungrafted, thanks to certified vines that are free of virus. There are a couple of thousand acres coming into bearing, to be doubled by mid-decade. Some are in the Tepusquet hills above the Sisquoc River, new names someday to be seen on bottles.

New York
and
Nearby States

The Great Grape Rebellion:
From Natives to Hybrids

Tantalus had an easy time of it compared to Eastern pioneers. He could never reach the grape above or the water below. The pioneers were glutted with both. Tantalus lost hope, but the pioneers never did. Wild and woolly dreams of liquid gold were surely closer to the national spirit than anything later manifest. They are still trying.

Grapes scraggled everywhere, from Nova Scotia south along the Appalachians; *labrusca* on the slopes, *riparia* on river banks, *rupestris* on stony ground, *rotundifolia* in the South, more in the Southwest, more up the Pacific coast. Grapes were everywhere. It was easier to swing from vine to vine to get to Fort Pitt than to walk the trails west from Philadelphia, said an early leatherstocking.

Not one of the pioneers made fit wine. All of it had a funny taste — foxy, it came to be called. The Indians never made wine, or if they did, there is no record; they were content with brews from herbs and roots or with various things to smoke, like tobacco and peyote. John Smith tried to make wine. Jefferson tried, as did homesteaders in Kentucky, Ohio, and Mississippi. The wine had a funny, musky taste. Why does one call it foxy? Skunky is a better word.

All of these native grapes produce strange wines that are quite different from the *vinifera* of Europe. Perhaps the most distinctive of these are the Muscadines of the South, one of this family being the Scuppernong. Wines from them were made throughout the South from earliest days, but it was made famous all over the country around the turn of the century by Captain Paul Garrett. He made a blend of Scuppernongs, naming it after the first child born to English colonists, Virginia Dare. Its sweet and musky flavor, muted with wines less pronounced, was a sensation in the South, so much so that prohibitionists got busy. As southern states went dry, Garrett moved north, using less and less Scuppernong in the blend and more and more *labrusca,* of which the most famous variety was Catawba. Catawba has a foxy taste.

Nicholas Longworth planted hundreds of acres near Cincinnati and made Sparkling Catawba. It was a sweet and nasty wine. He sent some to Longfellow, thus inspiring the worst verse extant on the subject of wine, which takes the name of two Champagne townships in vain:

> *Very good in its way*
> *Is the Verzenay,*
> *Or the Sillery, soft and creamy;*
> *But Catawba wine*
> *Has a taste more divine,*
> *More dulcet, delicious, and dreamy.*

None of the vinifera grapes of Europe would grow. Hopes soared with every grape that looked a little different. Lord Penn's gardener, Alexander, found a grape that later bore his name. He thought it might be a vinifera. It was not. There were hundreds — the Missouri Riesling, Dutchess, Isabella, Niagara, and Noah were the promising whites; Ives, Concord, and Delicatessen the promising reds. All make terrible wine. One white, the Delaware, makes something perfumed

Eastern Wines

The Finger Lakes

A. CANANDAIGUA
B. KEUKA
C. SENECA
D. CAYUGA
E. OWASCO
F. SKANEATELES

1 Gold Seal
2 Great Western
3 Taylor
4 Widmer
5 Boordy Vineyards
6 Renault
7 High Tor
8 Ohio Wines
9 Canadian Wines

0   20   40   60   80   100

LAKE ONTARIO

ONTARIO

NIAGARA PENINSULA

LAKE ERIE

OHIO

Sandusky
Cleveland

Chautauqua

Niagara Falls
Buffalo
Rochester
Hammondsport
Syracuse
Utica
Albany

N.Y. THRUWAY

HUDSON RIVER

Newburgh

New York

NEW JERSEY

Egg Harbor

Baltimore

and almost pleasing, not really musky. One red, the Lenoir, makes a dark red wine without much taste. Two others, the white Ellen Scott and the red Cynthiana, which is like a grape called Norton, have possibilities. To use the others, you have to blend.

Even skilled winemakers hired by colonial governors did not know what to do about it. When imported vines failed, the only thing to do was to try again — and fail again. Accidental crosses occurred. European vines would flower for a year or so before the phylloxera killed them, and the pollen would fertilize a native vine, producing seedlings, first the Alexandria, then the Catawba, and many other by-blows. Then Ephraim Bull produced a grape in Concord, Massachusetts, which he named after the town. It would grow anywhere. He exhibited it in 1852, suggesting it was a cross between a wild grape and Catawba. This was the needed clue.

Grape growers began trying all sorts of crosses, naming them after towns like Delaware in Ohio; or the grower, one being Moore's Diamond. They were less foxy than the Muscadines and Scuppernongs, and even drinkable.

Not that all of them were so bad once you got used to them. Just because they do not taste like European wines is no reason for blanket condemnation. You have to watch the muskiness, of course, but some of the native white wines are fair, something you cannot say for the reds. But the only eastern reds you are likely to come across are blends that fill out a line, that curse considered a need in most wineries. The New York State law helps, permitting the addition of as much as a quarter of out-of-state wines, and the soft bulk wines of California nicely counteract the thin acidity of the native New Yorkers. New York is called the Switzerland of America, because the white wines from upstate are supposed to show a similarity. There is a second similarity; Swiss law requires that reds imported from neighboring countries must contain a percentage of Swiss wines. Blending is a custom, not always a crime, by any means.

None of the native wines were much, but as winemaking improved, thanks to Pasteur's discoveries, they became drinkable. They offered a new range of aromas and flavors — as American as doughnuts and corn on the cob, says Philip Wagner in *American Wines & Wine-Making*. But they had to be more than that. It was Wagner himself who cleared the way to make them so. In a second book, Wagner explains just how to go about it.

As night editor of the *Baltimore Sun,* Philip Wagner had days to himself, not entirely filled with his hobby, which was refurbishing violins. To get out-of-doors more, he decided to plant some vines on the little farm where he lived in Riderwood. He was amused by the centuries of American failure and intrigued by the possibility of trying European hybrids, which were developed mostly in France in the wake of the phylloxera. His first book generally described his efforts and problems, and his second, *Wine Grower's Guide,* went into detail about managing a vineyard. Both were revised several times during the next twenty years and faithfully published by Alfred Knopf, so that anybody foolish enough could make wines, and if hooked, could raise grapes. Nobody paid him any mind, until Charles Fournier, up in Hammondsport, New York, tasted some of the wines made at Boordy Vineyard down in Maryland. No one else was growing hybrids or trying to develop new strains, and Fournier needed both to improve his blends of sparkling wines. His interest rekindled that of the experimental station at Geneva, which had done some basic research under U. P. Hedrick and had published one of the most beautiful books on grapes, one of a series on New York State fruits. Copies sometimes turn up in secondhand bookstores, but most have been torn apart so that the color plates could be sold separately to decorators for guest room walls.

In California, Amerine and Winkler, who were busily developing their temperature charts for vineyards and fermentations, began to take an interest. So did wine buffs throughout the South, Southwest, and Midwest. Every fall Wagner was busy on the phone answering questions and making suggestions, with scarcely time to handle his own vintage. The latest edition of the guide was published in 1969; during its first quarter century it has inspired more than 4,000 growers. During the seventies, the first wines from Boordy scions will become known, and Wagner has now set up a second winery in the Chautauqua country of western New York. Someday, there may be Rio Grande wines, Okefenokee wines, Ozark wines, Blue Grass wines, Nebraska wines, all courtesy of a night editor who felt that he should get out-of-doors more.

He even interested neighbors, including some Johns Hopkins professors like Dr. Charles Singleton, who has been maintaining his Caroli Vineyard north of Baltimore for more than twenty years. Up near the Pennsylvania border, a research psychologist, Dr. G. H. Mowbray, went off on a tangent and began planting vinifera as well as hybrids on his 5 acres of Montbray vineyard and is now offering Chardonnay and Riesling as well as Montbray Seyve-Villard and some blends. It's a long way from Catawba, which was cultivated for the first time in what is now Rock Creek Park in Washington, D.C. The grape was named Catawba by a major of the Revolutionary army, John Adlum, and he was the one who supplied Nicholas Longworth with cuttings for the first Ohio vineyards.

The introduction of Catawba, followed by Concord and Delaware, started a fever that only cooled with the distribution of California wines during the 1880s, squelching further development so effectively that eastern wineries subsided pretty much to the production of sparkling wines. Prohibition finished all but a few in New York and Ohio, Missouri and Michigan. Only the enthusiasm for still wines that began after World War II caused interest to be fanned again. With Wagner's hybrids and new techniques of vine management, new wines could be made. Fresh experiment with planting *vinifera* suggested they also had promise.

Even today, the few still wines produced outside New York come from a few vineyards around Sandusky Bay and the Put-in-Bay Islands in Lake Erie — North, Middle, and South Bass. Old-time wineries, like Meier's Wine Cellars do most of their business in sparkling wines. So does the American Wine Company of Missouri, with its Cook's Imperial, and the wineries of Michigan, little of whose wine gets out of the state. The industry at Paw Paw, Michigan, may stay alive only because of high taxes on out-of-state wines, although there is a little experiment with hybrids.

There is plenty of experiment in New York State. There is a small district up the Hudson from New York; Everett Crosby at High Tor began producing reds from hybrids and a white from Catawba. At Highland, the Hudson Valley Wine Company does most of its experimentation with new vinification techniques, and is content to produce mostly Delaware and Catawba.

Plenty of work is going on around the two most western of the Finger Lakes — Keuka and Canandaigua, where Taylor and Great Western, Gold Seal and Widmer produce the bulk of the eastern wines. Even an oldtime winery that produces only altar wines, O-Neh-Da Vineyard, after a century has begun experimental plantings of hybrids and vinifera to augment the native grapes in their hundred acres of vineyard.

The Chautauqua region, along the western border of the state, running south from Buffalo and along the shore of Lake Erie, is planted mostly in Concords. These are used primarily for producing Kosher wines, syrupy and sweet, although the Wagner presence may cause some changes. North of Buffalo, there are vineyards on both sides of the Niagara River, where hybrids are beginning to thrive, and we may yet see labels picturing Horseshoe Falls and the Maid-o'-the-Mist.

Something, but maybe not much, can be said for perseverance. Some remarkable and strange white table wines from native grapes are produced by Widmer's Wine Cellars. Gold Seal Vineyards makes some astonishingly good blends of white wines and sparkling wines in European style. Taylor and Great Western make some widely distributed blends, as well as sparkling wines. The state produces about twelve million gallons of table wines each year. Who knows what will happen when the acreage of hybrids increases? Will the Concords leave Chautauqua? Will Seibel replace Catawba? Will Ravat replace Delaware? What about Baco Number One, Landot 244, Seyve-Villard 5247? The names are interesting. During the seventies the wines will become so too.

SOME POPULAR HYBRIDS

The numbers simply wouldn't do. To say that Ravat 36 didn't have the full bouquet of Ravat 6 wasn't quite the same as talking about the robe of Chambertin and the depth of Richebourg, although equally boring to some. Names were better, and a decade ago the French devised some for twenty-five of the most popular hybrids, listed here for reference.

FRENCH NAMES OF HYBRIDS
RED WINE GRAPES

Baco Noir	Baco Number 1
Bellandais	Seibel 14,596
Chelois	Seibel 10,878
Colobel	Seibel 8,357
Couderc	Couderc 7,120
Chambourcin	J. Seyve 26,205
Florental	Burdin 7,705
Garonnet	Seyve-Villard 18,283
Landal	Landot 244
Marechal Foch	Kuhlmann 188.2
Leon Millot	Kuhlmann 192.2
Oberlin	Oberline 595
Plantet	Seibel 5,455
Seinoir	Seibel 8,745
Varousset	Seyve-Villard 23,657
Villard Noir	Seyve-Villard 18,315

WHITE WINE GRAPES

Ambror	Seibel 10,173
Baco Blanc	Baco 22 A
Ravat Blanc	Ravat 6
Rayon d'Or	Seibel 4,986
Roucaneuf	Seyve-Villard 12,309
Rubilande	Seibel 11,803
Seyval	Seyve-Villard 5,276
Valerien	Seyve-Villard 23–410
Villard Blanc	Seyve-Villard 12,375

Some of the French-American hybrids that do well here were not named but this was rectified by an association of New York wine growers. Among these hybrids are De Chaunac, originally Seibel 9,549, renamed for one of the pioneers of grape growing on the Niagara Peninsula; the red wine from it has a light and balanced taste. Other Seibels like Chancellor (S. 7,053), Rougeon (S. 5,898), Cascade (S. 13,053) and Verdelet (S. 9,110) all show promise as blending wines, if not as varietal bottlings. At experiment stations in Geneva and in Vineland, Ontario, other hybrids are being tried or developed — some with names, some with numbers. The aim is to find vines that withstand disease and winter kill and can produce wines of good quality in commercial quantities — maybe five tons an acre. Before the decade's out, you may be able to buy Cayuga White or Vincent, but meanwhile, look for the following:

REDS

BACO NOIR: Derived from Folle Blanche, this hardy, resistant vine produces wines with good acidity and a spicy aroma like that of the clarets of Bordeaux. A clean, light wine that improves with age. Originally Baco No. 1.

MARECHAL FOCH: An Alsatian hybrid derived from Pinot Noir and Gamay, early to ripen, producing a straightforward wine with an aroma like a Burgundy. Originally Kuhlmann 188.2.

LANDAL: A deep-colored wine, fruity and full, of good quality, like a Beaujolais. Originally Landot 244.

CHANCELLOR: Heavy producer of a sound and simple wine, extensively planted in France. Originally Seibel 7,053.

COLOBEL: A color grape, used as a *teinturier,* or dyer, to deepen the color of light reds. Originally Seibel 8,357.

CHELOIS: Late to bud, this vigorous vine produces a wine reminiscent of light Burgundies, with some spice. Originally Seibel 10,878.

CASCADE: Early, hardy, and resistant, producing a superior grape that makes an attractive rosé. Originally Seibel 13,053.

WHITES

RAVAT BLANC: A hybrid from Chardonnay, producing the best white wine of any hybrid, but the vine suffers from humidity, dampness, and intense cold. Originally Ravat 6.

AURORE: Has a distinctive bouquet and makes a soft, well-balanced wine. Originally Seibel 5,279.

VERDELET: Produces an outstanding table grape, rated by Wagner as far superior to those commonly available, at the same time producing a wine of good balance and a flowery bouquet. Originally Seibel 9,110.

SEYVAL: Superior sugar-acid balance. Rivals Aurore, according to Wagner. Originally Seyve-Villard 5,276.

VALERIEN: An offspring of Villard Blanc — grown widely in southern France, and is in turn related to Roucaneuf — which Wagner says is good to eat and good to drink. Originally Seyve-Villard 23–410.

The Hudson Valley

It looked like the Rhine and Huguenot settlers planted French vines three centuries ago, switching to wild vines when their cuttings failed. Not until the 1820s were there commercial plantings along the river, the first at Croton Point, and the first winery was set up at Washingtonville in 1839. It's still in operation as the Brotherhood Corporation, the oldest in the country, founded by the religious community that eventually established Fountain Grove in the Sonoma Valley. It's all history, now, for the birthplace of American wines is now planted mostly in Concords. What isn't, is due to Everett Crosby, who was so persevering at High Tor that other enthusiasts have come to the valley and there are signs of a rebirth. The first Hudson Valley Grape conference was held on the campus of the new university at New Paltz in the spring of 1973 and Concord growers went away wondering about the possibilities of hybrids and *vinifera,* if only to provide grapes for the hundreds of New Yorkers who have taken to making wine. Like Rip Van Winkle, the valley may be waking up after a long sleep. The early Huguenots would have been pleased.

The Brotherhood Winery makes blends, kosher wines, and sparkling wines, using some native grapes. The Royal Wine Corporation and Marlboro Industries make mostly kosher wines, and the Mandia Champagne Cellars follows the pattern, and insists that they were the first to bottle Cold Duck. Like the Hudson Valley Wine Company, the other old firms are beginning to turn to table wines. Hudson Valley was bought by Monsieur Henri, the New York importers, and hybrids were started in the 200-acre vineyard at once, their wines to be blended with those from native grapes. Of most interest in the region, though, is the small grower and the amateur.

One of these is Tom Clarke, who has been making wines for

years from a plot of Chardonnay near his home in New Canaan, Connecticut. He wanted more room so he bought a plot in Marlboro and began putting in Chardonnay, Riesling, and hybrids. Like others, he'd like people to get to know his wines, but the annual license fee to operate a winery is close to a thousand dollars. To solve the problem of costs, Mark Miller sells vines to friends from his Benmarl Vineyard, entitling them to a case of wine each year, as well as a chance to buy sections of contemplated vineyards, grapes from which would be taken by his winery. The laws keep the region from developing, but when they are liberalized, a new-old region will be in the making.

HIGH TOR

The crag above the Hudson is high enough for a climber to see the night glare from Manhattan and along its southern slope are the vineyards planted a generation ago by Everett Crosby. His city friends used to come out and help with the vintage and they still talk about the harvest picnics and dinners that Crosby would provide to pay them for their labors. Those times were the only ones that most of them got to taste the wines, for when he retired and sold High Tor Vineyards to Dick Voigt at the decade's turn, production of Rockland Red and White and Rosé was only 500 cases. There are 15 acres of vines now planted in French-American hybrids, with more to come on the 78 acres of land, so production will mount to maybe 5,000 cases by 1976. If Voigt and winemaker Tom Hayes can influence neighbors to put in hybrids there may be even more. Success on High Tor will come from encouraging people to rip up their Concords and find out what the new grapes can do.

Hudson Valley vintages are the country wines of New York City, but bottles are so few that only the most curious are willing to pay the three or four dollars to find out what the wines taste like. There's a soft white called Aurora, a light red called Rougeon, the fruity Cascade Noir and the full Chancellor Noir, hard to find even a hundred miles from the vineyard. New plantings may change all that by the end of the decade but until there's a chance to taste the wines, you might like to read how a new wine region has come into being in

Everett Crosby's book, *The Vintage Years*. The early days were marvelous times and in these first bottlings you can taste the beginnings.

BENMARL WINE COMPANY

Mark Miller is an illustrator who lived in Burgundy for five years, partly because it was a good place to work, but mostly because he wanted to soak up wine lore. When he returned in the fifties he went up the Hudson to find himself a vineyard. In the Gay Nineties there had been twenty square miles of vineyards, but it had dwindled to a tenth of that, all in Concords and native grapes except for a dozen at High Tor. The first acres were planted by a man named Caywood, an early experimenter in the development of new varieties. On stony ledges four hundred feet above the river he had produced Dutchess, a grape still grown in a few vineyards, mostly in the Finger Lakes. It was about the last vineyard Miller looked at, off a rocky road up behind Marlboro, a little town above Newburgh. It was just what Miller had in mind. He decided to call it Benmarl, which means Slate Hill in Gaelic, and he proceeded to plant a dozen acres of Chardonnay and the French-American hybrids, particularly Baco Noir and Chelois, Aurore and Seyval, followed by Chancellor and De Chaunac. The whole family pitched in. Help came from the Société of Vignerons, a group of friends that Miller organized into a cooperative. Members bought "Vinerights," which was title to a pair of vines, entitling them to a case of the Benmarl wines each vintage year. Miller's years in Burgundy had been rewarding, as had his frequent visits to fellow winegrowers in the East, and with the seventies, some of his wines begin to appear on the New York market.

The Finger Lakes

TAYLOR WINE COMPANY AND GREAT WESTERN

In 1829 the church brought the vine to the Finger Lakes, or at least to Keuka, in the person of an Episcopal minister named Bostwick. The cuttings came from the Hudson valley and they flourished in the rectory garden in Hammondsport. It must have something to do with the lake, people said, and they asked for cuttings. Fifty years later, there were enough vines to support a cooper, and Walter Taylor arrived from the East with his bride, bought a 7-acre plot, and planted vines. After all, he had the casks. Two years later, in 1882, he bought a 70-acre farm on Bully Hill. Today, there are ten times as much in vines, enough cooperage for fifteen million gallons of wine and annual sales of two million cases — must have something to do with the lake.

Grapes come from fifty miles around, and from as far away as Chautauqua and Niagara, almost 85 percent of them being supplied by some 270 growers. Receding glaciers formed the land, gouging long deep lakes, with hills rising high on either side. The morning sun catches the western slopes, the afternoon sun the eastern ones, warming the lakes in its daily swing, so that they freeze late and the ice melts early, tempering frosts. But hardy vines are needed to live through the freeze of winter. Growers dared not risk winter kill, limiting the varieties planted, so Taylor embarked on a development program twenty years ago to widen the range.

You have to be suspicious. A vine that looks good in an experimental plot — that has grown well for half a dozen years, borne generously, produced balanced wines — may peter out after a dozen years in a new vineyard. A vine can be expected to last for twenty years, even twice that, and should do so to be worthwhile. When most of your grapes come from growers who take your advice because you are going to buy their production, you tend to be cautious. The risk is less, though, when the worst that can happen is that the wine will be bland or the supply small. Even so, a third of the home acreage is now in hybrids, 2,000 acres among the supplying growers, and more to come. Eight of every ten tons of the new hybrids go to Taylor.

The founder's three sons took over operations, Greyton taking charge of Great Western when that was acquired in 1961, in time for Christmas. The following year the firm went public to raise money for expansion, and now the third generation is supervising the growth. A score of blends is marketed under the Taylor label, even more under Great Western, which offers a group of wines from hybrids, varietal bottlings called Aurora, Dutchess, Baco Noir, and

Chelois. The new wines go into Taylor blends, particularly the rosé, both still and sparkling, plus two others called Lake Country Red and Lake Country White.

A SELECTION
Taylor Lake Country White
Taylor Vin Rosé
Great Western Baco Noir

BULLY HILL

The little vineyard on the hill above the lake had sentimental attachments, the winery was still there, and Walter Taylor bought the property to see what could be done with it. The old winery he turned into a museum, naming it after his father, Greyton Taylor, who had taken over the Pleasant Valley Wine Company when the Taylors took it over. Walter had been an officer of the firm, but his heart was in the making of wines, not the marketing of them. Like many enthusiasts before him, he thought he could make wines better than had been done before, natural wines without any adulteration, amelioration or sophistication — an act that many winemakers liken to riding a bike with no hands.

Walter hated the idea of adding water and sugar to juice that had too much acid to produce balanced wines, he hated extensive blending, he hated the addition of preservatives and chemicals — and he hated Concords and all the other grapes that produced mediocre wines. The Finger Lakes was one of the greatest wine regions in the world. Bully Hill was licensed as a winery in 1970 to prove it.

While scouring the country for materials to put in the wine museum, Walter worked on a *Home Winemaker's Handbook* with Richard Vine, then the winemaker for Pleasant Valley, doing all the drawings for the book. When the museum was well underway, he opened a Winemaker's Shop and started a newsletter to carry his gospel and answer technical questions about wines and vines. He converted a barn into a winery and bought an old winery down the road where he could make sparkling wines. He set up Hermann Wiemer, a graduate of the German wine school at Geisenheim, as winemaker.

And he planted grapes — natives such as Delaware and Diamond, French-American hybrids such as Baco Noir and Seyval Blanc. He doesn't like to call them hybrids, arguing that all grapes are crosses, but prefers to call them direct producers because they don't always need to be grafted. His first wines were blends called Bully Hill White and Bully Hill Red and they were good, but in short supply. Today he has 200 acres and is producing a lot more wine.

GOLD SEAL VINEYARDS

It is all well and good to talk about the native taste of the wine — that distinctive tang not found in wine of the Old World, that not-so-elusive something that set York state wines apart. When Charles Fournier arrived in the 1940s, he knew he had to do something about the grapes. An early American chronicler, Robert Beverley, described the grapes of Virginia as having "a rank taste when ripe, resembling the smell of a fox." That was in 1722, and while getting foxed was slang for getting tipsy, and while legend is full of foxes eating grapes, the truth was in the tasting. Fournier determined to do something about both the taste and the grapes.

There were three ways. One was to find grapes with the least foxiness and propagate these; carefully vinified, they made suitable wines. Another was to try the hybrids, and Fournier was quick to enlist Philip Wagner, making the first plantings of those grapes in his own vineyards. The third was to try again with *vinifera,* and for this he turned to the skills of Dr. Konstantin Frank.

The last of the czars had inveigled Frank's German parents to settle in the Ukraine and use their German training to establish vineyards. When Frank arrived in the Finger Lakes in the forties, the problems seemed much like those his father had solved in the west of Russia. Fournier was inclined to agree, and willing to try once again. Three hundred years of failure merely showed what you should not do.

Dr. Frank believed that the secret was to have the vines enter the dormant period only after fully ripening, after a growing season in which the vine was quite free of disease. It was one thing to choose your clone from a particularly fine specimen, and propagate from this single bud, but it had to reach maturity in a completely healthy state to withstand winter freezes that go to twenty below, and then some. To do this, you needed root stocks that mature early so that the vine will develop its wood early. He took himself off to get root stocks from wild vines along the St. Lawrence, and began experimenting with all the hardy stocks at hand.

The big test came after two harsh winters in a row, 1962 and 1963. The young stocks of Riesling and Chardonnay came through well, and Pinot Noir and Traminer survived. In the years since, Gold Seal has occasionally offered small lots of Chardonnay or Riesling, to show what can be done.

The prime use for such wines is to balance the blends, and to make possible the marketing of Fournier Nature, a dry white wine made with Chardonnay, the still companion to the sparkling Fournier Blanc de Blancs. Three wines based on native grapes are lightly sweet — Catawba Red, Catawba White, and Catawba Pink. The newer hybrids contribute to a trio of soft wines called Carousel — white, pink, and red.

There are something like 500 acres of vines on three farms, one on each side of Lake Keuka, and a third new one over east, above Lake Seneca. This last is an extension of what has been generally considered the Finger Lakes region, which has been pretty much confined to the area around the two western lakes of the chain. There will be new plantings to augment the 25 acres of Chardonnay and the 35 of Riesling, 10 acres or so of the old vineyards being replanted each year in those grapes or in the new hybrids. Sales are approaching one million cases a year.

A SELECTION
Fournier Nature
Carousel Red
Gold Seal Rosé

VINIFERA WINE VINEYARDS

Dr. Konstantin Frank lives amid his vineyards above Lake Keuka in a farmhouse full of woodwork he carpentered himself.

The winery is a long, low shed out back, partly buried in the ground. Both are on the crown of a hill, the slopes of vines falling away to long views of the lake and the roll of hills, blowy in winter, breezily blazing in summer. Sitting on the crowded porch or in the still more crowded office, Dr. Frank pulls corks on bottles, holding them low and out of sight, so you cannot see the labels. He will say, "What do you think of that? Have you ever tasted anything like this one? Look at the color. Just note that bouquet." He gets more excited with each wine. He has earned the right.

Dr. Frank wanted his own vineyards so he could make wines just the way he wanted, and Charles Fournier helped him get a few acres in the fifties. In no time at all, it seemed, there were the bottles with a colored picture of a vineyard on the labels — Cabernet Sauvignon, Gewürztraminer, Pinot Chardonnay Natur, Johannisberg Riesling Natur Spätlese. There was even a Johannisberg Trockenbeeren Auslese, which sold for forty-five dollars a bottle.

This caused talk, some of it outraged, much of it confused. There was no longer any doubt that vinifera could be grown in the East, although, as English visitors were apt to say, they were a bit pricey. Everybody wanted to taste them, and those who did thought they were wonderful but that they were full of sulphur. Dr. Frank denied this out of hand, and said the wines were exceptional. They certainly were, and wine buffs had a fine time explaining to the curious what all the words on the label meant.

Spätlese is the German term for late-picked grapes, and *Auslese* means selection. Bunches were allowed to remain on the vines until some of the juice had evaporated, concentrating the grape sugar, then particularly raisinized bunches were selected to be made into wine. If wine was made from selected dried berries taken from these bunches, it was called *Trockenbeeren Auslese,* or dried berry selection. The wines were sweet, rich, and in the classic tradition.

Dr. Frank is tending nearly 60 acres of vines, all planted in European stocks. He offers wines from Pinot Gris, the only plot of that Alsatian grape in commercial bearing. There is also Pinot Noir, Gamay Beaujolais, some Aligoté (a lesser Burgundy grape that makes a light, fresh white wine) , and even some Sereksia, a Russian grape that makes a sweet wine.

Dr. Frank says that he will make no more Trockenbeeren Auslese. That was produced just to make a noise. People were forever being amazed at the mere existence of the wines, and he wanted to shift the talk to their excellence. He made the rarest of wine types and charged accordingly, neatly making his point. Still, you never can tell. If response is not what Dr. Frank thinks it should be, he just might let his Riesling raisinize again.

A SELECTION
Pinot Gris
Pinot Chardonnay
Pinot Noir

WIDMER'S WINE CELLARS

His brother said it was a great place, so, in 1882, John Jacob Widmer abandoned the Alps of Switzerland for the hills of Naples and borrowed money for some land, which he cleared and planted in vines. The hills of Naples were at the foot of New York's Lake Canandaigua, which is said to mean the chosen place in old Indian. It was a good place for Widmer, for there are now some 500 acres in vine, with another 50 being added each year, plus the grapes from 1,100 other acres owned by independent growers. He had three sons to take over the business, and the winemaker was Will, who was sent to Geisenheim for training and came back to make the best wines ever produced from native grapes. Will liked the taste and his wines taught thousands of others to like them, too.

The first wines were sold by the keg to other Swiss — in New York, Rochester, Paterson, New Jersey, and round about — and partly because of this, the idea grew up that the wines were Swiss in character. The similarity was slight, and as the land looks somewhat like the Rhineland, it came to be called this as well. When sparkling wines became popular, there was an effort to dub the region the Champagne Country of America, this having more pull in the marketplace than Rhineland of America or Switzerland of America. Similarities are mildly geographic, if you squint a little. The wines remain unique. Will Widmer liked it that way.

He felt that white wines from the native grapes were unique, desirable just because they did not taste like *vinifera*. Instead of one kind of vine, America had dozens, a vinous heritage unmatched anywhere. It should be taken advantage of, and the way to do it was to vinify carefully. But first you had to choose your grapes.

The native grapes were actually hybrids, accidental crosses with European varieties. Suppose such a scion was crossed with another scion that was also a cross. Suppose you took the French hybrids, those containing some American strain, and crossed them back again. One success out of a thousand was a good average. By tracking down various hybridizers, among them Phil Wagner, he came up with fine stocks. By vinifying with great care, he made some matchless wines.

Finger Lakes grapes need sugar, which comes from full maturity in the vineyard — just the reverse of the California problem. Grapes had to be bred for early ripeness, then vinified according to the newest techniques, many of which Widmer pioneered in New York State. He was the first to produce wines with grape names on the label, the first to install a solera system for his fortified wines. This last caused a sensation. The casks are laid out on the roof of the winery and exposed to the weather — a startling sight after a snowfall, but his Sherry types are unlike any other.

His varietal whites include not only Delaware and Riesling but also Moore's Diamond, Vergennes, and Elvira. The last three are available nowhere else, as are red Isabella and Seibel-Rosé. His blends include the sweet white Lake Niagara, which the firm says is the largest-selling vintage wine in the country, and the soft pink Lake Roselle. As a bow to tradition, there is Widmerheimer White and Red, both fruity, both light and fresh.

The taste of foxiness comes mostly from the skins, and even the Isabella is removed from the skins to ferment, so that wine is light in color, growing lighter with age. Will Widmer was one of the few who learned to love it. Moore's Diamond has a spicy taste, and sipping it makes one wonder what to serve with it. Like the other white varietals, it might go with fish or seafood, with a cold buffet, but then the idea comes that it is best by itself, to be drunk the way so many German wines are, apart from meals. It is best alone, at most with some fruit or mild cheeses for contrast.

The three Widmer sons had nobody to carry on the firm, so it was sold to a Rochester business group who subsequently sold the company to the makers of French's mustard. Installed as manager was Ernest Reveal, who supervises the expansion of the firm, sales of which are now more than one million cases a year. There is expansion in another direction, for Widmer's has purchased 500 acres of land in the Alexander Valley of Sonoma, which will come into bearing by mid-decade. Widmer's will be the first firm to market varietals from both districts.

A SELECTION
Moore's Diamond
Vergennes
Seibel-Rosé

CANANDAIGUA WINE COMPANY

Virginia Dare was the first child born to English colonists, legend has it, and her name was given to the first brand of wine marketed in the United States, back in 1835. It was made in Virginia from the Scuppernong, a native grape of the Muscadine family and grown most successfully at Mother Vineyard, which belongs to a winery so named in Petersburg. Virginia Dare, along with others from Catawbas and Niagaras and other native grapes, hybrids, and fruits, is produced by the country's largest wine firm outside California — Canandaigua. It is the third largest in the country, coming right after Gallo and Italian Swiss.

Canandaigua was founded in the town of that name in upstate New York to provide blends for bottlers, of which the company owns several, located from Maine to Texas. It also owns several wineries including the Hammondsport Wine Company for making sparkling wines; Tenner Brothers in the heart of the South Carolina peach orchards, where Richard's Peach Wine is made; and Richard's Wine Cellars in Virginia. When that last bright star was added to the crown — along with brands like Sun Ray, Suppertime, and Old Maude — the popularity of them all led to the purchase of Onslow Winery in Holley Ridge, North Carolina, and plans to plant thousands of acres across the South and into Texas. Scuppernong may someday reach the Pacific. One of the largest selling wines in the country is the company's Wild Irish Rose.

When Mac Sands started out as a bottler in Richmond, Virginia, right after Repeal, he knew where he was going but he didn't know how far the "scups" would take him. Scuppernongs are round grapes as big as olives, and they have a wild, sweet taste that makes a wild, sweet wine. Americans have always hankered after the taste, which is strong in Virginia Dare, but there's a different wildness in Wild Irish Rose, which includes Catawba, Concord, Delaware, Elvira, and Niagara. No other flavors are added. None are needed, say wine buffs, who think the musky flavor is out of place in wines. For some who feel the same, there's a new product called Aquarius containing blackberry, cherry, guava, passion fruit, pineapple, and raspberry. The company is expanding sales into Alaska and Hawaii. They might well do so, for they claim fifty million consumers for their bottlings each year.

Such wines may be the salvation of the South, which is slowly moving away from tobacco and cotton. A decade ago, farmers were also moving out of Concords, which were bringing $40 a ton. The popularity of Canandaigua's wines started a trend, for the company willingly pays upward of $300 a ton for scups, which average better than three tons to the acre; Catawbas are less but yield five tons. Mac's son, Marvin, now oversees the expansion of the company, which went public in 1973. A loyal band of managers from the member companies, several of whom have been involved for a quarter of a century, along with a gaggle of younger men trained in the various wine colleges and business schools, keep on the lookout for new opportunities.

Traditionalists may hold back when it comes to serving Scuppernong regularly, but an experience not to be missed is Muddled Colonial Punch. You boil three sliced lemons in three cups of water with six cinnamon sticks for half an hour. Take this off the fire and add a cup of light rum, along with a bottle of Mother Vineyard Scuppernong. Directions say, "Thrust a red hot poker into the punch (for authenticity)." Pour into mugs. And if you don't try that, here's another suggestion — try Old Maude.

Chautauqua and Niagara

In the western crook of New York State that borders on Lake Erie lies its largest grape growing region, more than 20,000 acres devoted to Concords. First cultivated by Ephraim Bull in Massachusetts, its producer named the grape after his home town and tried to sell its cuttings for five dollars apiece. Nearby nurseries propagated their own, ignoring Bull, who died penniless, perhaps the proper reward for the man who gave to the world one of the worst grapes ever grown. There's nothing wrong with it for jam or jelly, of course, and every American knows the taste of its juice and the alcoholic, syrupy version called "kosher wine." But there is no possible way to make a palatable table wine from it, or even to use it to make a blend. Perhaps its highest form is Cold Duck as spiked soda pop — fizzy with bubbles, sweet with sugar, and quite refreshing if you can bear it.

Concords came into their own in Chautauqua through the earnest efforts of a dentist named Welch, an early Prohibitionist who hated alcohol and one day happened to read Pasteur's experiments. In all likelihood he was seeking ammunition for attacks on the evils of drink. Instead, he got a subtler idea. Why not pasturize grape juice and get people to drink that instead of wine? He began his experiments in Vineland, New Jersey, but rot ruined the vineyards. Undeterred, he moved to New York State, eventually settling in Westfield in Chautauqua County just before the turn of the century. He picked the right spot, for the farm country was a hotbed of temperance from which tentfulls of uplifters were sent on lecture circuits each summer to bring culture and good thoughts to the sinners in the surrounding countryside. All the highflown thoughts generated thirst, and Welch's grape juice was just the thing to slake it.

Concords came long before Welch, of course, spreading like a plague deep into the South and the Midwest, where the grape was raised for eating. So many were marketed, though, that they became a glut. Pasteurized grape juice created a new demand which lasted until Prohibition, when suddenly there was not enough Concord to meet the demands of bootleggers and the hordes who made wines at home. The slump after Repeal was taken up in Brooklyn where a man named Star set up the Monarch Wine Company to make an extra-sweet alcoholic concoction for Passover. He called it "kosher wine." After 3.2 beer, the first thin and sour beverage marketed, Kosher wine tasted delicious. Star asked Manischewitz if he could use their name on the label and the house that matzos built agreed. Out in Chicago, Mogen David produced a copy with the shield of David on the label. The two began an advertising battle for the market that was one of the wonders of the late forties, with every company producing its own version. In a dozen years sales rose to a million bottles a week, where it stays. As public taste shifted toward dry wines, less-sweet versions were offered. Noting a good thing, Coca Cola bought Monarch and began its steady expansion into the wine business.

JOHNSON

Meanwhile, back in Chautauqua, things weren't going all that well. Demand had spread Concords to Michigan and beyond and the price of the grapes was steadily declining. Then somebody thought of Cold Duck and soon millions of bottles of that were being sold — all flavored with Concord. Observing the boom and bust cycle, though, some Concord growers took to wondering if Cold Duck might be a fad. Maybe it was time to get out of Concords.

One who thought so was a Cornell graduate, an expert in tropical agriculture, who had inherited 125 acres of Concords in Westfield. He began pulling them out, planting hybrids and Delawares and other varietals, setting up the Johnson Vineyards Winery. With the seventies, Johnson Estate wines — Seyval Blanc, Delaware, Dry Red, and others — began to pick up a following. Frederick Johnson had started the first new winery in Chautauqua in a generation.

SENECA FOODS

Hearing about prices for hybrids that growers were getting over in the Finger Lakes, some of those in Chautauqua began putting in a few rows. They were encouraged to do more when first Manischewitz and then Mogen David put in 500-acre plantings — Delawares and Catawbas, but also hybrids. Mogen David even put in plots of the top vinifera. The clincher came in 1968, when the president of Seneca Foods talked Phil Wagner into a joint venture. Big in juice and apple sauce, Arthur Wolcott saw no good reason why the company's juice plants — in Chautauqua, the Finger Lakes, and the state of Washington — couldn't make good wines. Wagner thought so too, bought some hybrids, and lent his Boordy Vineyards name to the wines he made, "produced and bottled at Westfield." The Seneca plant at the top of Canandaigua, in Penn Yan, was an old Garrett winery and the wines are now made there; a 500-acre block of new plantings was established in Prosser, Washington.

The trouble was that growers had a Concord mentality — wines at fifty cents a bottle — and had to begin thinking about the best grapes they could grow, not the most, from which to make wines that would cost two dollars a bottle and more. As the seventies began, a quarter of the acreage was out of Concords. Much of the 5,000 acres of better varieties were planted in hybrids. By the end of the decade Concords may account for less than half the acreage, as they do in the Finger Lakes. In 1972, nearly a hundred growers took a tour of West Coast vineyards, and more have gone since. There will always be Concords along the lake, say old hands, which is true, but there won't be as many. Even some of the young growers are holding out for Concords, not taking for granted the cliché that Concords make bad wines. Like musk in perfume, a little Concord adds a strange something to a blend, a mysterious quality that may be good. As the range of wines widens and are drunk at all times, not just at meals, new blends are in the making.

New England

The rockbound coasts and hardscrabble hills of New England are no place for vineyards, but slopes above the river valleys and along the Connecticut shore are another matter, and where there's room between people, wine buffs are putting in grapes. The marginal orchards, pastures, and tobacco fields are beginning to look good to farmers with an eye on grapes, and several shrewd New Englanders are thinking of vineyards as a secondary crop. All this, of course, is due to the success of Philip Wagner's hybrids, Konstantin Frank's vinifera, and the new vineyard and winery techniques coming out of California. Growing national thirst also has something to do with it.

WHITE MOUNTAIN VINEYARDS

Still, outlanders beyond the Hudson shouldn't spend much time seeking out New Hampshire vintages from the hundred scattered acres of White Mountain Vineyards. The wines scarcely get far from Laconia, where John Canepa opened a pharmacy after growing up in and around New York. Wild grapes grew so well that Canepa saw no reason why hybrids and vinifera shouldn't do the same, and in scarcely a decade he had talked some forty New Hampshire, Vermont, and Maine farmers into providing grapes for him. Canepa and neighbors talked the state into letting their wines be sold direct. In Vermont the winery license fee was reduced to $150 from $300, and various state agriculture stations are now taking belated looks at grapes. Now Canepa is talking to farmers in the big valley of Massachusetts. Don't miss the Canepa estate bottlings and New Hampshire Lakes wines if you ever get up that way. And peel an eye for the Lakes Region Dry White Dinner Wine; you'll have a nice surprise.

New Jersey

RENAULT AND NEIGHBORS

A mild and distinctive climatic zone runs up the Atlantic coast from the Carolinas to Cape Cod, and if it weren't so crowded with people and resorts, it would be a great place for vineyards. The glacial moraine of Long Island, turned to the east, is particularly promising, but potato farmers and dairy herds got there first, losing to this country a potential Bordeaux. The only place where wines have been made successfully is in New Jersey, back from the shore, and even there, truck farming has been more successful. Toward the pine barrens behind Atlantic City are a thousand acres of the Renault vineyards, a century-old company that made a name for itself with sparkling wines. Its headquarters are in Egg Harbor, the wine center of the state, and since being taken over by Universal Foods of Milwaukee, some hybrids have been planted to use in the blends and a white wine made from the prize native grape, Noah, is being offered. Others nearby include Gross's Highland Winery, with 60 acres; Tomasello Winery, with 50 acres; and John Shuster & Son, which buys grapes for its lines. Most of the wines are blends of native grapes or fruit wines, the most extensive line being that of Monte Carlo Wine Industries in New Brunswick. There are several large bottling plants that depend on California gallonage, among them Vermouth Industries of America, whose Tribuno brand is the most popular in the country; the company has been taken over by Coca Cola.

The oldest company in the state is Laird's, founded in 1780 to make cider and applejack. It still does, now producing apple wines in response to the demand for them created by Gallo's Boone's Farm. Laird's is the only applejack producer worthy of note that's left in a state once famous for Jersey Lightning. It is said that oldtimers in the apple country used to bury jugs of hard cider in the ground and after the first good freeze they poured off the liquid that wasn't frozen and tried to be patient while it aged in wood. Laird's uses modern distilling methods to make its apple brandy, patiently marketing a drink that's almost forgotten.

There are some small wineries, several amateurs grow hybrids and vinifera, and there's potential around the pine barrens in the southern part of the state, but little effort goes into reviving a once-thriving industry.

Pennsylvania

Lord Penn had vineyards planted around Philadelphia before 1700 but all that came out of them was the Alexander, cultivated from *labrusca,* which went west with settlers to the Ohio Valley and gradually disappeared. Religious communities and German settlers moved from valley to valley, finally making the area around Pittsburgh into vineyard country. A few went up to the shores of Lake Erie, but what was left after all the effort was mostly a sea of Concords — fifteen square miles of them. Amateur growers who had busied themselves with hybrids and vinifera finally got a law passed permitting them to bypass the state liquor stores and sell up to 100,000 gallons a year directly to the public, and wine makers were suddenly free to see what they could do. The liberating law of 1968 is such a boon to small growers, such encouragement to experiment, that neighboring states are being badgered to update their silly rules.

Drys, bureaucrats, producers of mass-appeal wines, and retailers fearful of losing some of their lucrative trade band together to keep the old restrictions. Table wines, at least, should be as readily available as beer, so that small growers can have direct access to the market — local groceries and wine shops — without going through the costly wholesaler-distributor systems. Many states still demand a thousand dollars and more each year to license a winery, further squelching small growers, many of whom feel they're doing well if they make a dollar a bottle profit. They need every cent they can get to plant new varieties and try new techniques in new locations, for their pioneering opens the way for commercial plantings. Decades of restrictive legislation has kept eastern plantings of vinifera to less than a thousand acres, the acreage in new hybrids is perhaps ten times more. Liberalizing the laws is the only way to get rid of the horrid Concords. Pennsylvania has shown the way.

CONESTOGA VINEYARDS, PRESQUE ISLE WINE CELLARS, AND PENN SHORE VINEYARDS

Ignoring all restrictions, a Philadelphian named Melvin Gordon got some grapes from Philip Wagner in the fifties and planted 10 acres at Birchrunville, up near Valley Forge; his Conestoga Vineyards now offers Rayon d'Or and hybrid blends to restaurants as far away as Philadelphia. The son of a Concord grower, Douglas Moorhead, came back from a tour of army duty in Germany and planted some Rieslings and hybrids in the family vineyard, joining forces in the early sixties with newspaperman William Konnerth to start Presque Isle Wine Cellars at North East, up on Lake Erie near the New York border. Their first customers were other amateurs, but now a few wines can be had from them; part of the grape supply comes from neighboring growers who have become interested. Another group of growers pooled their 125 acres in 1969, set up Penn-Shore Vineyards, and now markets a range of blends, including a sparkling wine. This is only the beginning, thanks to the new laws. Other vineyards are going in.

The Great Lakes and the Ozarks

Ohio

In the 1820s a lawyer who had made a fortune in real estate began planting Catawbas in what is now Cincinnati's city park. His name was Nicholas Longworth, and his wine was Sparkling Catawba. It came from two square miles of vineyard and was the most famous American wine of the century until disease attacked the vineyards. By the end of the Civil War, Longworth's Sparkling Catawba was no more.

MEIER'S, TARULA FARMS, AND THE EXPERIMENTERS

For the grape, that was only the beginning, and while plantings along the Ohio River disappeared, others around the Great Lakes and along the Mississippi flourished, fighting for vineyard space with Concords. Those planted on islands in Lake Erie even withstood

Prohibition; the popularity of Meier's Sparkling Catawba, not to say juice from the grape, kept the vineyards alive. Meier's had been taken over by Henry O. Sonneman even before Repeal, and to provide grapes for his winery he bought the vineyards on North Bass Island, now called Isle St. George. There are 350 acres of them — half the island — and there he began planting some hybrids. They were so successful that he encouraged the state to establish experimental vineyards all along the Ohio, buying 300 hundred acres along the river to see what he could do. One of the experimental vineyards has been developed into Tarula Farms; another of the farms has a 40-acre vineyard to provide the Valley Vineyards Winery; and Gast and Dilger winery has converted a Cincinnati brewery into Fountain Wine Cellars. Up near Cleveland, Cohodas Vineyard is going out of Concords and into Catawbas, and even oldtimers like Mantey Vineyards up near Sandusky are putting in hybrids. On the Lake Erie Islands, the wineries like Heineman at Put-in-Bay and Lonz and Bretz on Middle Bass, cater mostly to the boating fraternity in the summer.

Even including Meier's, Ohio production is so small as to make little impression beyond the neighboring states, but growers of Concords are beginning to eye the hybrids with interest. There are more than two hundred miles along the Ohio that can be planted in wine grapes, including the small Markko Vineyard that specializes in vinifera. A reborn wine region may be in the making.

Michigan

FROM COLD DUCK TO BRONTE WINES AND TABOR HILL VINEYARD AND WINE CELLAR

In the orchard country back from the shores of Lake Michigan, in the southwest corner of the state, are some 16,000 acres of vineyard, mostly producing grapes for juice and jam, with a little left over for Cold Duck, Kalte Ente. The name came from Germany, where it's common to perk up ordinary white wines by adding some sparkling wine, brandy, and sugar. The story goes that the first Cold Duck was really Kalte Ente, cold ends, made by pouring together what was left in the bottles after a night of drinking and adding sparkling wine to make a nightcap. A restaurateur from across the state liked it when he was touring Germany and began serving it in his Pontchartrain Wine Cellars in Detroit, mixing sparkling white from New York with sparkling red from California. Customers liked the name and the drink, so early in the 1960s the Michigan wineries began bottling Concord with bubbles, well stretched with bland white wines to mute the foxy taste. It looked pink and frothy in the glass.

California couldn't stand it. That state doesn't grow Concords. Their equivalent is the miserable Thompson Seedless, a three-way grape so-called because it can be used for eating, for raisins, and for producing a neutral white used for blending and making brandy. Much of this blending wine is shipped out of state for use in local brands and now these users were making a lot of money by adding Concord and bubbles. Soon everybody was bottling Cold Duck. In the state of Washington, which has about the same acreage as Michigan, mostly planted in Concords, growers began planting thousands of acres more.

All the competition hurt Michigan. Concord prices rose a little during the sixties, but then dropped back. By the turn of the decade, the number of growers was cut in half, to not many more than a thousand. What kept them going in the wine business was a protective tax. To satisfy the growing local demand for dry table wines, a few began considering the hybrids of New York.

The largest producer, Michigan Wineries, buys most of its grapes and vinifera concentrates to use in its blends, but its California-trained winemaker also uses hybrid grapes from a 500-acre plot owned by the director of the firm. These are marketed as Warner's Vineyards wines. The company also extracts methyl anthranilate, the ester that gives Concords their musty flavor, which is used in making grape soda pop.

Of the large wineries, the one most interested in hybrids is

Bronte Wines. They have 230 acres of vineyard and market a Van Buren County Aurore and a Baco Noir; they also make specialty wines, their brand being Rally. Two other producers also market specialty wines. Frontenac Wine Company is responsible for a line that includes Cherry Smash, Cola Smash, something called Bahama Mama, and Wild Goose; St. Julian Wine Company makes mostly sparkling wines and flavored fortified wines.

But most interesting of all is Tabor Hill Vineyard and Wine Cellar. Tabor Hill has 25 acres of vineyards — eight of them vinifera and the rest in hybrids. In addition to sparkling wines, Leonard Olson markets two hybrid blends from his own vines called Cuvée Blanc and Cuvée Rouge, and Baco Noir, a Trebbiano and a Chardonnay, among others. All are estate bottled. His success is influencing some of the growers to plant a few hybrids and an occasional row of vinifera, but it will be years before the wines get far beyond the state.

Illinois and Indiana

The corn begins in Ohio and reaches across the plains for a thousand miles, across Iowa, across Nebraska — most of it feed for cattle and pigs. There's grain above and range below, the land shaped by what we eat. Along the rivers and the flooded valleys made by dams, the waters temper frosts so grapes can thrive, but pesticides kill the vines. Only where people and industry have pushed out the silos and the granaries is there room for orchards and vineyards, much of it in rural Indiana and Illinois.

The first vines were cultivated by French colonists who came down the rivers from the Great Lakes, by the religious sects that set up communities after crossing the Alleghenies and fanning out into the plains and on the river bluffs, by succeeding waves of Swiss and Gemans who pushed into the Ozarks. Prohibition ruined most of them, leaving only Concords for juice and jelly and a few Catawbas, but with the success of hybrids and vinifera in New York, interest has revived, sparked mostly by amateurs turned semipros.

FROM OLD NAUVOO TO THOMPSON WINERY
AND TREATY LINE WINE CELLARS

Treaty Line Wine Cellars is beginning to offer blends from 20 acres of hybrids that are being increased to 90 by an optometrist named D. L. MacDaniel and a group of friends. The vineyard is east of Indianapolis, near the Ohio border. A similar development south of the city near Bloomington is the wine company headed by William Oliver, a professor at the University of Indiana Law School. Carl Banholzer, one of the founders of Tabor Hill in Michigan, is planting both hybrids and vinifera on the Indiana side of the border. Vineyards are being planned along the Ohio near Vevay, the town founded by Swiss settlers, and vinifera are going in across the river in Kentucky, planted by an enthusiast named William Schwerin.

The same kind of development is taking place in Illinois, whose vineyards, like those in all the nearby states, have mostly been providing Concords for juice, jelly, and kosher wines. Along the Mississippi River at Nauvoo they used to do better than that but the cellars are now used mainly for ripening cheese. An experimental vineyard an hour out of Chicago was set up to produce sparkling wines but pesticides killed the vines. Replanted by a physiologist who owns the adjacent farm, the Thompson Winery is beginning to market wines from hybrids and vinifera.

If it weren't for the amateurs, there would be no vineyards in the corn belt, but the struggle continues, even up in Minnesota and out in the Dakotas. Eventually, wines will come from the prairies, but until they do, country wines of the Midwest will come from vineyards in the Ozarks, Missouri, and Arkansas.

Missouri and Arkansas

Missouri was famous for wines in the last century, even naming a grape that people still argue about, the Missouri Riesling. First cultivated at Hermann, the wine center up the river from St. Louis, the grape is most likely a cross between *labrusca* and *riparia* although the taste indicates to some that a little of the true Riesling got into it. Today it is called the Elvira and it still grows in Missouri; much more is expected from the hybrids and vinifera that are coming into bearing.

FROM BARDENHEIR'S TO PEACEFUL BEND

A grand old winery that was begun in 1847 has been rescued from mushrooms and is again producing wines at Hermann. Stone Hill Wine Company makes blends from its own 20 bearing acres, which it is expanding, and it encourages others to extend their plantings by agreeing to take their grapes. Nearer St. Louis, in Augusta, the Mount Pleasant Vineyard has been revived and is producing Emigré wines from a dozen acres, some planted in vinifera. In a sea of Concords to the south, on the Ozark Plateau near St. James, Stoltz Vineyards added some 20 acres of native grapes and hybrids to improve its blends. The St. James Winery started by James Hofherr is offering Cascade and is planning to plant viniferas. Over on the Meramec River is a pediatrician's hobby — Peaceful Bend Vineyard — where Dr. Axel Arneson is making blends from hybrids obtained from Philip Wagner over twenty years ago. His red is Meramec, his white is Courtois, and any day now he may branch out.

St. Louis was once the wine capital of the country, but its most famous wine, Cook's Imperial, is now made by Guild in California. Both the brand name and the company were purchased by the Hecks in the thirties and called The American Wine Company. When they needed capital, they got it by selling stock to a Swiss company, which turned out to be controlled by a former wine salesman named von Ribbentrop. The company was seized because of the German connection, the Hecks moved on to greener pastures on the Russian River at Korbel, and the only relation that Cook's Imperial now has to Missouri is a little Catawba in the blend.

The largest winery in Missouri is Bardenheier's, founded a century ago in St. Louis. They had been happy to blend local wines with California blends until the sixties, when they discovered that most of the Catawbas in the state were being bought by eastern wineries. Now they have 75 acres in bearing down by the Arkansas border on Lost River Ranch, where they are beginning to think about vinifera to perk up the hybrids. For now, there's Ozark Mountain, Rosie O'Grady, and Frisco, among many others.

Arkansas is a land of lakes these days, like Nebraska and Tennessee, Oklahoma and Kentucky, created by the great dams that stem the various river systems. Those in the Ozarks are becoming resort areas, but there have been vineyards in the hills ever since Swiss and German settlers tamed the Scuppernongs and began planting Concords. Biggest of all is Wiederkehr Wine Cellars, founded in 1880, which now has more than 400 acres of vineyards and buys from other growers. Some of the vines are vinifera and hybrids, thanks to the generation now running the winery, some of whom went to Davis and studied winemaking in Bordeaux. Founded the same year, but maybe a few months earlier, is the Post Winery, which has a substantial proportion of hybrids on its 200 acres of vineyard. Next door is Mount Betherl Winery, run by one of the family, one of several wine cellars (others are Cowie, De Salvo, Heckman, and Sax) set up when the dry state passed a law permitting native wines to be served in the state's restaurants.

This is the Bible Belt, which extends into Oklahoma and Kansas, much of it stubbornly dry to this day. Times are changing slowly, and in Oklahoma a vineyard project has been set up by the Office of Economic Opportunity. Some acres of hybrids have been planted on a quarter-section in the hopes that a family tending a dozen acres can generate a living income. Plans for settling 300 families on the vineyards are going ahead slowly. The dry belt runs down into Texas, but there have been dreams for decades of wines from the valley of the Rio Grande. A particularly vigorous local vine is called the Mustang, and a sorghum and cotton grower named Norman Willms has crossed Mustang with hundreds of other grapes, with little success so far. The grape that does well for the Val Verde Winery down near the Mexican border at Del Rio is the Lenoir. Called the Black Spanish there, it makes a dry or sweet red. The vineyard was started in the 1880s by the Qualia family and the wine from it is so popular that another vineyard has been started nearby — for a grand total of 14 acres. Even larger are the Corrales Bonded Winery and the Gros Winery in New Mexico, whose vineyards were planted before those of California. Gros even has some Pinot Noir, agreeing with the state university and various hobbyists that vinifera and hybrids may be the grapes to grow. You hear the same talk in Arizona and Utah, where test plantings have proved successful, but wines from the Southwest are for the future, and development remains in the hands of enthusiasts and the state universities.

The
Northwest

Lying back from the coast the Cascade Mountains push two miles and more above the long valleys. The high range running from British Columbia down into Oregon forces clouds upward so that they dump rain on the seaside flanks but the inland vales are desert unless water is run in from the Columbia and Snake Rivers. The first grapes were planted by builders of Fort Vancouver at the mouth of the Columbia from seeds picked from the tablecloth at the farewell banquet for the adventurers given by the Hudson's Bay Company in London in 1824. Maybe the first wines came from cuttings from the vines planted by the first settlers, down in Oregon's Willamette Valley or on the Washington side of the Columbia, but Concords and fruit wines won out, until just yesterday. Now a trickle is made from noble vines, perhaps to become a freshet before the end of the decade.

Oregon

HILLCREST VINEYARD AND EYRIE VINEYARDS

Oregon's Willamette is too rich for good grapes, but the soil thins out on the slopes down around Roseburg and in feeder valleys like the Umpqua, where mild winters lead optimists to believe that 10,000 acres could go in, mostly Rieslings and Gewürztraminers to start. There are 100 acres now, 20 of them at Richard Sommers's Hillcrest Vineyard, where he began setting out vines in the early sixties. His enthusiasm led Paul Bjelland to buy a couple of hundred acres, 30 of which are in production. There are 10 more at nearby Eyrie Vineyards, some 35 at Coury Vineyards in Forest Grove, and the beginnings of scattered plantings that will provide grapes to the four wineries. The rest, a handful, stick to Concords and fruit wines, although one makes dandelion and another makes rhubarb wine.

Washington

BOORDY VINEYARDS, VEREDON VINEYARDS, AND OTHERS

Things are different up in Washington, east of the Cascades, in the Yakima Valley. Most of the valley is Concords, including the largest vineyard of that grape in the world, which is five square miles. But on the slopes of the Columbia, Snake, and tributaries, potential for a third of a million acres is claimed. A thousand of them may be bearing noble vines and hybrids by 1976.

American Wine Growers is marketing its Ste. Michelle varietals in the western states; and Seneca Foods Corporation is doing the same with its Boordy Vineyards wines, the production and the planting of some 500 acres being supervised by Phil Wagner. Veredon Vineyards has a quarter of its 760 acres producing wines from varietals, a similar percentage of 350-acre Sagemore farm is offering wines, and an associated partnership called Bacchus is planning a couple of hundred acres, half in Cabernet Sauvignon. George Stewart, a doctor with 10 acres bearing in Sunnyside, has plans for 160 acres on the Wahluke Slope, at a bend above the Columbia River. An economist at the University of Washington, Lincoln Wolverton, has 27 acres of noble vines in a former pasture at La Center, thirty miles north of Portland, and is setting up a winery. Associated Vintners is marketing some varietals from its own vineyards and is on the lookout for grapes from other growers.

It's like Bordeaux, say the Washington growers, with lots of light and a good growing season. It's like Burgundy, say Oregon growers. Both think the potential for quality is superb. If so, there's a new region to be heard from.

Like their neighbors in Washington and Oregon, British Columbia growers are planting vines in the valleys flanking the Cascades, some 3,000 acres of them, many in vinifera and hybrids. The wines may be the surprise of the decade.

Eastern winemakers argue that California weather is too mild to force noble vines to do their best, so that the wines lack acid. Western growers argue that Eastern growing seasons are so short that grapes do not build up enough sugar, and that vines do not flourish because of severe winters. Northwesterners say that vineyards to the south don't get enough light. The Canadians point out that their latitude is right, that valley winters rarely have zero temperatures and then only for a day or two, giving them a climate like the Rhine or Champagne or Burgundy. Optimists everywhere say that all these variations can be attended to. Pessimists say that may be so, but all that's known isn't consistently applied to vineyard problems, and decades will pass before the right grapes are in the right places to produce many sound wines at reasonable prices. Wine lovers taste wines from the Northwest every chance they get, hoping for the best.

Neighbors North and South

Canada

Canadian wines? You're kidding. Look at any map; it is white above the border, which means there is snow in Canada. All they have is beer and whiskey.

A German named Schiller planted the first vines in 1811 in Cooksville, outside Toronto, and there were 5,000 acres by the end of the century on the Niagara peninsula. The tip of the peninsula is as far south as Pennsylvania, the growing season is almost six months long, and the Great Lakes on three sides keep most winter days above freezing. Most of the wines come from native grapes or hybrids, but there are some noble vines, though not many, among the present 22,000 acres. The pioneer who planted the first of these was a Frenchman named de Chaunac, the technical director of Bright's Wines, who made some remarkable wines out of some of the Seibels. Most of the grapes, alas, were Concord, Niagara, and Delaware; Château Gai made a sparkling wine from the Delaware grapes that has been praised. Danforth and Jordan wines are well known.

There are several good bottles among the more than eleven million gallons produced each year by the eight wineries of the Niagara peninsula. There are six more in British Columbia, handling the production of some 2,200 acres of grapes in the Okanagan Valley, planted in California varieties.

With such faint praise does a reporter from one region damn another. So speaks the Californian about New York wines, the German about the Austrian, the Italian about the Swiss. The Burgundian speaks thus of Bordeaux, and both of them look down on the Rhone. And all of it is ignorance.

People drink the wines they can get. The famous districts produce a few great bottles, but most of it is ordinary, at best. Given grapes, man makes wine.* If he is lucky, his region will have a dozen great vineyards and several score that are good. If he is not, his region will have a few good grapes, and a few bottles that are good. But those few will be unique, unlike wines anywhere else, worth finding, worth drinking. Such, at the moment, is the case with Canada, which exports no wine to the United States.

Mexico

The first vines in the New World were planted in Mexico, scarcely a quarter century after the first voyages of Columbus. When Cortez ruled, every holder of a Spanish grant was ordered to plant vines, ten of them for every Indian living on the land, for five years running. The plan failed, and it was not until the last days of the seventeenth century, when the first of the missions was founded in Baja California at Loreto, that wine came to be made regularly. The vines moved north with the missions, reaching the twenty-first and last of them in 1823, at Sonoma.

Most of Mexico is too hot for the vine, but along the northern

---

* In Canada, kits for making wines from concentrates of grapes and other fruits are offered by a company calling itself Wine Cellar, whose mailing address is Vineland Station, Ontario. The results have not been tasted by the author.

border and in the highlands grapes can grow to make bland and generally undistinguished wines. The best of them may be the reds from around the old Mission of Santo Tomás at Ensenada, on the Pacific. Going east from Lower California, there are vineyards in the border states of Chihuahua and Coahuila, and further south around the towns of Aguascalientes and Querétaro.

The town of Parras, on the uplands west of Monterey, is the leading vineyard center and claims to be the first. A vineyard was planted there in 1593 by Don Francisco de Urdiñola; still in production, it is the property of Bodegas del Marqués de Aguayo. Other firms include Casa Madero, Delfin, Rosario, Perote, and Vesubio. Bodegas de Delicias is the leading firm of Chihuahua, and Compañía Vinícola de Saltillo is the main one in Aguascalientes. The best-known wines are from Bodegas de Santo Tomás, near Ensenada, where Dmitri Tchelistcheff is supervising vineyard development.

Mexico has some 30,000 acres of vineyards and produces in excess of three million gallons a year, much of it distilled or made into fortified or tonic wines. No imports of any significance are made to the United States.

South America

South America bottles and drinks twice as much wine as the United States, most of it from Argentina, the best of it from Chile, with some from Brazil and a little from Uruguay. We see practically none of it, except once when an electric company took payments for equipment in wine, and there was a little red and white around for a while. Chile Riesling comes in sporadically, always cheap and often good, shipped in flasks patterned after the German *Bocksbeutel,* so named because of its resemblance to the nether parts of the goat. Yanquis would drink untold quantities of Chilean wines if the good ones were exported and became known, but they do not, and are not, which is a sad example of Pan-American misunderstanding.

Spanish Jesuits brought the first vines to the Continent in the wake of the conquistadores, but it was not until the nineteenth century that Italian immigrants set the patterns for wines in Argentina, the French doing the same for Chile, the Portuguese for Brazil. The best vineyards lie along the spine of the Andes and produce from the noble vines of Europe. Everything else is common wine, drunk as it comes to hand.

Chile

Chile has more than 275,000 acres of vineyards and less than 6,000,000 people, who drink 125,000,000 gallons of wine a year, permitting not much more than 500,000 cases to leave the country. This does not work out, because per capita consumption is restricted to a scant 16 gallons, so the rest is distilled. Spasmodic attempts are made to increase exports, and the laws are designed so that only good wines can leave, but wine growers of the Northern Hemisphere zealously guard their markets. A trickle comes to the United States.

The best vineyards lie south of Santiago, in the valley of the Maipo, although good vineyards extend from the Aconcagua to the Maule, with still others north and south. These names will be famous someday. In the middle of the last century, Silvestre Ochagavia caught the wine fever and induced French vignerons to supervise the planting of their noble vines — Cabernet Sauvignon and Cabernet Franc, Merlot and Malbec, Sémillon and Sauvignon, Pinots Noir and Blanc. They even planted Riesling, but this proved to be a shy bearer and expensive to grow, and the grapes of Bordeaux are predominant. The wines are noted for a certain finesse and balance, with good bouquet. They mature faster, it is said, than similar reds from France or California, and they could find a sizable niche in North American cellars, given a good chance. Phylloxera is not a problem. The high Andes and strong Pacific breezes guard against Argentine infection, the northern desert of Atacama bars the way from Peru. There are more than 30,000 separate vineyards, well over half of them less than 10 acres, so the government is developing winery cooperatives and marketing groups.

Export laws are strict; wines called *Gran Vino* must be six years old, those labeled *Reservado* must be four. Those classed as *Special* must be two years old. Tourists returning from summer skiing sojourns and those invited to embassy activities report velvety reds, silken whites, and big sparkling wines among the confusing scatter of labels, but few seem to get much beyond Valparaiso — as legendary as Incan treasure, as lost to us as El Dorado.

Argentina

Italians from the Piedmont invented ways to tap the snowfields of the Andes and direct the melt to the arid highland plains of Mendoza, the western province that produces over two-thirds of Argentine wine. San Juan province to the north produces a hefty quarter of production — heavier and coarser wines. Rio Negro to the south produces lighter wines, the best, but only 3 percent, with the rest of the 740,000-plus acres scattered wherever grapes will grow. Production is nearly three-quarters of a billion gallons a year, per capita consumption being well over twenty times that of the United States.

Mendoza produces wines in a big way, using enormous vats that can process as much as a quarter of a million gallons at a clip. When phylloxera bothers the vineyards, irrigation sluices flood the land, drowning the louse. The Spanish grape called Criolla, descendant from the vines of the missionaries, produces most of the rosé, various French and Spanish grapes produce the whites, and the Malbec of Bordeaux produces most of the reds. Wines are marketed under regional names and a visitor to Buenos Aires would be making a mistake by not trying the special bottlings from Rio Negro.

Brazil

There are 170,000 vineyard acres in Brazil, mostly in Rio Grand do Sul on the Atlantic coast, bordered on the south by Argentina and Uruguay. Production approaches forty million gallons, from hybrids and odd grapes like Isabella and Concord. A few wines from noble vines are marketed under the Granja União label by Brazil's largest winery, which produces some seven million gallons a year. The wine most prized in Brazil is the Espumante, sparkling wines from grapes called Moscatel and Malvasia. A few thousand cases come to the United States each year but they are not appreciated.

Uruguay

There are some 50,000 acres of vineyard, mostly in the country-side around Montevideo, producing almost twenty-five million gallons a year. A little reaches Rio. This is no great loss, although some Italian and French grapes are said to do well. Much of the common wine is made into brandy, and some of it is made into *Vino Seco,* a strongly fortified blend of white and red that is allowed to oxidize into something tonic and strong of taste. None of it is imported to the United States.

PART THREE

The Kinds of Wine

Sparkling Wines

America is having a love affair with sparkling wines, and it doesn't hurt a bit to have them called Champagne. Everybody knows what Champagne is — it's what you drink out of slippers, what tickles your nose, what you launch ships with, what you get at weddings, what pops when you pull the cork. No movie about the good old days, no story about the gay life, no grand victory of any sort, is complete without the bubbly foaming in the glass. A toast is no toast at all unless it is drunk in Champagne.

Champagne is less than this, and more. It is truly the wine from the Champagne district of France, which lies east of Paris. It is made from the grapes of Burgundy, which lie just south — Pinot Noir and Pinot Blanc and Chardonnay. The grapes are pressed, and the juice is quickly removed from the skins; when fermentation is complete, it is bottled with a dosage of yeast. It ferments a second time in the bottle, the sediment is removed, then the bottle is refilled with the same wine plus a little dissolved sugar. If this dosage is less than 1½ percent, it is called Brut; if less than 2 percent, it is usually called Extra Sec; if less than 4 percent, it is called Sec. Champagne Nature is not supposed to have any sweetening added at all, but Brut is plenty dry enough, and quite the fashion, although most people really prefer Extra Sec, which means Extra Dry. Some wine is made only from white grapes and is called Blanc de Blancs, although the traditional blend, or cuvée (which means vat), contains wines from black grapes, which lend body and fullness. It is wine from the Champagne district, fermented a second time in bottle. This is the least Champagne can be, and the most, as well.

Wines can be made sparkling in other ways, but none of them can be called Champagne — at least, not in France. Wine can be fermented a second time in large tanks, for instance, not in the bottle. This is called the Bulk Process, developed by a Frenchman named Charmat, and it is sometimes called by his name. The wines are bottled under pressure and can be excellent. The Transfer Process calls for bottle-fermenting the wine, emptying it into vats that retain the carbon dioxide, then filtering, and these wines can be good. Still another way is to carbonate the wine, like soda water, and such wines are poor. A Californian has devised the Millerway, named for himself, whereby open bottles are put in canisters pressurized with CO_2 for forty-eight hours while the wine absorbs bubbles. His winery is just above Oakville in the Napa Valley, where you can buy a bottle to try. The owner wants to get the law changed to cover his methods so he can sell his wines as Champagnes.

None of these sparkling wines should be called Champagne, but they are. The United States has never been party to the international wine laws that reserve the right of the name to the French district. Every producer will publicly state that the name is certainly the property of the district called Champagne and that wines not made by the bottle-fermentation method are not properly entitled to the name, but he is privately delighted that he can use the word, because it sells a lot of wine. Every major wine-producing country has foresworn calling its sparkling wines Champagne except the United States.

Wine called California Champagne comes from every district and is made from just about every grape available, including the

Thompson Seedless, which is good to eat. The most common grape used is the French Colombard, variously blended with others; in the North Coast counties some traditional grapes are used to lend character to the blends. New York Champagnes and those from other states depend heavily on native grapes, principally *Vitis Labrusca*, which has a distinctive quality all its own. Much wine is shipped East in bulk and blended with that of *Vitis Labrusca* to mask this distinctiveness. Such blends will carry on their labels only the name of the place where they are bottled. To be called California (or New York) Champagne, at least 75 percent of the wine must come from that state.

Champagne became popular in the 1800s, and the Burgundians could not stand the competition, so they began sparkling their lesser red wines to win back some of the market. Sparkling Burgundy became successful outside France after World War I and attained some popularity here during the Depression, and more since, no matter how often wine buffs look down their noses at it. After all, bubbles are cheery, and while there are outrageous state, federal, and local taxes on them amounting to almost a dollar a bottle, the sparkle and pop may be worth it — fireworks in a glass, or stars, as the originator is supposed to have said.

There is no reason at all why any wine cannot be made sparkling, if people are willing to pay the price. They seem to be, for there are many sparkling wines.

Bubbles in wine are rarely accidental, except in the spring, when wines have a tendency to work, and many may show some bubbles if the wine has not been heavily filtered. If a wine is bottled before all the fermentation is over, some carbon dioxide will be captured. The Swiss wine Neuchâtel is purposely bottled to catch a few bubbles, which are called the "star." When Chianti is made, some wine from raisinized grapes is added to the fermentation. The process is called *governo*. The gas is allowed to bubble off, but there is generally a prickly quality left behind, called *piccante*, noticeable in the wine. Wines made from the Muscat grape can be slowly fermented so that some gas remains and the wine — called *Moscato Amabile* — is said to shimmer or smile. Similar wines are said to be *spritzig* in Germany; *perlant* in France. When there are quite a few bubbles, the wine is called *pétillant* in France, *frizzante* in Italy and *perlwein* in Germany. International agreement says such wines should not have more than two atmospheres of pressure, and an example is Vouvray. *Crémant* is the word the French use for wines that are in between *pétillant* and *mousseux,* the term used to designate wines that are fully sparkling and foamy. All sparkling wines, including Champagne, are classed as *vins mousseux* and must have a pressure of four atmospheres. Champagne often has six.

People do all sorts of things with sparkling wines, and a current American fad is Cold Duck, originally a wine heavy with the taste of red Concord grapes, and now almost anything. Eastern wineries have been making sparkling wines from the beginning, because bubbles added a certain charm to the odd, wild taste of native grapes and because white varieties were the only ones that produced well. The exception was the Concord. When sparkling Burgundy began to seduce the innocent, winemakers asked themselves why they didn't try the Concord. They did, but without much success. It was not until someone out in Paw Paw, Michigan, thought of naming the wine Cold Duck that Concords became prized instead of despised, in Michigan at first, then throughout the country. Now Concord concentrate is imported from Canada to eke out the erstwhile superabundance.

Eastern Sparkling Wines

Eastern winemakers have always been successful with sparkling wines, blending local ferments with California gallonage shipped East in bulk and marketing the blends as American Champagne. Once there were dozens of brands. Today only one winery in New Jersey is prominent — Renault in Egg Harbor, an area once covered in vines. Missouri was once a famous wine-producing state, particularly the area around the town of Hermann, where the American Wine Company once produced Cook's Imperial, which even came to be known in Europe. In Ohio, along the shores of Lake Erie, near Cincinnati, the American horticulturist Nicholas Longworth began planting Catawbas — called cats — in 1825, and a flourishing industry sprang up. Sparkling Catawba became North America's first truly successful sparkling wine. Versions are still being made by Meier's Wine Cellars, located near Cincinnati and Sandusky, where National Distillers also has a winery producing Bellows Brut and Lejon Vermouth.

The Finger Lakes region in central New York State is by far the most important wine-producing area in the East, and was the first to make sparkling wines of much distinction. The largest producer is the Taylor Wine Company of Hammondsport, which now also owns the Pleasant Valley Wine Company, whose Great Western was one of the early names to gain fame; it is operated as a separate firm. The town lies at the foot of Lake Keuka, and is also the home of Gold Seal Vineyards, the outstanding producer of sparkling wines.

After training in the Champagne district of France, Charles Fournier was persuaded to come over to see what could be done with Keuka vineyards, and for twenty-five years he set standards for all the rest. He was a pioneer in planting hybrids whose wines could balance the pungency of the native grapes. His meticulous winemaking practices brought out the best in both, and in that short span of time, New York wines came of age. There was steady experiment with Chardonnay and Riesling and other white wine grapes, with initial assistance from Konstantin Frank, a postwar emigré from the Crimea, where his parents had gone from Germany to develop vineyards. His knowledge, out of Germany via Russia, coupled with Fournier's Champagne background, brought excellence to the sparkling wines of New York. From such international backgrounds come local delights. The taste of the native grapes is still prominent in many of the sparkling wine blends, but it has become attractive, producing a new kind of sparkling wine that can share the stage with Champagne. Gold Seal offers a Brut and a Fournier Blanc de Blancs to head their line of sparkling wines.

The leading producer using native grapes is Widmer Wine Cellars, and its sparkling wines have a definite taste from these grapes, but are so well made that they can be a pleasure to drink. They are certainly the best sparkling wines made with that dominant taste, and are probably the ones that someone unfamiliar with New York State wines should start with. Too great a familiarity with Champagnes and European still white wines is apt to get in the way when trying to taste such wines simply. The taste is unexpected and different, but the wines deserve judgment not clouded by preconceptions. The most difficult wines to taste without prejudice are those that are unfamiliar or unknown. Widmer's wines, especially, call for an unprejudiced palate.

A SELECTION
Gold Seal Fournier Blanc de Blancs
Widmer Extra Dry
Great Western Brut

California

Sparkling wines came to California early, Paul Masson being among the first to gain something more than local success. Many followed his lead, among them Korbel, which began concentrating on such wines and was making nothing else when the Heck brothers bought the firm in the fifties; still wines began to be produced again as the market expanded, and while Korbel continues to be noted for its sparkling wines, its varietals and other still wines have gained national attention. Weibel followed a similar pattern, establishing its reputation with sparkling wines, which is now extended to a score of others.

These three gained such acceptance for their wines that other firms began to pay attention to what they were offering in their foil-wrapped bottles. Almadén produced a Blanc de Blancs, a high-priced wine that competed with French Champagnes. Others like Buena Vista and Weibel began doing so as well. Korbel and Mirassou offered Nature, sparkling wines with no sweetening dosage added at all; Concannon offered one with a dosage of less than 1 percent. Two new firms began marketing nothing but sparkling wines, Hanns Kornell and Schramsberg, which deserve special attention. Today, there are dozens of sparkling wines on the market. Expert opinion lists the following as outstanding:

BRUT	EXTRA DRY	BULK PROCESS
Schramsberg	*Kornell*	*Christian Brothers*
Kornell	*Korbel*	*Weibel*
Almadén	*Weibel*	*Almadén*
Korbel	*Mirassou*	*Italian Swiss Colony*

SCHRAMSBERG VINEYARDS

Robert Louis Stevenson came to visit in 1880, talked of the wonder of it all in *Silverado Squatters,* and made the fame of Jacob Schram, who had founded the winery in 1862. The spirit of the winery died with Schram, and periodic resuscitations failed to bring the hillside to life until 1965, when Jack Davies decided to give up managing money and take up running Schramsberg. Los Angeles was one thing, sparkling wine was another; Davies and his wife much preferring the latter. He decided to manage a little money to see if he could turn it into wine.

So much for replanting the vineyards, so much for rebuilding the winery, so much for getting it on the market, so much to produce sixty thousand bottles by 1972, then double it in five years. "With the resources available we have to concentrate," says Davies, "we can't afford to have a line, but there is always a corner for excellence."

He started working himself into the corner when Martin Ray wanted to expand his vineyards down on Mount Eden, above Saratoga and the Santa Clara Valley. Davies joined the group that financed the venture, learning some of the intricacies of producing fine wines, then withdrew and began looking for his own vineyards. When he found Schramsberg, he set up the winery so that he could place his sparkling wines on the national market, however broad and thin the initial distribution must be. California has to make wines for the whole country, Davies believes, not just for enthusiasts in the state. European wine regions make a point of seeing that their best wines get on the world market, and California must do the same or the market will never become large enough to support the many good wines that can be made. Good wines tend to raise the level of all.

An old road cuts up onto Schram's hill, the berg being a lesser rise of the Mayacamas range. It opens on a clearing — cellars to the right of you, cellars to the left of you, dug into the slopes by Chinese laborers. The one on the right is faced with a glassed front and topped with a shed roof that follows the hill pitch, enclosing the winery. Ahead is the stone base and wooden frame of the house, surrounded by gingerbread porches. Behind is a ramshackle barn that someday will be a tasting room. The road curves around the winery dugout, past a long shed that was a dormitory for the tunnel diggers, and up to an avenue of olive trees, 30 acres of Chardonnay on one side, 30 acres of Pinot Noir on the other, nicely come to bearing.

"I need all the help I can muster," says Davies. "There's just so much you can learn by reading and talking, but I got a lot of coaching and practical help from Dmitri Tchelistcheff, Andre's son."

The making of bottle-fermented Champagne is an intricate but straightforward process. The second fermentation in the bottle can take years, the dosage of yeast and sugar producing a sediment that must be shaken to the neck and then disgorged, the bottle then being refilled with the same wine to get it ready for shipment. There is a trend to lightness in Champagne, but many prefer the fuller wines, those called *franc et loyal*. Some firms, like Krug and Bollinger and Charles Heidsieck, stay close to the long tradition, which is the one that appeals to Davies. He also likes Champagnes like Roederer Crystal and Lanson, and is partial to those that contain a goodly proportion of Pinot Noir.

Davies takes issue with the current enthusiasm for Blanc de Blancs, believing that blending is vital because it excludes the possibility of any one particular variety dominating the blend. Champagnes should be blended, he feels, and he is not trying to make a sparkling Chardonnay or a sparkling white Burgundy. Lightly pressed juice from the Pinot Noir, fermented away from the skins, is needed for body and balance, Davies feels.

"Our wines are first made as if they were going to be still wines, and the base wine is of critical importance," Davies says. "If there is anything off-taste in the base wines, then a large dosage is needed to mask it. This is particularly true with sparkling wines made by the

Bulk Process, when grapes like Thompson Seedless and French Colombard or others that have distinctive tastes are used. We want to use as light a dosage as possible, but we use ones that suit the wines. We don't designate a wine as Brut or Extra Sec on the label, simply making them as dry as we think they should be, which is often a lot drier than many."

Davies makes no Bulk Process sparkling wines, but he is admiring of the Christian Brothers, who do. "They make a fine wine," he says. "All of us should be grateful they are around. They have a special place in California, and they perform a great service by setting an example of long-range thinking. They take a permanent view, and this is a great strengthening force for stability in an industry that has had its ups and downs."

Davies has certainly been encouraged, thinking about the long range from the beginning. "We want our wines to become known all over the country, and we want to get them around so that people can drink them. We can't hope to be America's finest sparkling wine and not have it available everywhere."

There is a certain assurance at Schramsberg these days, with everybody taking plenty of time to do things right and being meticulous about detail. To design the labels, for example, all the empty bottles that could be found were lined up, and what were considered to be the most attractive elements of what is called the dressing were chosen — the foil, the way of capping the bottle, the size of label, the type, the color. It was decided to use engraved labels, just because it looked nice and had a nice feel to the hand — a wine to rub, as it were.

Perhaps the most surprising thing of all about Schramsberg is the way its capital is being managed. So many dollars were needed to launch the wines, so many bottles needed to be marketed; once a reasonable profit is being made, there will be no attempt to keep increasing it each year. The idea is to make a sensible investment with adequate return, over the long term, an economic entity that will continue to be valid into the next century. Everybody will share in the profits, measured in a long continuity of excellent sparkling wines. Maybe, even, the best.

HANNS KORNELL

The third generation of winemakers in his family, Hanns Kornell left Germany in 1939, landed in New York broke, hitchhiked to Sonoma, then worked his way east making wines, then west again via Ohio and Missouri, and finally opened his own winery back in Sonoma. The vagabond voyage took a dozen years, during which the journeyman winemaker found out pretty much all there was to know about making sparkling wines in North America.

His first job was at Fountain Grove, a famous California winery on its last legs. It had been founded in the 1870s by a small band calling themselves the Brotherhood of the New Life, who eventually planted 2,000 vineyard acres. The war finished off the winery. After a stint making Sparkling Catawba and such in Cincinnati, Kornell moved on to become production manager of Cook's Imperial in St. Louis. He saved enough to rent a winery in Sonoma, then bought the Larkmead Winery from Italian Swiss Colony in 1958, a functional old building above St. Helena, where the Napa Valley narrows. Production is nearing half a million bottles a year.

The wines are made in the old-fashioned way and all are bottle-fermented, after which they are placed in riddling racks, where each bottle gets a shake and a turn and a tilt each day, until the sediment is in the neck. The various steps are laid out so that a visitor can follow along from the blending of the cuvée to the disgorging of the sediment. From the beginning, he has made sparkling wines for various firms that want them for their lines, the wineries supplying the wines, already blended in most cases, but sometimes even leaving that step to Kornell. Other firms buy his own wines for marketing under their labels, for the Kornell expertise is appreciated. Until he came along, few sparkling wines came from the Napa Valley.

As so often happens in wine country, everybody helped him get started, lending him equipment and supplying him with wines. He still buys most of his grapes, although a vineyard program is being developed. He is of such a size now that he has begun to market some table wines under his own label, and as his winery's silver anniversary approaches, he is preparing to offer a complete line. It is now his turn to watch the newcomers, helping out with a filter, with a cask, with a truck, as help is needed. That, too, is part of the tradition. There is only one criterion for admission — you have to make good wines. More people are part of that tradition every year.

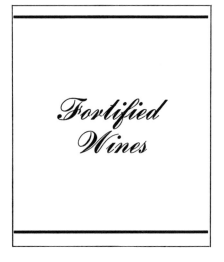

Fortified Wines

Vineyards in hot climates produce wines with a lot of sugar and little acid. They are usually sweet, because when the alcohol reaches around 14 percent during fermentation, the yeasts die. The wines vary; hence the practice of blending to an acceptable taste. The wines also have a tendency to change in taste, but this was corrected when knowledge of making brandy, the distillate of wine, became widespread. Brandy was added to fortify the wines against change, to hold them to a taste. Eventually, mostly for tax purposes, wines containing between 14 percent and 21 percent alcohol came to be considered as a group and were dubbed fortified wines. Anything more alcoholic was considered to be in the realm of spirits because the taste of brandy dominated, while anything less was considered light wine, or table wine.

Two kinds of fortified wine — Sherry and Port — quickly became famous. In Jerez, in southern Spain, the wines from white grapes were permitted to ferment completely — to dryness — then brandy was added. Since Britain was the largest market for Jerez wines, the name was Anglicized, and they became known as Sherry. If sweet wines were wanted, sweet wines were added. In Portugal, the red wines from grapes grown along the river Douro had brandy added to them before fermentation was complete, thus stopping the action and leaving the wines with some natural grape sugar — and a natural sweetness. Shipped from Oporto, the town at the mouth of the river, the wines became famous under the Anglicized name of Port. The Portuguese island off the bulge of Africa, Madeira, settled on a third method, allowing the wines to heat in hot rooms during the day and cool at night. The action gives the wines a "baked" taste, and the addition of brandy keeps them from deteriorating, so that they become more intense with the passing years. The secret of their success was skilled blending, wines too intense with age being refreshed from time to time with a little young, fruity wine. One or another of these three methods is used in hot-climate vineyards around the world, to make the wines drinkable.

None of these wines is really good with meals. All taste better before and after — sweet ones by themselves or with desserts, dry ones as apéritifs, alone or with hors d'oeuvres or a soup course. Good fortified wines are hard to make, and expensive. As with all kinds of wines, poor specimens greatly outnumber the good, flaws being easily masked by sweetness. They can be produced in enormous quantities because hot-climate vines are heavy bearers and consequently the cheapest form of alcohol.

Perhaps the worst of the fortified wines is Muscatel, sweet and bland, made from various table and raisin grapes that have "Muscat" as part of their names. The commonest and poorest of these may be the Muscat of Alexandria, while the best may be the Muscat de Frontignan, named after the town in which the best French *vin de liqueur* is made. The Gallic term is the most precise description of such wines, but it sounds bad in English. "Fortified" is the British euphemism for "spiked," a term that is banned under U.S. regulations. Americans euphemistically refer to dry versions as "appetizer wines" and sweet ones as "dessert wines," further confusing the issue. Slangy Americans have dubbed them all "Sneaky Pete," particularly Muscatel, most of which is sold by the pint or half-pint, ranges in color from gold to red, and is as much as 15 percent sugar.

None of the words is satisfactory. And calling something California or New York Sherry is misleading, because the wines are rarely like the originals, and because the English word properly refers to the wines of Jerez. Despairing of getting their word back, the Spanish have taken to calling their wines Spanish Sherry, the way the Swiss call their cheese Switzerland Swiss. The Portuguese are calling their wines Porto, for the same reason.

A buyer scarcely knows which way to turn. Half the wines made in America are fortified — it used to be three bottles out of every four — while fortified wines account for less than a quarter of consumption in wine-drinking countries of Europe. As more good table wines become available, sales here of ordinary fortified wines will doubtless continue to fall.

There are still those who like to drink Sherry and Port, and many Americans prefer the U.S. versions to the more intense European ones. The occasional producer will make efforts to produce satisfactory other types, like Paul Masson's Tinta Madeira, but few U.S. producers bother much with Angelica, Malaga, Aleatico, or Tokay, these being little more than names for inferior wines.

The main regulation in the United States concerning fortified wines is that they must be no more than 1 percent away from 21 percent alcohol. This law — a particularly idiotic one, because many of the drier types taste extremely alcoholic at that percentage — is being changed to permit wines of only 17 percent, so that the alcohol will not mask their character.

There are no U.S. regulations at all about the grapes used for making fortified wines. Any at all can be used, and are. Until other uses are found for the thousands of acres of table, raisin, and inferior wine grapes planted in California, there will be no change in the law. As a result, most American fortified wines bear no relation to the European types after which they are named, nor do they have any interest to the drinker, except as a source of cheap alcohol.

The few fine Sherries and Ports are thus faced with almost insurmountable difficulties in the marketplace. As the market for fortified wines shrinks, there is less and less incentive to find new names for wines that may be distinctive on their own, however different in taste they may be from the European types.

SHERRY: The best Sherry is made from Palomino grapes, the variety used in the Jerez district of Spain. The wines are fermented until they are dry, then divided into three distinct classes: Fino, which has a distinctive yeasty taste caused by the development on the surface of the fermenting wine of a yeast the Spanish call the *flor;* Amontillado, which develops a nutty taste with age; and Oloroso, or Cream Sherry, which has a rich and even nuttier taste and is usually sweetened. The Finos are generally called Cocktail Sherries in the United States, the dry versions having less than 2 percent sugar. Amontillados are generally called simply Sherry and may have as much as 4 percent, and Cream Sherries contain more.

In Spain, casks of young wines are put in tiers — called *criaderas,* or cradles — for some years, perhaps three or more. Wines are drawn off from the oldest tier, which is replenished from a younger second tier, which is replenished from the youngest tier, which is then filled with new wines. The wines taken from the *criadera* then go into a similar system called the *solera;* wines for bottling are drawn off the oldest tier, and so on. Blends can be made up from the wines of a single solera or several.

Most of Spain's soleras were begun before the turn of the century, and there is always a minor portion of extremely old wine in a Spanish Sherry. Rarely is as much as 10 percent of the wine from a solera drawn off each year, so that the minimum age is usually ten years. Finos average about seven years, however; Amontillados average more than ten, and Olorosos even more.

Similar systems are used in the United States, the largest solera being that of Almadén. Most of them were begun in the last couple of decades. To make some dry Sherries, a submerged *flor* method is used. The yeast is periodically stirred into the wine, producing a superbly characteristic yeasty taste, but without the complementary, desired woody taste obtained in Jerez. The resultant wines are used in blending. The most usual way of making Sherry in the United States is by heating and then cooling the wine a number of times, imparting a "baked" taste rather similar to that of Madeira.

Sherries vary so widely that it is difficult to make a selection, but since most wineries offer a complete line of all types, it is sensible to try those from producers whose other wines are found pleasing. It might be noted, though, that Almadén, Paul Masson, the Christian Brothers, and many smaller quality producers take pains in making their Sherries.

With the seventies, the system of making Sherries by the submerged *flor* process had been pretty well mastered, while the Michigan law permitting 17 percent wines was gradually being extended to other states, broadening the market. Some splendid dry, light Sherries are being made and may revive the dying interest in a kind of wine that can be remarkably appealing. One of these comes from Concannon and it's called Prelude. It tastes good with salty and spicy things before dinner, well-chilled, on the rocks, with soda.

The various apéritif wines continue to be drunk in the cities, so someone soon is sure to use dry Sherry as a base for one, maybe adding something bitter or something lemony. Until then, you can do it for yourself, using a bitter Vermouth, or lacing some dry Sherry with tonic and adding a slice of lemon or sliver of cucumber.

PORT: The best Ports are produced from grape varieties originally grown along the Douro river in northern Portugal, and the best among these are Tinta Madeira, Tinta Cao, Touriga, plus a few others. American regulations specify no varieties for fortified wines, and many inferior grapes are used in U.S. versions.

Young Ports are blends of fruity wines, called Ruby because of their color. Older blends acquire an amber tinge and are called Tawny. Tawny Port retains some of this fruitiness and acquires a taste of raisins.

Almadén, Paul Masson, the Christian Brothers, and many of the smaller quality producers take pains in making their Ports. For years, the outstanding Port made in America has come from the California winery of Ficklin.

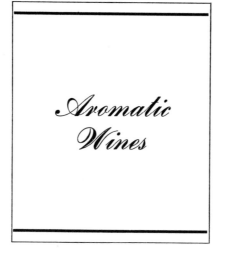

Aromatic Wines

Wines from warm climates are changelings, tasting one way one moment, another way the next. This has been noted above. Lack of acid gives them a bland taste; excess of sugar makes them sweet. When air gets at them, they tend to take on the taste of straw — a brackishness, as if they had been cooked or baked — and a brownish color that ranges from that of tarnished silver through amber, copper, even bronze. With age, the wine may oxidize, or rust, taking on a metallic taste and a tonic dryness. This is called maderization, because the taste is like the basic quality of the wines of Madeira. It is a strange taste, sometimes almost parching, and often — when it suits the wine — pleasant. When it is not suitable, it is just plain unpleasant, and the winemaker has problems.

Fruit acid gives wine freshness; tannin lends a tartness that cuts too much sweetness. Without them, a vintner has to think of something else. Sweetness is a dominating taste that hides unpleasant qualities. The Persians added honey to their wine, going along with its sweetness; even blossoms, too, to add a flowery quality. The Greeks, who used pitch to seal the pores of their earthenware vessels, added some of the resinous stuff to their wines, minimizing the sweet taste by hiding it under another one. Aromatic herbs and spices were used by the Romans, to such an extent that mixing became a special craft. Cold mutes sweetness, and the Phoenicians employed runners to bring snow from the mountains down to Tyre.

Winemakers everywhere lay awake nights, thinking of ways to make their wines taste good. When an idea flashed, the winemaker would try it out, doing a little steeping or adding so much of this or that — macerated dried fruits perhaps, or a mixture pounded to a powder in a mortar. Time was needed for everything to marry; then the first taste. Sometimes it was not half bad.

An eighteenth-century Italian of Turin thought of bitterness. What better way to mask sweet than with bitter? He added the flowers of *Artemisia absinthium* to some wine and let it steep. Not bad at all. Quite refreshing. Germans thought it was marvelous and called it *Wermut,* their name for the herb we call wormwood. Vermouth was born.

Vermouth was the first aromatic wine to become popular around the world. The Italians made it with white wines, dark and sweet, even red wines, developing a masterly control of the bitterness that delighted the British, who took it all over the empire. Sometimes they added gin, and Gin and It — short for Italian Vermouth — became one of the first cocktails.

The French used wormwood to flavor thin, acid wines, inventing Vermouth *sec,* which became a fashionable apéritif. There was also quinine, and along with various herbs this bitter bark was used to balance the sweetness of fortified red wines, and brandy was added to hold the taste. Apéritifs became the rage in turn-of-the-century Europe, the perfect drinks to have while dawdling at sidewalk cafes — something French, at last, to compete with the Sherries from Spain and other foreign concoctions. There was finally a good use for mediocre wines.

Aromatic wines are made in every wine region, and nowhere more than in the United States. In recent years Vermouth was reduced to use in Martinis, becoming paler and drier and less flowery as the fashion for ultra-dry Martinis spread. But as drinking tastes broaden, Vermouth is being drunk again as an apéritif, a mild drink before dinner, served cold or on the rocks. People are varying what they sip, and the way is clear for experiment.

The generation that grew up after Prohibition was set in its ways, and in general, not too fond of the taste of spirits, which accounts for the popularity of cocktails, ever-milder whiskies, ever-blander gins and rums, and almost tasteless vodka. The once-countless concoctions have been reduced to a few staples, and bartenders who once could make perhaps one hundred drinks based on gin alone now mix Martinis and an occasional Tom Collins or Bloody Mary or Daiquiri or Whiskey Sour, and not much else. The following generation, brought up on fruit juice and soda pop, is even less interested in cocktails, but it shows a cheerful readiness to experiment, which amounts to an astonishing thirst for the exotic.

There is practically no such thing as serious drinking any more. Drinking has become a form of play, reviving a tradition that is as old as wine itself. The Germans, in particular, have always been ones to make drinks based on wines, and the British, especially during Queen Victoria's reign, added all sorts of things to wines in pitchers and bowls. The sign of a good host was a well-made punch, and his performance while making it, like that of tossing a salad or flaming something in a chafing dish, was something to behold.

Today the ever-ready winemakers of California, the birthplace of fads, the mother lode of whatever is far out, are doing more than playing around with wine-based drinks. The trick is to catch a fashion, start a fad like that for Cold Duck, and as one fades, start another. California comes up with new ones each year, and one of the first was Thunderbird, a sort of bland and spicy Vermouth launched by Gallo in 1956. It was quickly followed by Silver Satin, a somewhat more lemony version from Italian Swiss Colony. Then there was Golden Spur, as well as Ripple, Vermouth drinks, and soon almost too many to count. Vermouth accounted for sales of a couple of million gallons in 1950; with these new wines added, sales rose to ten million gallons in 1960.

Wine lovers snorted. These things were not really wines at all, certainly nothing to drink with meals, and they were not even like

European apéritifs, or meant for leisurely sipping in cafes or bistros. Exactly. But for Americans who went to picnics and beach parties, who drove around on motorbikes and skimobiles, and who had a style all their own, the drinks were tailored to suit, and the less like things Continental they were, the better.

You could add fruit flavors. Italian Swiss Colony offers Bali Hai and Swiss-Up; there is Swizzle, Rose Swizzle, Half & Half, and even an Apple Wine. Gallo came out with Spañada. In fact, there were all sorts of wine blends, not much like the originals, such as Rhinegarten, Barberone, White Port, sauterne without the *s;* those needed no flavoring at all. Still, the wine was new and different.

You could make berry wines, which have a long tradition, but they could be made less syrupy — or more so — than their European counterparts. Kosher wines are a class apart, tasting of the Concord grape. These became a special category all over the country; a trade journal lists thirty brands, Manischewitz, Mogen David, and Schapiro's prominent among them.

You could add bubbles, to offer people the frivolity of Champagne, as the Burgundians did when they put sparkle in their ordinary wines. All sorts of grapes could be used for sparkling, and you could bubble them in bulk by the vatful, or simply carbonate them. And you could add just enough bubbles to make the wine shimmer, thus avoiding the sparkling wine tax.

All of this has led to a breaking down of distinctions between wines. The result is confusion, but a playful one. The drinks may not appeal at all to people who fix their attention on traditional table wines, but those not used to having wines with meals, who are the majority of the population, seem to be intrigued.

Most of the new wine drinks are made by combining various classic winemaking methods with techniques borrowed from soft-drink manufacturers, and they have two major flaws. All of them are too sweet, and most of them have unpleasant taste qualities — of vegetables, of grasses, of chemical fruit essences. They are generally made from young wines from undistinguished grapes, and few of them are a nice balance of flavors, tasting too much of one thing or not enough of another.

But this, too, will change, for like the Persians, the Greeks, the

Romans, and every generation of winemakers since then, U.S. wine-makers are constantly fooling around with the old problem, trying to make something better out of what's on hand. During the decade, some excellent aromatic wines should emerge, neatly flavored with fruits or berries, herbs or spices, barks, seeds, peels, blossoms. The result may not appeal to all, just as there are those who cannot abide the resinous wine of Greece, the rice wine of Japan, the palm wine of India.

With all those vineyards in California, all those orchards from coast to coast and all the way to Hawaii, there just may be something good coming up. Any day now, some modern wizard may, with serendipity to help him, come up with a present-day Falernian, a latter-day Vermouth.

PART FOUR

Exploration

Finding Wines Around the Country

An innocent European touring North America has a bizarre time finding wine to drink. Restaurant glasses range from thimbles with thick lips to pretentious balloons. In Canada and more than a dozen states in the U.S. he would have to go to government stores and perhaps fill out a slip to buy a bottle. Many counties and some states are completely dry. Many cities ban sales on Sundays. Some parts of the country sell wines from under the counter with a leer and a wink, or with silent disapproval. Familiar European names might spark a gleam in a thirsty man's eye, but the taste would have nothing to do with what comes from those regions. Following the maxim of drinking the wine of the country, he would be most apt to find something sweet in the South or Midwest, certainly something bland elsewhere. Surprised waitresses in country inns would ask if he was sure he wanted a whole bottle and if he wanted the red wine chilled; half the time the white wine would be warm. A traveler from our biggest cities, used to a generous supply, would have as much trouble as a foreigner. Like the foreigner, he might settle for beer.

There's a thin skein of stores and restaurants everywhere that have good bottles at reasonable prices, but in most places wine is rare and very expensive or very cheap. In fact, the good wines go to the best places, for wine is still mostly considered the drink of the rich and the sophisticated. Much of the dearth is due to the American wine industry, which has miles and miles of vineyards that produce tons and tons of Concords and Thompson Seedless that have to be made into wine. This production is what gets around.

Three bottles out of every four come from California and most of that comes from the Great Central Valley. Gallo, all by itself, produces close to 40 percent of all California wine, and while they market skillfully made "Burgundy" and "Dry Chablis," their volume and their advertising goes into Boone's Farm Apple Wine and Pink Chablis. Heublein has perhaps 20 percent of the market with its United Vintners brands like Italian Swiss Colony, Roma, and Petri, but much advertising focuses on Annie Green Springs, which comes in assorted flavors. Through its Inglenook holding, good half-gallons are produced from North Coast grapes, and that success has influenced other bulk producers (who sell by tank car and truck to local bottlers across the country) to produce jug wines under new labels. Guild, which has 7–8 percent of the market, sells its Tavola and Cribari labels most widely. Franzia, which has 6–7 percent of the market has a multitude of brands, best identified by the post office address of Ripon, found on the bottom of the label. These names, and local bottlings, are what are most widely distributed.

There are four large producers of "premium wines" — The Christian Brothers, Krug, Paul Masson, and Almadén. They account for 15 percent of the market. Their distribution is spotty in the sense that any one store may have a wine or two from each, perhaps even several from one of the producers, but these wines seem to be high-priced, compared to others on the shelves, and there simply isn't room for all of them. A store has to display its imported wines because of their snob appeal.

Imported wines account for one bottle out of five, but only a small fraction of that, perhaps 10 percent (and all expensive) are as good as or better than the wines of premium producers. The cheap imports, those under two dollars, rarely match the wines from the Great Central Valley. Three dollar imports rarely compare with bottlings from the four big premium producers. When in doubt, too many people buy the cheap imports, discouraging the shopkeeper from stocking the American wines.

Altogether, the giants of the Great Central Valley and the four "premium producers" account for 90 percent of American wines available, and much of this is hidden under counters and on inconspicuous shelves because most of the good shelf space is devoted to imports and to spirits.

The distinctive wines, unique and often splendid, so extensively identified in this book (in the same way that books on European wines spell out the bottlings from Bordeaux and Burgundy and the Rhine) — all that are so often called the fine wines of America — account for less than 10 percent of production. They have to be sought after. They are worth the seeking.

America's fine wines are in every market, some in one shop, a few in another. Most of them are in the warehouses of distributors. Your local shop can order them by the case and will be pleased to do so. To buy them by the bottle, you may have to search the shelves or ask for them by name.

In restaurants, American wines are relegated to the back of the wine list, a page or less, if any are listed at all. What's there is usually something from Paul Masson or Almadén. Restaurants that feature "all the wine you can drink" with steak or spaghetti most often buy jugs from Gallo or the United Vintners part of Heublein. Those that offer wine by the glass or carafe may buy jugs from the four "premium producers." A few restaurants, still mostly in California, feature American wines; most good restaurants have a few good bottles from North Coast and South Bay vintners, left over from a wine society dinner or for sampling by the owner. It never hurts to ask.

Good bottles are easy to find in New York, Chicago, and Washington, D.C. There are a few to be found in cities like Boston and Detroit, Denver and Houston. Resorts in Florida and Vermont keep stocks. Some are to be found in *the* wine shop that's made a name for itself in nearly every city and suburb. But mostly, you'll have to order.

In the fifty major markets, distributors will have limited stocks of wines from Beaulieu Vineyard and Louis Martini, Korbel and Sebastiani, Wente and Mirassou. Spottily available are Robert Mondavi and Beringer, Buena Vista and Concannon. Soon to come are wines from Sterling Vineyards and Souverain Cellars, Windsor Vineyards and Oakville Vineyards. All of them can be ordered through local shops, although they are sold by quotas because supplies are short. You may have to wait for months unless you order right after the first of the year.

You may have to get on the mailing lists to get the wines of Heitz and Freemark Abbey, Mayacamas and Parducci, and the rest. If you're lucky, a local shop may have made the effort to get stocks of Schramsberg or Hanns Kornell, but in all likelihood such wines have to be ordered. You don't have to wait for the release dates announced to the mailing lists each spring. You'll do even better by sending a check for fifty dollars and reserving a case to be shipped when ready. That won't be enough, perhaps, and you will get a bill for the remainder; when paid, the wine will be shipped to a local distributor or to a shop in your neighborhood. You can arrange to pick up the wine or have it delivered.

After your initial purchase, you will automatically go on the mailing list and if you order promptly you will get some of the wines. Don't be greedy, though. Be satisfied with a case or two. Joe Heitz has scarcely 20,000 cases for the whole country, and he has distributors in something like a dozen states who are constantly badgering him to increase their allocations. It takes an effort to obtain the fine wines made in America, but they are worth it.

Tomorrow's Wines

One of the most ancient branches of agriculture is becoming one of the most sophisticated. Wines and the vineyards behind them have been on a boom-and-bust cycle for centuries, expanding with world trade and prosperity, contracting with war and depression. But a portion of the market has been impervious to such fluctuations — production of fine wines has progressed steadily since the Romans. There has never been enough good wine to go around.

The making of wine is a craft that approaches art and a fine bottle certainly is a work of art. It's consumed, of course, hopefully at its peak, and not in the way that a building or a painting is consumed by the ravage of time. Permanence, though, is not necessarily a criterion. Excellence is, and people of all ages seek involvement with whatever is excellent. Those unable to make a work of art themselves can make it possible for others to do so, and the well-to-do of today are becoming patrons of vineyards as did the nobility of the past, as a way to create something that will live after them.

Developing vineyards is an old tradition in Europe. A wealthy merchant or manufacturer would buy run-down or deserted land and set out a vineyard. The vine thrives in soil suited to little else, particularly slopes hard to farm for crops where high yields are needed. There's satisfaction in taking marginal land and causing it to produce wonders, few things are lovelier than a vineyard in flower or leaf, and with patience you can drink the fruit of your labors.

Many California vineyards began this way — Inglenook, Beaulieu, and Cresta Blanca are examples — and others were rescued from decline, like Buena Vista and Almadén. Still others were expanded, like Paul Masson and Krug. By the 1960s, though, cost for development became too great for one man's fortune and corporations began taking over the estates or the marketing of the wines, or both.

Some individuals saw a way of developing vineyards by assuming the responsibility for investing the money of friends. Several such limited partnerships and group ownerships came into being, among them Schramsberg, Freemark Abbey, and Oakville Vineyards in Napa. Others went public, selling shares in the winery and estates, like Windsor Vineyards in Sonoma. The world of wines took on a new look.

Not only well-to-do partners became interested in wines, but also friends and acquaintances — doctors, lawyers, architects, builders, engineers — all those people whose talents are used in the complex matters of establishing a vineyard and marketing its wines. Stockholders were customers, partners wanted to come see what was happening, everybody wanted to taste the results.

A generation ago, when wines were novelties, the wineries established tasting rooms where visitors could be introduced to the wines. A way to spend a weekend was to tour the wine country, tasting as you went. It got so that wineries were built not only to handle so many gallons of wine but also to handle so many visitors per day. Buying wine at the winery became the thing to do, and being on the mailing list for release dates of bottles from the small wineries was a sign that you had reached a level of sophistication. With so many people becoming financially, professionally, or socially involved with the wineries, suddenly the wine business had a wealth of knowing kibitzers.

No other business is likely to get so much free advice, much of it professional, much of it good.

As for tasting rooms, they are no longer places where you get a sip of wine from a thimble-sized glass. The more sophisticated of them have fully staffed kitchens catering lunches, dinners, and picnics. Several museums have come into being, most notably that of The Christian Brothers. Paul Masson began concerts in the vineyards, and there are similar music seasons at Krug, Mondavi, and Windsor. Dance recitals, plays, pageants, chorales, exhibitions — any aspect of art now takes place at that new center of culture, the winery. All of it is humanized by food and drink. And it's taking place at a time when many gloomily maintain that we live in a hamburger-and-French-fries society that is the lowest common denominator yet achieved by any civilization. The wineries and their audience may be merely a paramount sign of the counter-culture, but their effect is deep.

Smart money is coming into the business — from the Texas oil fields and the Wall Street banks. Big money is coming in — from Schlitz and Pillsbury, following Nestlé and many of the food and drink conglomerates. The liquor business, in and out of wines ever since Repeal, is back in wines for good. Land developers are planting vineyard acres by the thousand and selling shares or limited partnerships and other forms of participation. Some think we are in a decade of boom, to be followed by one of bust.

But a bottle of wine is a work of art and an appreciative audience doubles in size every five years or so. No doubt some of the large thousand-acre developments have been poorly conceived and the investment will be as disastrous as the wines. But there will be scarcely 12,000 acres of Cabernet Sauvignon in full bearing by the end of the decade, half as much Pinot Noir and Chardonnay, half that of White Riesling, of Sauvignon Blanc, of Sémillon. There may be 20,000 acres of Grenache Rosé by decade's end, nearly as much Chenin Blanc. Of the 24,000 acres of Zinfandel, scarcely half produces fine wine — from the vineyards around San Francisco Bay. The new grape crosses, among them Ruby Cabernet and Emerald Riesling, are going into new vineyards and replacing many of the nonwine grapes planted in the Great Valley and Cucamonga, but wines from most of them may be good only for blending.

In all, there will be a scant 100,000 acres of grape varieties able to produce fine bottlings. Maybe there never will be enough good wine to go around.

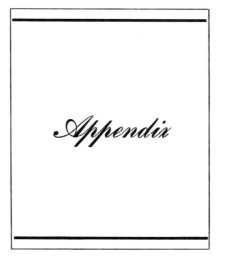

Tasting Notes, and a Glossary of Tasting Terms

Drinking is the only way to become familiar with wines, and the best way to do this is by comparative tasting — one wine against another. This is a slow but effective test. A tasting of three similar wines is interesting, but it gets monotonous. The most satisfactory method is to select a wine to taste, and to try the bottlings of two different producers, tasting the preferred one against a third one at a later time. Notes help; at the moment, you are always sure you will remember, but a day later you are likely to be confused. A sure sign of the experienced wine taster is that he remembers the wine he tastes, even if he has to refer to notes to recall what was what.

There should be some distinctiveness in the nose, a pleasant floweriness or fruitiness, not of grapes but of wine. There should be no off-smells — of straw or vegetables or chemicals.

The taste should also be sound in the same way, and it should not be watery or too acid. It should taste of wine and not of fruit juice. It should not be harsh or insipid.

There should be a balance between the smell and taste. There should not be a big bouquet and a small taste, or the reverse. And the taste should not vanish instantly from the mouth, but continue after swallowing. This aftertaste may be short, but there should be a suggestion of it, a variation of the smell and the first taste.

The best way to taste wine is with food, and one of the simplest and most satisfying of meals is wine accompanied by the two other basic foods that are products of fermentation — bread and cheese.

All the cheeses should be fairly mild, nothing much sharper than a good Cheddar or Monterey Jack, the various blue cheeses being too strong for most wines. There should be two or three kinds, for a wine tastes differently with each cheese. Crusty French or Italian bread is best, but crackers that are not too salty or buttery will do. Salami and other cold cuts add to the variety.

The wines should be as close together as possible — a Mountain White or a Chenin Blanc, say, from two Napa producers, or one each from Napa, Sonoma, and Santa Clara. A Mountain Red or Zinfandel might be tried in the same way. Two bottles of wine will barely do for four people at such a lunch, the general rule being that a bottle serves four people twice. A simple dinner of a roast, something from the grill, or a stew, may well call for a third bottle, particularly if the French custom of serving cheese after the salad is followed.

It is quite simple, of course, to have as many as a half-dozen wines at a tasting, but that may be confusing, and it requires many glasses. At a dinner for six or eight, a pair of white wines might be served with a first course, a pair of reds with the main course, the wines acting as foils for each other and complementing the food.

Most wine tastings present too many wines, too far apart — a miscellany of reds and whites with little relation to each other, from various vintages and various districts. For a crowd, the most casual way to have a tasting is to serve a buffet, with perhaps four different but similar wines presented. Anybody who wants to try each one can then do so by pouring a tablespoonful or so of the wine into his glass, swirling it, then drinking or pouring out the sip before pouring a different wine. At table, it is pleasant to have two different wines poured at the same time. One wine may taste better with the main course, the other with the cheese.

Once you are familiar with a few wines from a district, you are ready to try those of another. In California there are a dozen districts to choose from, and at least a dozen wines from each district.

Some Tasting Terms

The vocabulary of taste is meager and inadequate, and the wine world uses a sort of shorthand language tested by time to express the almost indefinable subtleties of taste. The language sounds precious to the uninitiated, but the terms are quite straightforward and unforgettable once the characteristic has been tasted. There is no reason why one cannot make up one's own tasting language; in fact, this is one of the pleasures of wine drinking. In describing taste there is a tendency to make analogies, saying a wine tastes like raspberries, or whatever. Another tendency is to personify the wine, likening it to gentle maidens, hearty cavaliers, or whatnot; others find similes from the world of music. All these impart a certain comprehension, but, finally, a Cabernet tastes like a Cabernet, a Chardonnay like a Chardonnay, and awareness comes only from tasting.

Acidity — The fresh taste of fruit acids keeps a wine from tasting flat or insipid. Volatile acidity occurs when there is too much acetic acid in a wine, turning the wine sour — *vin aigre* in French — so that it is spoiled and tastes of vinegar.

Aroma — The smell of fruit or flowers in a young wine. As the wine ages aroma tends to be replaced by a more subtle collection of smells called the bouquet.

Astringency — A combination of sharp and bitter tastes in a young wine that tends to make the mouth pucker, coming from tannic acid, which disappears as the wine ages. Pleasant in young wines when not too pronounced.

Balance — Said of a wine whose various qualities are poised and in equilibrium, so that none is overpowering.

Body — Alluding to wateriness of a wine, one that is light in body having a pleasant liquid quality, one that is full in body seeming to fill the mouth and not tasting watery at all, but "winy."

Bouquet — The collection of fruit and flower smells in a wine, from the fruit acids and alcohols, becoming more complex with age, notable in wines from cool vineyards whose grapes develop much fruit acid.

Corky — A wine that has the smell and taste of the cork, masking its qualities, a flaw called *bouchonné* in French.

Depth — Related to body but suggesting a complexity of taste, one lasting into the aftertaste and seeming to be an echo of the first sip. The taste is long and subtle.

Earthy — Called *goût de terroir* in French, this taste of the soil is something like the smell of clay or loam or earth found in coarse wines from alluvial soils. It is not quite the same as the mossy, spring earth smell that is in the taste of some wines, like Cabernet Sauvignon, reminiscent of mushrooms and more pleasing.

Flowery — The various alcohols and fruit acids have floral smells in young wines, which gradually develop into a perfume that is a composite of them, eventually becoming the more subtle bouquet. Some floweriness has a sappy, green character; others may have the scent of blossoms.

Maderization — A smell like the wines of Madeira, occurring when a wine is in contact with air, causing it to oxidize or rust, turning it brown and giving it a strawlike, musty taste. Also noticeable in Sherries, where it is pleasant, and in white wines that are too old, where it is not.

Nose — Taster's term for a developed bouquet.

Rounded — A mature wine without sharpness, all of whose elements balance one another.

Soft — A wine without sharpness, where tannin and acid is less noticeable than sweetness or lightness. A poor example might taste flat or empty, while a good one would taste pleasing.

Tart — A wine in which the acid is noticeable, often pleasantly.

Storing Wines

The best storage for wines is a place free from vibration, with a stable temperature somewhat less than 55 degrees. Failing that, a space where the temperature is not much more than 70 degrees, which varies little from week to week, will serve nicely. Most people make do with part of a closet, stacking partitioned shipping cases on their sides with the flaps folded back. The cartons provide some insulation, from both vibration and temperature change, the two enemies of wines that cause them to age quickly or fall apart. Sooner or later, most people begin thinking about racks or bins or some sort of place where the wines are easy to get at and the labels are easy to read.

Small racks holding a dozen bottles or so are fine for keeping a few bottles on a shelf or in a cupboard near the kitchen or the dining table. Assemblages of these, or larger racks holding 60 or 120 bottles, are much more convenient because they put at hand a large assortment and provide space for extra bottles.

But best of all are bins, the simplest being cubbies about a foot square, each large enough for a case. Bottles roll in such a space unless cradled with slats or cutouts shaped to hold the bottle or its neck, and so the traditional bin is usually triangular in shape. These are made by making square cubbies about two feet on a side, then inserting a partition on the diagonal. The two isosceles triangles thus formed are considered an ugly shape by some, although a second row can be fitted with a diagonal partition angled from left to right instead of right to left, which forms a diamond shape that is pleasing to the eye. Any existing cupboard may be binned in similar fashion and will hold a surprising amount of wine. Bins should be on the small side, made so as to hold not much more than a dozen bottles. There should not be more than two wines to a bin; when there are more, the bottle you want always seems to be on the bottom. Tags help. Wise keepers of a cellar soak the label off the first bottle drunk, tacking or taping it onto the bin with the remaining bottles to make easy subsequent identification.

Stocking a Wine Cellar

How much wine should be kept on hand depends on how much is customarily drunk, an obvious consideration usually ignored in the enthusiasm of stocking a wine cellar. Someone who drinks two or three bottles a week and gives a dinner party perhaps once a month, during which three or four bottles may be served, will use about one dozen cases of red and white table wines a year, on the average. Three bottles out of four are apt to be red wines, the basic amount augmented by the odd case of sparkling wines, of rosés, and of apéritif and dessert wines. A useful rule of thumb is to keep on hand a year's supply, to be replenished each season, in which case the cellar should be able to store some 150 bottles and might occupy a space about four feet wide and six feet high. The space would be smaller if the wines were put in racks or bins.

The size of a cellar depends on how old the wines are when they are drunk, something like a dozen years being about right for Cabernet Sauvignon, about half that age for Pinot Noir and Zinfandel, between two and four years for most white wines. For laying away wines, a second rack capable of holding some 150 bottles might be needed, although most wine drinkers are content to keep wines for current consumption in their shipping cases, using a single rack for bottles that are set aside for future drinking.

In any event, the way to get a wine cellar started is to buy perhaps a dozen cases of red wines and set them aside for at least a couple of years, and to buy six cases of white wines and set them aside for at least a year. Once that is done, wine for present drinking is needed.

The most casual way to buy wines for current drinking is to order two or three cases at seasonal sales, which are customarily held right after the first of the year, after Lent, before summer vacations begin, and early in the fall. Mixed cases — pairs of six different wines — offer a pleasing variety, and when any particular wine proves especially attractive in taste or price, an extra case can be laid away for later drinking. Wine drinking is most pleasant when it is not an expensive luxury. At least one of the cases purchased each season should cost less than twenty dollars, and the second case should not be much more than twenty-five. Wines for laying away should cost under forty dollars, even though they may be worth thrice that when you get around to drinking them. Wines costing over four dollars a bottle are extravagant luxuries, to be reserved for special occasions, like Friday, or a rainy day.

Here is a list of wines to put away, to be replenished case by case, as the seasons turn:

6 cases *Cabernet Sauvignon*
2 cases *Pinot Noir*
2 cases *Zinfandel*

2 cases *Chardonnay*
2 cases *Pinot Blanc*
2 cases *Johannisberg Riesling*

2 cases *mixed reds and whites*

The two mixed cases of reds and whites, one of each, are for sampling, and might well include some rosés. Red wines to try might include Barbera, the two Gamays, Petite Sirah, Grignolino, Ruby Cabernet, and the various generics from top producers. White wines might include Sauvignon Blanc and Sémillon, Chenin Blanc and Folle Blanche, Sylvaner and Gewürztraminer, Emerald and Gray Riesling, as well as the generics of leading producers.

The cost of such a cellar might well exceed five hundred dollars, but there is no need to build up a complete wine cellar all at once. A practical plan might be to spend perhaps one hundred dollars each season for a couple of years, buying only one or two cases each time for storing away. By so doing, prices and the way they rise become matters of familiarity, as do the various wines available. In the beginning, purchased wines can be left with the wine merchant, who will often store them for a year without charge.

Hidden Wines and Where to Get Them— California and New York

By January the vineyards are streaked with mustard, the cover crop bright yellow against the sodden earth and dark trunks. In yards, mimosa glows under a weak sun, oranges gleam to brightness behind dark and shiny leaves. Palm fronds clatter in the winter rains. Mists drift over the hills to give them the look of Chinese brush paintings. It is a fine time to drive around, before work has begun.

Or maybe the other side of Christmas is better, before the rains, after the vintage, in the lull between the holidays. August may be best, before the vineyards quicken, when other fruits are ripe and the air is full of drying apricots and plums.

Release dates for new wines are usually in the late winter, when the last vintage has been racked into vats and casks, when there is time for bottling. Room has to be found for new wines, so bottles of an older vintage are offered.

The way you find out about the releases is through the mailing lists. Sometimes all the wines are gone the first day. If any are left, the only way to get them is to go and pick them up. Shipments can be made to states where producers have wholesalers, but the small vintners scarcely bother with such formality.

Here is a list of small wineries with little distribution, plus larger ones that have special reserves or limited bottlings that may not be widely distributed. Those marked with an asterisk do not regularly receive visitors; appointments should be made by letter in advance. At such places a sure way *not* to get any wine is to barge in without warning.

NOTE: A touring guide listing all wineries open to visitors, *California's Wine Wonderland,* is available without charge from the *Wine Institute, 717 Market Street, San Francisco, California 94103*

CALIFORNIA

* FICKLIN VINEYARDS
30246 Avenue 7½   (209)
Madera, Calif. 93637   674–4598
Walter C. Ficklin, Jr., *Vineyardist*
David B. Ficklin, *Winemaker*

FREEMARK ABBEY WINERY
3022 St. Helena Highway North   (707)
St. Helena, Calif. 94574   963–7106
William Jaeger, Jr., *Partner*

HANNS KORNELL CHAMPAGNE CELLARS
P.O. Box 249   (707)
St. Helena, Calif. 94574   963–2334
Hanns J. Kornell, *Owner*

* HANZELL VINEYARDS
18596 Lomita Avenue   (707)
Sonoma, Calif. 95476   938–4370
Mrs. Douglas N. Day, *Owner*

HEITZ WINE CELLARS
500 Taplin Road   (707)
St. Helena, Calif. 94574   963–3542
Joseph E. & Alice M. Heitz, *Owners*

* LLORDS & ELWOOD WINERY
1150 S. Beverly Drive   (213)
Los Angeles, Calif. 90035   274–5916
J. H. Mike Elwood, *Chairman of Board*
Richard Elwood, *President*
    1250 Stanford Avenue
    Mission San Jose, Calif. 94538

* MAYACAMAS VINEYARDS & WINERY CO.
1150 Lokoya Road   (707)
Napa, Calif. 94558   224–4030
Robert B. Travers, *General Partner*

NICHELINI VINEYARD
Chiles Valley Sage Canyon Road   (707)
St. Helena, Calif. 94574   963–3357
James E. Nichelini, *Owner*

NOVITIATE OF LOS GATOS
P.O. Box 128   (408)
Los Gatos, Calif. 95030   354–4137
Father Francis J. Silva, S.J., *President*
Sheldon St. John, *General Manager*

PARDUCCI WINE CELLARS, INC.
Route 1, Box 572   (707)
Ukiah, Calif. 95482   462–3828
John A. Parducci, *President*

J. PEDRONCELLI WINERY
1220 Canyon Road   (707)
Geyserville, Calif. 95441   857–3619
John A. Pedroncelli, *Partner*

*RIDGE VINEYARDS
Cupertino, Calif. 95014   (408)
D. R. Binnioh, *President*   867–3233

* SCHRAMSBERG VINEYARDS CO.
Calistoga, Calif. 94515   (707)
Jack L. Davies, *Managing Director*   942–4558

SPRING MOUNTAIN WINERY
2867 St. Helena Highway North   (707)
St. Helena, Calif. 94574   963–4341
Michael Robbins

* STONY HILL VINEYARD
P.O. Box 308   (707)
St. Helena, Calif. 94574   963–2636
Frederick H. McCrea, *Partner*

WINDSOR & SONOMA VINEYARDS
P.O. Box 57   (707)
Windsor, Calif. 95492   433–5545

THE COMPLEAT WINEMAKER
(For grapes and equipment)
P.O. Box 2470 (707)
Yountville, Calif. 94599 944–2626
Robert Ellsworth, *Owner*

NEW YORK

BOORDY VINEYARDS
Westfield, New York

WIDMER'S WINE CELLARS (315)
Naples, New York 14512 374–6311

BULLY HILL VINEYARDS
Hammondsport, New York 14840

HIGH TOR VINEYARDS
New City, New York

BENMARL VINEYARDS
Marlboro, New York

NOTE: Widening interest in small wineries has encouraged an importer—Bon-Vin of Houston—to contract for distribution of some producers that scarcely receive passing mention in general accounts. Made by wine buffs, even hobbyists, and those who used to sell to big firms, the wines are ones to grab whenever you see them. Here is a sampling from the Bon-Vin offerings:

Kenwood Vineyards, Sonoma—*Zinfandel*
ZD, Sonoma—*Pinot Noir*
Dry Creek Vineyard, Sonoma—*Fumé Blanc*
Cambiaso Winery, Sonoma—*Petite Syrah*
Woodland Vineyards, Lodi—*Zinfandel*
Husch Vineyards, Anderson Valley, Mendocino—*Gewürztraminer*
Edmeades Vineyards, Anderson Valley, Mendocino—*Chardonnay*
Fetzer, Redwood Valley, Mendocino—*Carmine Carignane*
Joseph Swan Vineyards, Forestville—*Zinfandel*

Château Vintners, San Leandro—*Pinot Blanc*
J. Mathews Winery, Napa—*Chenin Blanc*
Pope Valley Winery—*Zinfandel*
Varietal Vintners, Santa Clara—*Bonesio Grenache, Pedrizzetti Barbera*
D'Agostini Winery, Plymouth—*Zinfandel*

Index

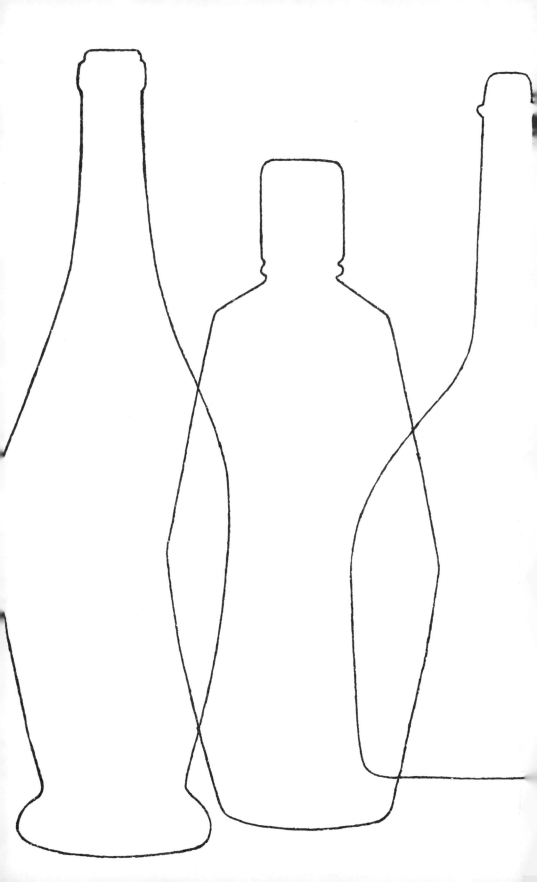